If you are at the beginning of your writ  in
your hands. Joyce K. Ellis's brilliant, inf n-
dreds of hours of learning everything t ·r,
this book is guaranteed to teach you thi ;e
you to keep this book on your shelf, rig.
It's that good.

ROBERT HUDSON,
author, *The Christian Writer's Manual of Style: 4th Edition*

I have read Joyce Ellis's writing tips for many years with appreciation and, well, envy. She is so doggone entertaining and helpful, which makes me jealous. The wisdom she shares in *Write with Excellence* has guided me in my own writing, so you should buy it, read it, and heed it.

BOB HOSTETLER, author of more than forty books,
including *The Bard and the Bible: A Shakespeare Devotional*

Joyce Ellis serves up a feast of sound, practical advice to energize and enrich your writing. Whether you're crafting your first manuscript or your ninety-first, *Write with Excellence* will help you get it right.

DAVID HORTON, VP editorial,
Bethany House Publishers

From her many years as a freelance writer, editor, writing teacher, and speaker, Joyce Ellis has learned much about using the proper voice and tone, choosing the precise word, and structuring grammar for maximum impact. Her quirky sense of humor often shows up but never intrudes. This is a keeper. Until there are major shifts in English language usage, this guide will be a handy reference that writers keep at the ready for many years to come.

TERRY WHITE, EdD,
journalism educator, author, publisher

When Joyce Ellis leads a workshop for writers, she is always upbeat, encouraging, insightful, and current. Her writing book provides that same spirit of motivation for students, while also giving them pragmatic lessons that help them write, proofread, and edit meticulously.

DENNIS E. HENSLEY, PhD, author and educator, Taylor University

What writer (or editor for that matter) doesn't need help from time to time sorting out the complexities of the English language when it comes to grammar, punctuation, and style? Joyce Ellis's *Write with Excellence* provides just the right guidance any wordsmith might need in order to write clearly and effectively.

RODNEY L. MORRIS, senior editor,
Harvest House Publishers

This user-friendly guide with touches of humor explains the important rules writers need to know about grammar, punctuation, and style with examples to help you apply them. It's the kind of book you will want to read through, as well as use as a reference.

LIN JOHNSON, managing editor, *Christian Communicator*;
director, Write-to-Publish Conference

Joyce Ellis is a trusted colleague who has assisted me with editorial work on three magazines over the course of two decades. She is gifted at making me and many other writers read much better with her tweaking of our work. This book makes even the driest grammar rules much more understandable—even interesting! Other grammar books on my shelf will just need to move over to make room for Joyce's refreshing work.

CAROL MADISON, editor,
Prayer Connect magazine

Joyce Ellis's wisdom on the craft of writing will save you time, money, and embarrassment. Anyone considering independently publishing, especially, would benefit from this resource. Add *Write with Excellence* to your reading list today. You can't afford not to!

ATHENA DEAN, author and publisher,
Redemption Press

Joyce Ellis became one of my favorite people years ago as my editor. This book's content reminds me fondly of her—fun, insightful, practical, winsome, clever, precise, and full of heart.

RUSTY WRIGHT, international lecturer, author,
syndicated columnist, www.RustyWright.com

Joyce Ellis has succeeded in creating a practical and entertaining book to boost any writer's skills. Her illustrations are lucid and gripping, her guidelines concise, and her exercises enable immediate application. This title will undoubtedly result in the creation of better books and articles for years to come. I recommended it to our staff this morning during our break.

DAWN JEWELL, communications manager,
Media Associates International (www.littworld.org) and author of
Escaping the Devil's Bedroom: Sex Trafficking, Prostitution and the Gospel's Transforming Power

In twenty years of writing professionally, I can't remember ever laughing out loud while reading a grammar book and wanting to keep reading. But in *Write with Excellence* the personal anecdotes and humorous examples illustrate the importance—and impact—of good writing.

ANN-MARGRET HOVSEPIAN, author of
Restore My Soul: A Coloring Book Devotional Journey

Don't read this book straight through! Read a small portion, digest it, and practice it. Then move on to the next point. When you've finished the book, start over, and review the points you need help with. This is a handy desk reference you'll return to over and over in the writing process.

DENNIS TUCKER, PhD, adult services librarian,
Stockton–San Joaquin County Public Library, California

Through entertaining anecdotes and compelling examples, Joyce Ellis masterfully explains the reasons behind the rules, which means you won't have to memorize them; you'll remember them and apply them correctly because you'll understand them.

DAN BROWNELL, editor,
Today's Christian Living

WRITE WITH EXCELLENCE

201

WRITE WITH EXCELLENCE

201

A lighthearted guide to the serious matter of writing well—
for Christian authors, editors, and students

JOYCE K. ELLIS

Foreword by JERRY B. JENKINS

For Sherrie,
Happy writing!

Joyce K. Ellis

credo
house publishers

Lovingly dedicated to all my writing and editing mentors over the years

and to all the writers I've had the privilege of mentoring—

including my own children, who "do their mom proud."

Onward!

Give of your best to the Master;

Naught else is worthy His love; . . .

Give Him your heart's adoration;

Give Him the best that you have.

—HOWARD B. GROSE[1]

And, we might add, "Give Him the best you can *learn*."

Contents

3 Style, Usage, and Other Considerations

Appendices

Foreword

Linger on the word *Excellence* in the title of this book.

My long-time friend and colleague, Joyce Ellis, is known for her humor and for her attention to exhaustive detail. She uses both to maximum effect here, which makes this book a treasure for us *bona fide* wordophiles.

But *excellence* is her bottom line—as it has been for her in every area of her life since I've known her: mom, wife, grandmother, homemaker, freelance writer, speaker, churchwoman.

We met in an unlikely fashion. My humor from the platform of a writers conference 40 years ago resonated with her, and Joyce's laughter cascaded over everyone else's. Later she introduced herself and asked me to speak to the Minnesota Christian Writers Guild.

Seeing her in her home, interacting with her husband, Steve, and their kids, I saw a side of Joyce that made me trust her to become a mentor for my writers guild down the road.

Write with Excellence 201 is a comprehensive volume non-word-lovers might call excessive. But Joyce layers in just enough fun to make it a delight for those of us who ply our trade with words.

And in the end, it's all about excellence. Some neophyte writers wring their hands over the details of grammar and spelling and punctuation and wonder if it can really be all that important.

It can. Details matter. If you want to write with excellence, you must know this stuff. Consider it a gift from Joyce.

JERRY B. JENKINS
novelist and biographer
owner, The Jerry Jenkins Writers Guild

Start Here

(an introduction to this quirky book, which we won't call an introduction because many people don't read introductions—and we want you to read this!)

One day I heard a writer say, "My husband says I read grammar books as if they were novels."

At that moment fireworks exploded inside my head. I said to myself—maybe even out loud (I do that sometimes), "Why *couldn't* a grammar book 'read' like a novel? Why couldn't I use my editing skills and a little humor to make the nuts and bolts of writing more fun?"

See how quickly I took personal responsibility for this goal?

For decades I've been teaching and mentoring fledgling writers at conferences and through the Jerry B. Jenkins Christian Writers Guild correspondence courses, trying to infuse in other writers my passion for *excellent* writing. So a fun grammar book could encourage *more* writers, especially Christians, to write with excellence: "It is the Lord Christ you are serving" (Col. 3:24).

The *Christian Communicator* magazine needed a grammar columnist at the time my mind was whirling with this notion, and editor Lin Johnson graciously let me run with my idea. The end game would be a book. But a regular column would give me monthly deadlines to actually write the thing. I'm so grateful for Lin's belief in me and her encouragement along the way.

Learning the Craft

We probably all picked up a pencil in first grade, or before, and scrawled letters onto a piece of paper—and maybe a few walls. We strung them into words and sentences we called writing. But sometimes we forget that "writing for public consumption" takes work. As with any apprentice in any craft, we need to learn to use the tools.

Somewhere along the way, we may have concluded grammar was too dry or too hard to learn. Or we may have become lazy. But you'll hear one principle over and over in this book. If we're writing for our Master, we'll want to invest time in learning to write with excellence.

Investing Our Master's Gold

Want biblical justification for this pursuit of excellence? Consider the parable Jesus told about the talents, or bags of gold, in Matthew 25. For writers, those bags could represent various types and quantities of writing projects.

The bags of gold the master gave his servants were not *gifts* for their own use but rather "capital" for them to *invest* on his behalf while he was globetrotting.

As Christian writers, we have a Master who brings projects our way and plants ideas in our hearts. They are not our own. He's *entrusting* (I do love that word!)

these responsibilities to us. And our Master expects us to invest them for the purpose of growing his kingdom, for bringing him glory.

And for what did the parable's master praise the first two servants? Their commitment to excellence and their faithfulness.

When Jesus delegates kingdom work to writers, he *expects nothing less* than excellence and faithfulness.

That's what makes me passionate about writing well and even using correct grammar and punctuation. If I'm communicating faithfully and *clearly*, the Master can take it from there to accomplish his purposes.

Heeding the Danger Zones

Through more than four decades of writing Christian material, I've learned that whenever we faithfully try to write for our Master, the Enemy delights in derailing us through procrastination, self-doubts, guilt over past failures, laziness, pride, and more.

Be prepared.

But God's Word declares that "he who is in you is greater than he who is in the world" (1 John 4:4 ESV). Although writing for our Master is a danger zone, it's also a "no-fear" zone. I'm amazed at how often in Scripture God says, "Don't be afraid" or "Do not fear." So I've started sketching in my Bible's margin the word *fear* with a red circle around it and a red slash through it: my no-fear sign.

Understanding the Changing Landscape

Here's another caution: Beware of the battle zone of grammar purists versus language evolutionists (so to speak). I tend to be more of a grammar purist, but in this book the editors and I have tried to straddle the fence a bit, allowing for the evolution of language and what's now acceptable.

Note: *Readers of my columns may notice some differences between advice given there and the advice here.* These changes reflect either changes in "rules" as I understand current language conventions or else input from editors I respect. I have also corrected some previous inadvertent errors (for which I throw myself down on my arthritic knees, begging forgiveness).

Getting the Most from This Book

As much as I hope this grammar book's approach entices you to read it like a novel, I hope you'll also slow down and allow these guidelines to sink deep into your "little grey cells"[1] so that they become second nature as you write.

We might compare ourselves to a carpenter's apprentice, learning how to use our tools effectively and applying what we learn as we build our writing projects—so we don't end up with the literary equivalent of lopsided kitchen cabinets. Review this book often, and keep it handy as a reference guide.

You will find repetition in this book because some topics overlap, and I suspect few people will read straight through from front to back. Consider repetition an opportunity to review and further cement these principles in your mind.

Our "Style" Authorities

The editors have used as the authorities for this book two complementary resources. One is *The Chicago Manual of Style, Sixteenth Edition* (*CMoS 16*), the standard used by most book publishers and many magazine publishers. The other is *The Christian Writer's Manual of Style, Fourth Edition* (*CWMS 4*), based on *CMoS 16*. *CWMS 4* also addresses specific issues pertinent to writing Christian material. Where applicable, we have provided references to these and other helpful resources.

We also occasionally mention differences in Associated Press (AP) style, used primarily by newspapers and some magazines. Where appropriate, we'll also reference other style manuals, such as the *MLA Style Manual* (the Modern Language Association), used in many academic settings and the *Publication Manual of the American Psychological Association*.

The authorities we have used for dictionaries are *Merriam Webster's Collegiate Dictionary, 11th ed.* (print version) and www.m-w.com.

Exploring the Benefits of Critique Groups

Throughout the book—especially in the quizzes designed to help readers put into practice what they're learning—I have mentioned *critique groups*.

What are they? Small groups (often three to five writers) who meet regularly—or exchange manuscripts via email—to provide skill-sharpening feedback, encourage one another, and suggest outlets for each other's work.

The group I have participated in has been working together for decades. And I believe this accountability and feedback have been the greatest influences on my growth as a writer. (To learn more, see "How to Grow a Critique Group" on my website: www.joycekellis.com.)

If you can't pull together a group, at least seek out a critique partner for constructive criticism—even via email. If using this book in a classroom setting, perhaps your instructor will help you create study groups that can serve the same purpose.

Poor writing quality is one of the chief reasons that writing projects fail to communicate well. So my prayer is that you'll learn or relearn some principles here to help you engage your readers and faithfully honor the Master.

—JOYCE K. ELLIS

"Be sure to fear the Lord *and serve him faithfully with all your heart; consider what great things he has done for you."*

—*1 Samuel 12:24*

Grammar and Related Matters

grammar \gra-mər\ *n* — the stuff you need to know to keep from sounding ignorant when you talk or write.

Defibrillate Your Verbs

You've seen it on TV (however inaccurate it may be).

An ambulance whips in front of the hospital's emergency entrance. One paramedic leaps from behind the steering wheel. Another jumps out the back, dangling an IV bag above the head of a lifeless patient on a gurney.

Inside the ER, Nurse Bella quickly takes vitals while other staff connect the patient to monitors. "I can't get a pulse," she says.

Dr. Guapo grabs the paddles from the crash cart and places them on the patient's chest. "Stand clear," he orders.

Zap! No response.

"Again!"

Another zap. No response.

(Pardon the soap opera, but the mere appearance of defibrillator paddles grabbed your attention, didn't it?)

In storytelling's perfect timing, on the third attempt the heart monitor's flatline leaps into those crucial jagged peaks and valleys. Another life saved!

Many a "mostly dead" manuscript arrives at a writer's conference or on an editor's desk. The writer may not know the gravity of its condition, and editors don't play ER-doc roles. Instead, they reject that type of manuscript.

But with a little training, writers can often bring manuscripts back to life by defibrillating the verbs—choosing more active, specific, accurate, and interesting verbs. Strengthening our verbs can't help but improve the rest of our writing.

We need to develop ER-style life-giving skills for our own writing and for helping others.

Perhaps you've seen the automated external defibrillators (AEDs) found in shopping malls and other public venues. We see them as lifesavers that enable

Ms. Average Citizen to jump-start Mr. Flatline's heart. A critique group or writing buddy can serve as an AED, reviving a manuscript by resuscitating its verbs.

When critiquing a manuscript printout, first I circle all the *to-be* and passive verbs on the first page. (For electronic files, I highlight them in yellow!) When circles or yellow highlights dominate the page, that manuscript needs the intensive care unit. What are some symptoms to look for, along with their treatment protocols?

To Be or Not *to Be*

What exactly are *to-be* verbs, and how do we strengthen them? *To be*, a state-of-being verb, hides in manuscripts in many forms and tenses: *is, am, was, were, will be, had been, were being*, and more. (See sidebar for more forms.) These verbs play an important role, but we default to them too often. A writer striving for excellence searches for more vivid ways to convey the scene or concept.

Go back and reread this chapter's opening. That scene contains no *to-be* verbs. And you probably didn't even miss them.

When we find those weak *to-be* verbs, how can we revive them? Sometimes the sentence doesn't require drastic changes, only a little more thought.

> LIFELESS: **Judith was unable to find many writers who followed her publication's guidelines.**
>
> DEFIBRILLATED: **Judith found few writers who followed her publication's guidelines.**
>
> OR: **Few writers followed Judith's publication's guidelines.**
>
> WEAK: **After seventy-two rejections, the author's hopes were gone.**
>
> MORE POWERFUL: **After seventy-two rejections, the author's hopes disintegrated.**

Especially watch for *there is, there are*, and *there were*.

> FEEBLE: **There were no words that could describe . . .**
>
> STRONGER: **No words could describe . . .**
>
> COMATOSE: **There are three categories of doubters that people fall into.**
>
> MORE ALIVE: **Doubters fall into three categories.**

See how strengthening verbs makes us write better? And eliminating needless words creates a more engaging read.

Beware of *to-be* verbs hiding in contractions too. Though less noticeable, they still rob us of opportunities to use precise, strong verbs.

> WEAK PULSE: **I'm [*I am*] fearful spring will never arrive in Minnesota.**
>
> RESUSCITATED: **I fear spring will never arrive.**
>
> ON LIFE SUPPORT: **It's [*It is*] dangerous in that neighborhood.**
>
> BREATHING UNASSISTED: **Danger skulks around that neighborhood.**

In dialogue, of course, stay true to a character's speech patterns. One might say, *I'm fearful*. Another, *I'm afraid*. Still another, *I shudder at the thought that . . .*

To-be verbs can also alert us to our perpetual nemesis: telling instead of showing. In a novel, we may be tempted to characterize a hero this way:

> He's [*He is*] ruggedly handsome.

Don't do it! Bring out the AED paddles. Show us what makes him handsome, or let the heroine's thoughts indicate what attracts her:

> SHOWN (NOT TOLD): **Jeff's curly black hair kept falling down over his eyes, and Cheri melted at his self-conscious attempts to smooth it back in place.**

In a profile I wrote of Christian musician Phil Keaggy, I could have told readers his mother was kind and loving. Instead, I briefly related something he shared in our interview: *She warmed his pajamas on the radiator every night before he dressed for bed.* That little detail showed her loving heart and kindness. No need for telling.

The *to-be* helping verbs, partnering with other verbs, indicate continuous action: *I was parasailing. She is snorkeling. We were rappelling. They will be bungee jumping.* However, we often insert unnecessary helping verbs. Do we need to say the bird on the balcony *was singing*? Or would the bird *sang* convey our meaning? Could we say the children *played* well for about an hour instead of *were playing?* Chop unnecessary words.

I met a writer whose high school English teacher required the students to write entire compositions without even one *to-be* verb. Extreme assignment! But challenge yourself. Try it. Yet avoid sounding awkward or unnatural. The more we employ active, precise verbs, the more we'll strengthen the whole manuscript.

Common *To-Be* Verbs

I: *am, was, will be, used to be, am being, have been, will have been*

We/you/they: *are, were, will be, used to be, are being, have been, will have been*

He/she/it: *is, was, will be, used to be, is being, has been, will have been*

Activate Passives

Active verbs engage readers more than passive verbs do. Can you recognize passive verbs in your writing?

> PASSIVE: **Randall and Frank were invited by editors to submit their book proposals.**
> ACTIVE: **Editors invited Randall and Frank to submit their book proposals.**
> PASSIVE: **Absalom's rebellion was caused by David's inattentiveness.**
> ACTIVE: **David's inattentiveness ignited Absalom's rebellious spirit.**

Monitoring the vitality of verbs—and substituting active verbs for passive ones—creates opportunities for vivid word pictures.

The word *by*, as illustrated above, sometimes betrays a passive verb. If you know who did the action, tell readers beforehand.

> DOWNRIGHT PATHETIC: **A loud belch was emitted by the conference speaker.**
> SLIGHTLY LESS EMBARRASSING: **The conference speaker belched loudly.**

Avoid passivity as you write and edit. Keep verbs alive and active whenever possible.

Use Passives Appropriately

If we never used passive verbs, however, they wouldn't exist in our language. So how can we use them appropriately? Two primary situations:

UNKNOWN DOER: **The murder was committed last night.** (Cops don't know yet who whacked the guy.)

UNIMPORTANT OR DEEMPHASIZED DOER: **The film was shown in its entirety.** (Monsieur Projectionist doesn't expect credit.)

The word *by* doesn't always appear, though.

AILING: **The editor's advice was ignored.**

MORE HEALTHY: **The newbie writer ignored the editor's advice.**

Avoid Other Weak Verbs

Other weak verbs that clog the arteries of our writing include *had, got, experienced,* and *went.*

Had: Instead of saying, *In the movie* Tangled, *Rapunzel had extremely long, flowing, blond hair,* why not "activate" that verb and give her hair something to do? *Rapunzel's blond hair tumbled from the tower window to the ground, and she often cracked it like a whip.* See how much fun we can have when we're playing with active verbs?

And the following use of *had* is one of my pet peeves:

INCORRECT: **Richard had his dog die of food poisoning.**

Richard seems somehow complicit here. We might consider it an active verb, but this usage makes it sound like a mob hit—e.g., *The Godfather* had *his competition offed.*

Instead, use an active verb; and we feel sorry for Richard instead of infuriated with the "canine-icide."

CORRECT: **Richard's dog died of food poisoning.**

Got: Which of these choices might impact readers more: *Maddie got angry that the editor at the conference marked up her manuscript?* Or *Maddie's anger smoldered when she saw all the editor's red ink?* And instead of writing *Dennis got vengeance,* narrate how he evened the score.

Experienced: Instead of writing *Reginald experienced depression,* give his depression an action: *Reginald's depression robbed him of his appetite.* Don't go bonkers with a thesaurus and say his depression *burglarized* his appetite. Use strong, appropriate verbs. If we choose our words thoughtfully, they won't interrupt the smooth flow of the manuscript.

Went: Watch for substitutes that create word pictures. *Lawrence went down the street* doesn't show us anything. No impact. Did he dash, limp, amble, hobble, strut, shuffle, saunter, or maybe even bebop down that street? Huge difference!

Run Diagnostics

After we finish an article or book chapter, the work has only begun. Examine *all* the verbs. Run diagnostic tests. Print out a hard copy and highlight all the weak verbs discussed here. Run your word-processing program's Find and Replace features, searching for at least the most common *to-be* verbs: *was, were, is, am*. Those may signal passive verbs as well. Then bring out the AED paddles for those flatlining verbs.

The cardioversion will take longer on manuscripts than it does on TV-drama patients. But, one by one, you can shock your verbs—the heart of your writing— back into healthy rhythm.

Zap! Another manuscript saved.

Chapter 1 Quiz

Read the beginning of this ridiculously boring scene. Highlight all the *to-be* verbs, passive verbs, and other weak verbs. Rewrite to defibrillate as many verbs as you can, bringing the scene to life. Feel free to omit some details. Encourage your writing buddy or critique group to do the exercise as well. Then compare your results. See a possible rewrite in appendix A, but you may find better ways to wake up this piece. Give it a go.

> Many years ago there was a little old widower who lived above a shoe-repair shop. He went by the name of W. E. Kling. He was seventy-six years old and only five feet tall. He had mustard-colored hair, his eyes were tired-looking, and he was always talking in hushed tones. He had a boring wardrobe and an equally boring dog that was always lying around on the couch. It wasn't playful at all. In one corner of the apartment was a comfortable dog bed that was donated by a neighbor; but the dog was happier, it seemed, on the couch. There wasn't much going on in the little man's life, but he was usually in fairly good spirits.
>
> One morning, as he walked down the stairs to his shop, his shoulders were rather low. When he sat down at his cobbler's bench, he had a gloomy look on his face. He was often teased by his sole employee, his granddaughter, Felicity. She had experienced these moods of his before, and she knew there was only one thing to do.

References

To-Be Verbs
   The Chicago Manual of Style, Sixteenth Edition: 5.98–99, 5.151–52

Passive and Active Language
   The Chicago Manual of Style, Sixteenth Edition: 5.18, 5.115
   Publication Manual of the American Psychological Association, Sixth Edition: 3.18

Resuscitate Your Nouns

2

In my early days of writing, my children learned their letters from my typewriter. They grew up with the sound of my old Remington manual typewriter's keys, then my hot new Smith Corona electric, and finally the more muffled sound of my huge dedicated word processor. They were grown before I bought my first laptop, but my offspring clearly knew words were my occupation and delight.

Consequently, they still love to torment me when I can't find the right word in conversation. One day when my daughter and I were working in the kitchen, I said, "Please hand me that . . . that . . . [searching for the word . . .] cut thing."

"Oh, you mean the knife?" my daughter teased.

Highly technical term. So this mind glitch has become a family joke.

I've discovered I'm not the only writer with this malady. One writer friend said she told one of her children to put something in "that . . . you know . . . that big box in the kitchen . . . the thing that keeps stuff cold."

My editor friend Andy Scheer has also self-diagnosed the condition, calling it *disnounia* (dis-*noun*-ia)—the inability to find the right noun and spit it out at the appropriate time (my definition).

In writing, we have more time to deliberate over the right word than we do in spoken communication. But do we take that time? Or do we whip out a manuscript without ensuring we're using the best word in any given situation?

In chapter 1, I wrote about how to defibrillate verbs, but here I'll discuss a treatment protocol for "disnounia" in your writing—resuscitating weak nouns you find during your revision process. It's worth the work to select the right nouns that will best communicate with your readers.

Diagnostics

If we want to avoid putting readers to sleep, we need carefully chosen and crafted words—down to the last verb and noun. Today's electronic submission process allows us—if we choose—to work right up to a deadline, then click a button and send it off.

But if we allow cooling time after finishing a manuscript, we can revise more objectively. Well-crafted, precise writing shows respect for our readers.

So, how do we diagnose weak nouns that need treatment?

Common nouns. If your nouns are too common, that may be a symptom of weakness. Of course, a noun is a person, place, or thing. But how precisely do your readers see what you see as you're writing?

For example, what do your readers visualize when you write that a bird flew overhead? Do they see a cardinal, an owl, or a yellow-bellied sapsucker? What do your readers visualize when you write that your character runs out onto the dock and hops into a boat? Do they see a fishing skiff, a pontoon, or a yacht?

What kind of teenager do your readers visualize when you write that a teenager chased your "story person" into an alley? Do you want them to see a jock, a gang member, or a drug dealer? It makes a difference. Be precise.

Adjectives nearby. If you need to prop up your noun with a lot of adjectives (or even a few), this could be a symptom of a weak noun. For example, few of us would write that someone was wearing pants made out of a heavy blue-denim fabric. He wore jeans, even Levis. Or, if you want to characterize him further, you might write about his 501s. Don't be afraid of using brand names. (Despite ads you may have seen in writer's magazines and elsewhere, you don't need to use a trademark symbol either.)

Examples: *He glanced at his Rolex* shows us more than *He glanced at his expensive watch. The scent of White Diamonds* means more than *the scent of alluring perfume. Neighbors blaring loud music* means something entirely different if they're blaring Aerosmith than if it's Slim Whitman.

Whether you're writing fiction or nonfiction, using precise nouns engages the readers' senses as well, transporting them to the scene.

Proper nouns. A proper noun is a particular person, place, or thing and is always capitalized—e.g., not a boy, but Timmy; not a weekday, but Wednesday; not a tall obelisk in the nation's capital honoring a president, but the Washington Monument.

Even ill-chosen proper nouns can be symptoms of weakness. During your planning, writing, and revisions—especially in fiction—have you taken advantage of little nuances of meaning you could convey in the names you choose?

In contemporary novels and short stories we don't use overt character names like John Bunyan's Christian, Mr. Worldly Wiseman, and Mrs. Light-Mind. Nor do we create obvious place names like Bunyan's Doubting Castle and Slough of Despond. But we can browse a baby-name book or website to determine the place of origin and meaning of a character name.

We can also convey character traits with the sound of a person's name. And we can create a mood with the sound of a place name.

Often the hard consonants (such as the sound made by the letter *g* in *go*, the sound made by the letter *k* and sometimes by the letter *c*) give strength to a name. For instance, many of the strong leading men of Hollywood in the 1940s and '50s, especially, took stronger stage names, so Archibald Alexander Leach became Cary Grant, and Roy Harold Scherer Jr. became Rock Hudson.

Gone with the Wind author Margaret Mitchell, at first, named her heroine Pansy. Can you imagine a Pansy making it through all Mitchell's heroine endured in that Civil War saga? But with a name like Scarlett . . . !

And what about place names? If you make up the name of a town, building, or geographical feature, think about how you can convey a feeling about the place. The hard-consonant principle could apply here too. The classic *Murder, She Wrote* TV series took place in Cabot Cove, a made-up small but strong fishing village in Maine. Softer consonants and sibilant *s* sounds can convey a more peaceful image. Personally, someday I would like to set a novel in a town called Heather Shores.

Caution: If you're writing fiction, think through the names you give even minor establishments in your novel. For instance, if you decide to use the Yellow Pages (as some writers do) to find actual names for restaurants and other places of interest in a particular city, be sure you investigate what that place is like.

I once read a novel set in Minneapolis, where I live. The author, apparently with telephone directory in hand (before computers), chose The Embers restaurant as a cozy place for a couple's romantic candlelight dinner. The name suggests warmth, doesn't it? It creates a picture in our minds.

However, my hubby and I often ate at The Embers when we were dating; and it was a well-lit family restaurant—hardly the intimate setting portrayed by the writer. Because of that slipup, I put the novel down, never to pick it up again.

Treatment

The number-one treatment protocol for weak nouns is this: Be specific.

Don't write *A dog bit him.* Tell us what kind. And don't tell us it was a dachshund-Chihuahua hybrid. A dachshund-Chihuahua mix is called a Chiweenie.

Don't leave a fuzzy impression by saying, *He brought her flowers.* Tell us they were daffodils, and you won't even have to tell us it's springtime.

Don't lull us to sleep by writing, *Brandt got into his car.* Tell us that *Brandt hopped into his MINI Cooper* or *his Lamborghini* or *his Jeep Cherokee.* Then we'll not only be able to visualize the scene instantly, we'll know a lot more about Brandt's personality.

The best cure for weak nouns is the use of vivid picture-painting words—not being satisfied with the first thing that comes to mind but crafting the specific image you want your readers to see, hear, feel, smell, and even taste.

Breathe life into your writing by resuscitating your nouns. Then your readers will know that the "cut thing" wielded by someone in your article or murder mystery isn't just any knife—but specifically, a dagger, a switchblade, or a machete. Have fun with specificity.

Chapter 2 Quiz

Identify the weakling noun(s) in each of the following sentences, and resuscitate them by using more specificity. (Feel free to defibrillate verbs as well.) Compare your answers with critique group members, and brainstorm other interesting possibilities. Obviously, answers will differ; but see some examples in appendix A.

1. Herkimer was proud of the fish he caught at the lake.

2. Patti always wanted a light-blue gem in her engagement ring.

3. Ellen unscrewed the fancy brass thing that held the lampshade in place.

4. The bad storm left us without power for a long time.

5. The woman discovered she was allergic to the artificial sweetener in yellow packets.

6. The wings of the tiny multicolored bird beat wildly, suspending him in air like a helicopter.

7. The Mendozas surprised us by bringing Chinese take-out food to our neighborhood potluck.

8. In the long-abandoned kitchen, there were bugs everywhere, looking for food.

9. In a huff the girl picked up her purse and went out of the house.

10. The bed-and-breakfast owners turned an old run-down house into a lovely, elegant showpiece painted in bright pinks and blues.

References

Common Nouns
> The Chicago Manual of Style, Sixteenth Edition: 5.5

Adjectives
> The Chicago Manual of Style, Sixteenth Edition: 5.66
> The Associated Press Stylebook: See Adjectives

Proper Nouns
> The Chicago Manual of Style, Sixteenth Edition: 5.6, 7.8
> The Associated Press Stylebook: See Capitalization
> Publication Manual of the American Psychological Association, Sixth Edition: 4.16

Peacemakers who sow in peace reap a harvest of righteousness.
—JAMES 3:18

The Match Game
Subjects and Verbs

3

When I attended my first Writing for Publication class at a local college, the instructor said that if we wanted to get published, we needed to pay attention to our grammar when we talk as well as when we write.

As a child of the rebellious '60s, I rankled at that. I had done well in English, but I didn't want to have to think that hard while talking.

I made the mistake of telling her so.

She lit into me as though she had been saving up all her "lighting into people" for years. Properly chastised, I've been learning, through more than four decades in this business, the wisdom of her pronouncement.

Similar to the way many pianists play by ear, many writers write by ear—by what sounds right. If we reinforce bad grammar by the way we speak, we're not training our inner ears to the good-grammar "tuning fork."

Negotiating Peace

One of the most common battlegrounds in everyday speech is the grammar principle of subject-verb agreement, the tried-and-true writer's device that matches a singular subject with a singular verb and a plural subject with a plural verb.

Most of us wouldn't say or write this: *The sopranos sings high*. The sentence subject is *sopranos* (a plural noun), so it sounds right to use *sing* (a plural verb): *The sopranos sing high*.

If we're compelled to discuss the stratospheric vocal range of one particular soprano, we would say or write this: *The soprano* [singular subject] *sings* [singular verb] *high*.

Elementary, my dear Watson, right?

Publishing conventions have been changing in recent years to accommodate modern speech patterns that do not harmoniously match subjects and verbs (as I'll describe below). But I encourage writers to strive for excellence here too. Other languages observe these same principles. So why not be a standard bearer?

Actually, the greater the distance between subject and verb, the more likely we'll miss the match. Often we hear sentences like the following (and the discrepancy spills into our writing):

> DISCORDANT (BUT NOW ACCEPTABLE BY SOME PUBLISHERS): **The band of "musicians" scream their lyrics.**
>
> HARMONIOUS: **The band** [singular subject] **of "musicians" screams** [singular verb] **their lyrics.**
>
> ALSO AT LEAST GRAMMATICALLY PLEASANT: **The "musicians"** [plural subject] **scream** [plural verb] **their lyrics.**

It sounds right (to some) to say, *The band of musicians scream.* However, *band*, not *musicians*, is the subject of the sentence. The words *of musicians* create a prepositional phrase modifying the subject. (See sidebar on page 15.) So the singular subject and the plural verb don't match. They fight like preschool siblings, and writers must negotiate a peace process.

I am about to promote a handy negotiating tool that could incite stone throwing from some writers and readers. But I trust you can find more constructive uses for nearby rocks. Many students have dreaded employing this tool, but writers can increase their CQ (communication quotient) by—Are you ready?—diagramming sentences.

This process can be fun, like assembling a jigsaw puzzle. Among other things, diagramming can build confidence that our subjects and verbs coexist peacefully, improving our writing.

Assembling the Puzzle

In its simplest form, diagramming starts with a horizontal line. Think of it as a fireplace mantel. We display our most important items there. The subject (often the actor of the sentence or what's being discussed) goes first on that line. A vertical line crosses the horizontal one, separating the subject from the verb (the actor's action or state of being):

subject	verb

If the verb has a direct object (a word or phrase that often answers the question *What?*), such as the "musicians" sentence does (the word *lyrics*), we draw a short line, like a bookend, and place the direct object to the right of it:

subject	verb	direct object (What?)

band	screams	lyrics

Anything else that describes or modifies the subject or verb hangs off the mantle like a Christmas stocking:

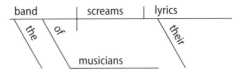

Finding a sentence's bare bones and pushing modifiers out of the way can help us see whether we need a singular or plural verb—and avoid other errors. Always, our primary goal is to communicate as clearly as possible.

Compounding the Problem

Compound subjects result in less-straightforward situations. If a sentence has more than one subject (a compound subject), we need a plural verb, right? Not necessarily.

A compound subject using the conjunction *and* generally needs a plural verb. This one's obvious:

> CORRECT: **Tom, Dick, and Harry write under the pen name Tracy Trey.**

However, the following example may challenge some writers.

> CORRECT: **The discovery of the Dead Sea Scrolls and the unearthing of Hezekiah's Tunnel testify** [not *testifies*] **to the Bible's accuracy.**

With modifiers pared away, we see the subjects: *discovery* and *unearthing*. That plurality calls for a plural verb—*testify*—no matter what comes afterward. To double-check, try replacing a compound subject with the plural word *they*.

A compound subject using the word *or*, on the other hand, generally calls for a singular verb. Is the following sentence grammatically correct?

> **Every week Jay or Linda bring donuts to the OH (Overeaters Hopeless) meeting.**

This compound subject with two elements (*Jay* and *Linda*) joined with *or* (another conjunction) requires switching to a singular verb because it applies to one person at a time. So that example is not correct.

> CORRECT: **Every week Jay or Linda brings donuts.**

In an either-or sentence with two singular subjects, an easy way to double-check the verb is to vote one of the OH members off the island—er, off that metaphorical fireplace mantle I mentioned earlier. *Jay brings…donuts.* Or we could amplify: *Either Jay brings donuts or Linda brings donuts.*

What if we have a singular subject linked to a plural subject with *nor* or *or*? Match the verb to the closest subject.

> CORRECT: **Dorothy or her quirky cohorts, at one time or another, need** [not *needs*] **help to follow the Yellow Brick Road** [cohorts *need*].

Heeding Red Flags

Watch for these danger zones:

1. Beware of prepositional phrases. (See sidebar.)

2. Beware of contractions, especially for *there is* and *there are*.

    DANGEROUSLY INCORRECT: **There's lots of shoes in our foyer to trip over when grandkids visit.**

    SAFELY CORRECT: **There are lots of shoes.** (Lots of shoes are there.)

3. Beware of plural subjects not normally considered plural.

    CORRECT: **"The media are [not *is*] biased," the commentator griped.**

    CORRECT: **The eerie phenomena have [not *has*] given her middle-of-the-day-mares.**

4. Pay attention to red-flag words and phrases that may need singular verbs.

    - *None/no one, anyone, everyone, etc.* For generations, students have been taught to use a singular verb with *none* (meaning not one) and similar words under the above category heading:

        MOTIVATINGLY CORRECT: **None of us wants [not *want*] it. But to finish a writing project, we may need a swift shoe imprint on the derriere.**

        However, as culture changes the English language, *The Chicago Manual of Style* now sanctions the colloquial rendering below:

        NOW ALLOWED: **None of us want it.**

        What I have labeled "motivatingly correct" may be considered, by some, stilted or archaic. However, many journalists still adhere to the first option.

    - *Each.*

        HUMOROUSLY CORRECT: **Each of the big-cat trainers clamors [not *clamor*] for the lion's share of circus profits.**

    - *As well as, together with, in addition to.* These words create parenthetical expressions, so when choosing the verb, we pretend the phrase is not there.

        A BAD PUN, BUT CORRECT: **Robin Hood, as well as his merry men, commits [not *commit*] highway robbery.**

    - *Collective nouns (e.g., majority, herd, association, infantry).* These words take singular verbs only when acting as a single unit.

        JUDICIOUSLY CORRECT: **The jury, frustrated with the judge's conduct, wants [not *want*] to sentence him.**

        FAMILIARLY CORRECT: **The majority understands [not *understand*] why the young mother craved adult conversation.**

Retuning the Ear

Diagramming, in all these cases, retunes the ear to find the best verb. Admittedly, the process gets trickier in more complicated sentences. But these tips offer a good foundation.

Remember, when in doubt, look it up! (We recommend *The Chicago Manual of Style* and the more easily accessible companion guide, *The Christian Writer's Manual of Style, Fourth Edition*, as your go-to style guides unless the publication you're writing for uses a different style guide. See the Resources section in appendix C for more guides.)

Grammarian Robert Pinckert wrote, "You're expected to have lots of time to do things right."[1]

If you want to be a *writer*—not someone who dabbles in writing—correctly use the tools of the trade. Search bookstores, libraries, and online sites for a grammar book that hasn't given up on this extremely useful sentence-diagramming tool, presumably because kids bellyached about it. You might start with Deborah White Broadwater's book *Diagraming Sentences*, a concise and relatively inexpensive resource.

Start putting the writer's tools to work in your written—and spoken—words.

Watch for Tricky Prepositions

Prepositions such as these, followed by nouns, can lead to misidentifying a sentence subject and, consequently, using an inferior verb:

in	on	for	of	by	to	under	over
down	beside	before	during	after	up	into	upon
from	with	near	above	about	except	until	

Chapter 3 Quiz

Below, if the sentence's subject and verb are in agreement, put a C by it. If any sentences are not harmonious, rewrite to make them so. Then try your hand at diagramming sentences 3 and 10. Defend your answers.

_____ 1. Einstein's $E = mc^2$ and the ubiquitous chicken-and-egg controversy—as well as Darwin's attempt to make monkeys out of us all—zooms right over my head.

_____ 2. Each year on April Fool's Day in Halfwit, Idaho, 1,823 "eggs" of Silly Putty mysteriously cover the school playground.

_____ 3. The call of loons are beautiful.

_____ 4. Bonnie or her daughter usually win the Book Lover's Scrabble game.

_____ 5. None of us want to make editors tear their hair out.

_____ 6. TV ads for stupid movies have been increasing.

_____ 7. Most of us hope that advertising stops.

_____ 8. There's tons of reasons to quit procrastinating and just write!

_____ 9. Either nuts or chocolate send Ruth into sneezing attacks.

_____ 10. Each of the boys wants his own room.

References

Subject-Verb Agreement
    The Chicago Manual of Style, Sixteenth Edition: 5.131

Prepositional Phrases
    The Chicago Manual of Style, Sixteenth Edition: 5.169, 5.173, 5.183–87

Contractions
    The Chicago Manual of Style, Sixteenth Edition: 5.103
    The Associated Press Stylebook: See Contractions

Singular and Plural Nouns
    The Chicago Manual of Style, Sixteenth Edition: 7.5

Compound Subjects
    MLA Handbook for Writers of Research Papers, Seventh Edition: 3.2.2j
    Publication Manual of the American Psychological Association, Sixth Edition:
        3.19, 4.12

Getting Tense?
Avoiding Verb Tense Errors

4

A distraught-looking man walked into a psychiatrist's office. When ushered in to
see the doctor, Mr. Naylebighter kept repeating, "I'm a wigwam. I'm a teepee. I'm
a wigwam. I'm a teepee."

The doctor made him comfortable on the couch and then patted the man's
shoulder. "Calm down, Mr. Naylebighter," he said. "You're two tents."

Ba dum pum!

What do some writers get *tense* about? Verb tenses.

Other writers may not even know their verbs tenses can send editors and readers running to a psychiatrist's couch.

I won't try to cover all the verb tenses here. I'll zero in on some potential anxiety-
producing errors and cover some terminology along the way—in the most entertaining way I can manage.

Differentiating Tenses

Verb tenses, in effect, allow a type of "time travel" within a story. Readers learn
whether some action exists in the past, present, or future. And within each of those
categories, we can express more precise time frames.

The foundation is the infinitive—the "to" form. Think, in the words of Buzz
Lightyear, "<u>To</u> infinity—and beyond!" Infinity . . . infinitive.

We'll use the infinitive *to write* in many of our examples. Quick review of "simple" tenses:

PRESENT: **I write today.** (That's what I do if I'm a writer. You may quote me.)

PAST (AT A SPECIFIC TIME): **I wrote yesterday.** (Whew! I can say that
honestly—today!)

FUTURE: **I will write tomorrow, good Lord willin' and the creek don't rise.**

"Elementary, my dear Watson," you say? Just wait.

"Name That Tool!"

In chapter 11, I talk about *-ing* verbs. There I don't use their precise name, but here we'll play "Name That Tool!"

1. ***Present participles and the progressive tense.*** Reaching into our writer's toolbox, we pull out an *-ing verb*, labeled *present participle*—e.g., *writing*.

This tool, when used with a handy-dandy to-be-verb attachment in the present tense (*is, are, am*), creates the *present progressive* tool. (We're not talking politics here, but something *in progress*.)

PRESENT PROGRESSIVES: **I am procrastinating. He is tinkering. We are pontificating. They are finagling.**

In case you run across the term *continuous tense*, it's the same as progressive. But I'll stick with *progressive* here because of its in-progress clue.

Progressives sometimes present a spelling challenge. Most writers wouldn't have a problem dropping the *e* in *procrastinate* to get *procrastinating*. But anxiety may rise over whether to write *bingeing* or *binging*, for example. Neither produces red squiggly lines from the spell-checker, so let's look at the online entry of *Webster's Collegiate*, the dictionary used by many publishers and the one we're using as our standard for this book.

I admit that entry only frustrates me more. It gives *binging* as the first-listed *-ing* form (progressive) of *binge*. But to me, if I see the word *binging*, it looks like it should rhyme with *ringing*.

Although I have to make up a word (I do that a lot!), I could envision Buzz Lightyear making a "bing" sound repeatedly, and I would say he's *binging*. Since we always want to avoid reader confusion, in this case, it would be better—in my opinion—to use an "allowed" spelling (though not the first one listed) to describe a writer *bingeing* on chocolate near a deadline. (I know many do. Who, me?)

My bold recommendation: use the first-listed spelling entry unless it could cause confusion or awkwardness.

What about doubling the ending consonants? Most writers could correctly write about an attorney *betting* [double *t*] on a witness's *compelling* [double *l*] testimony in court. But is the judge *travelling* or *traveling* to court via limo? In older published works and British writings, you will see the ending consonants doubled in words such as *travelling* and *worshipping*. But in the United States today, the preferred spellings are *traveling* and *worshiping*.

Rule of thumb in each of these situations: if the meaning, spelling, or pronunciation could create confusion, eliminate that confusion. For instance, if we didn't double the ending consonant in *slop*, this misspelling would give us *sloping* or *sloped*—an entirely different meaning. But few would mispronounce *traveling* as tra-VEE-ling, for example. Of course, make sure you're consistent in the way you treat each occurrence within a given manuscript.

Other cases may not be as clear cut. So, you know what I'm going to say. When in doubt, look it up!

The same principles apply to past actions. Using the present participle *writing* and a *to-be* verb in the past tense (*was/were*), we create *past progressives* such as these: I *was writing* ("in progress") and you/they/we *were writing*.

2. *Past participles.* Let's pull Mr. Useful out of our writer's toolbox. The past participle is often identical to a simple past-tense verb:

> INFINITIVE: to bake → PAST TENSE: **baked** → PAST PARTICIPLE: **baked** (we use it
>   with helping or auxiliary verbs—e.g., *had baked*).
> SIMPLE PAST TENSE: **baked** [completed action at a particular time—done!]
>   **I baked a black birthday cake for my friend's fortieth birthday.**
> PAST PARTICIPLE (A SINGLE WORD): the same word: *baked*
>   (We'll look at ways to put it to work below.)

Many "design variations" (some might say "design flaws") of this past participle tool exist.

Irregular verbs, in particular, present challenges. For example, instead of *writed*, the past participle of *write* is *written*. Other irregular examples include *heard* not *heared*, *gave* not *gived*, and *went* not *goed*. (For other potentially entertaining specimens, listen to a preschooler talk.) So, what is the past participle of *dive* or *show* or *dream*? If you're not sure, look it up!

3. *Perfect tenses.* I have scoured many grammar books and websites, and I confess I have never found a definition of the perfect tense that satisfies my little grey cells.[1] Some sources don't even attempt a definition. They simply give examples. I learn better from examples anyway. So hang on—let's go!

Past perfect verbs employ the past participle tool we saw above (an *-ed* form for most regular verbs) combined with the tool attachment *had*:

> SIMPLE PAST TENSE: *gave*
> **Cindy *gave* her race car a little more gas.**
> PAST PARTICIPLE (A SINGLE WORD): *given*
> PAST PERFECT TENSE: **Cindy *had given* her race car a little more gas before she crashed.**

Note the way the past perfect sentence example inserts the helping verb *had*. This tense indicates a relationship between two points in time—in this case, giving the car more gas and the car crashing.

> SIMPLE PAST TENSE (IRREGULAR VERB): **spoke**
> **The dude spoke for five minutes.**
> PAST PARTICIPLE (A SINGLE WORD): **spoken**
> PAST PERFECT TENSE: **The dude had spoken for only five minutes when we realized he
>   was a dud.**

Do you get that sense of traveling to various points in time? We use progressive and perfect tenses often in the English language, so we need to master these precise nuances. For more help with these verb tenses, I recommend *The Writer's Digest Grammar Desk Reference* listed in appendix C.

More Irregular-Verb Challenges

The irregular verbs—with their (okay, I'll just say it: *goofy*) past participles and perfect forms—can give writers "two tents" attacks. Here are a few we might use when writing Christian material:

- to *bear*: Jesus *bore* our sins. Jesus has *borne* them.
- to *lay*: God *laid* our sins on Jesus. God has *laid* all our sins on Jesus.
- to *lie* (down): Jesus *lay* dead in the tomb. He had *lain* there for three days when . . .
- to *sink*: When Peter saw the waves, he *sank* [or *sunk*]. He had *sunk* only a few inches, I think . . .
- to *swim*: After the miraculous catch of fish, Peter *swam* to his Master on shore. Peter had *swum* many times before.
- to *drink*: Eli *drank* in the scene. He thought Hannah had *drunk* too much wine.
- to *lead*: God *led* me to pray. He had *led* me that way so many times.

Google the term *irregular verbs* for other examples.

Avoid These Errors and "Awkwardisms"

Awkwardisms is a term I made up. But here are some common errors I must mention:

1. Sometimes writers use the simple past tense when they need the past perfect.

   INCORRECT: I never went to college before I started writing for publication.
   CORRECT: I had never gone to college when I started writing for publication.

2. Some errors are a by-product of English-language acquisition coming more often "by ear" than by reading.

   INCORRECT: Doris could of slapped her brother. She would of if she thought she could of gotten away with it.
   CORRECT: Doris could have [or *could've*] slapped him. She would have [or *would've*] if she thought she could have [or *could've*] gotten away with it.

I would recommend not even using *could of* or *would of* in fiction to indicate how a character speaks. Avoid reinforcing the error, especially for young readers. In dialogue, *could've* and *would've* can work well.

3. Sometimes writers pull the old switcheroo with verb tenses. They begin in one time frame, usually past tense, then switch into another, giving us whiplash. Editors see examples of "erroneous time travel" more often than we might think.

INCORRECT: Mr. Barto was so angry about the bully's repeated student attacks that he pins the guy down and shaves his head.

CORRECT: Mr. Barto was so angry about the bully's repeated student attacks that he pinned the guy down and shaved his head.

INCORRECT: I had an exciting job change that year. I remember feeling scared, but my performance review goes so well that I get a promotion.

Here we start out in past tense, but what throws off the writer is probably the present-tense *remember* (and *feeling*). The whiplash jerks us into the present with *goes* and *get*. We don't need the *remember* at all because the scene obviously comes from one's memory. So . . .

CORRECT: I had an exciting job change that year. I felt scared, but my performance review went so well that I got a promotion.

We need to use past, present, and future tenses to orient readers, but make sure to use (and switch) tenses purposefully.

Important note: At times, we *can* (*and should*) switch from past perfect to a simple past tense. "When?" the curious writer asked.

The past perfect is cumbersome to maintain:

Karen *had* literally *clowned* around for as long as anyone could remember. She *had been* the class clown from kindergarten on. And she *had learned* some basic techniques from her uncle Wayne, who *had been* a professional clown in a touring circus act. After Karen *had put* much thought and effort into her character and costume, she *had begun* her own party business called Seltzer Face.

So, once a few past perfect verbs have established that time frame, we can move forward with a simple past tense this way:

Karen *had* literally *clowned* around for as long as anyone could remember. She *had been* the class clown from kindergarten on. And she *had learned* some basic techniques from her uncle Wayne, a former professional circus clown. After Karen *put* much thought and effort into her character and costume, she *began* her own party business called Seltzer Face.

Maintaining a consistent tense—at least within a scene—can keep our readers oriented.

Now, remember Mr. Naylebighter in the psychiatrist's office? If by now he finally *has perceived* himself as something besides a conically shaped domicile for indigenous people erroneously thought to be from India, maybe his crisis *will have been* worth the heap-big-wampum psychiatrist bill.

Chapter 4 Quiz

In the following sentences, correct all errors. If you find any correct sentences, mark them with a C. Then label the tense of each underlined verb, after correcting if necessary. (See answers in appendix A.)

_____ 1. All her life Dabney <u>has dreamt</u> of bungee jumping from the St. Louis Gateway Arch.

_____ 2. Raúl <u>could of</u> eaten the whole garlic-and-anchovy pizza if his wife <u>hadn't intervened</u>.

_____ 3. The parrot desperately <u>wanted</u> <u>to sing</u> "Melancholy Baby."

_____ 4. Jane <u>was intending</u> <u>to repair</u> her Suburban's crankshaft herself, but then she <u>says</u> to herself right out loud, "<u>Have</u> you <u>lost</u> your mind?"

_____ 5. We <u>had worshipped</u> together many times.

_____ 6. Jethro <u>shows</u> good progress, but he <u>has shone</u> us better work in previous semesters.

_____ 7. Lisabeth <u>is serving</u> kumquats à la mode for dessert.

_____ 8. Paul <u>wrote</u> that "God <u>has</u> not <u>given</u> us a spirit of fear" (2 Tim. 1:7 NLT).

_____ 9. The gutsy politician <u>was travelling</u> on horseback for a while.

_____ 10. The clown <u>dove</u> from the high platform into the kiddie swimming pool. He <u>had</u> already <u>dived</u> many times that day.

References

Tenses and Participles

    The Chicago Manual of Style, Sixteenth Edition: 5.122–28, 5.136–39

    The Christian Writer's Manual of Style, Fourth Edition: p. 329

    Publication Manual of the American Psychological Association, Sixth Edition: 3.06, 3.18

Have the same mindset as Christ Jesus: . . . He humbled himself.

—PHILIPPIANS 2:5, 8

"Moody" Verbs

Using Verb Mood Correctly

With apologies to Jeff Foxworthy and his redneck stand-up routines, I offer this quip: if you cringe at the first few lyrics of the old Southern anthem "Dixie," you might be a grammar purist.

Why? Grammatically, the lyrics should say, "I wish I *were* in the land of cotton," not "I wish I *was*." This may sound strange to our ears; but, yes, it is correct.

Again, why? Most writers know verbs can get "tense"—the basic tenses of verbs being past, present, and future. (See chapter 4.)

But did you know verbs also get to be "moody"? In the English language, verbs come in three primary moods: indicative, imperative, and subjunctive. In "Dixie," the verb should reflect the mood we call subjunctive. Writers please editors more when they know how to use all three moods.

It's Indicative

Most of what we write falls into the category of the indicative mood: straightforward statements of fact, narration, or questions.

Think: Indicative = indicates what's happening or what's being asked. Here are some examples of verbs in the indicative mood:

1. **Ben's publishing house does not publish children's books.**
2. **Do you know any agents who handle books in both general and Christian markets?**

It's Imperative

When someone's getting a little bossy—giving instructions or commands—that's the imperative mood.

Think: Imperative = command. There's an understood subject in these sentences, the word *you*. We understand that the "commander" is essentially saying to the "commandee," "Hey, you! Do this!" Examples:

1. [You,] **Always use proper manuscript format when submitting your articles.**
2. **Quick!** [You,] **Get the barf bucket!**

The command form of the verb we use in an imperative sentence is generally the same as the verb we use in an indicative sentence with the subject *you*.

INDICATIVE: **You serve the Lord with your writing.** [statement of fact]

IMPERATIVE: [Hey, you,] **Serve the Lord with your writing.** [command—Get at it!]

One type of writing that consistently uses the imperative mood is the how-to article. We're talking to readers as if we were sitting across the table from them, demonstrating how to do something, make something, or grow in their Christian lives. To write an article titled "Five Ways to Instill a Love of Scripture in Your Children," we would take an authoritative tone and put the steps in command (imperative) form:

1. [You,] **Let your children see you consistently enjoying your time in God's Word.**
2. [You,] **Read the Scriptures aloud to them early.**

Three types of writing in which we *don't* generally use the imperative mood are personal experience articles, devotionals, and expositional/teaching articles (e.g., explaining the truths of a particular Scripture passage).

"You" language in those types of articles gets preachy—something we want to avoid. So to make an application—to give the reader takeaway value—in these articles, use the indicative mood. And use "we" language. Show readers the positives—the wonderful possibilities and good outcomes—of doing what you're advocating, rather than pointing your finger at your readers and telling them to shape up.

PREACHY, using the imperative mood and an understood *you*: [You,] **Read the Bible every day. It will make a big difference in your spiritual growth.**

Actually, this sentence shows good outcomes of doing what we're advocating, but first they preach at readers.

Instead of finger-pointing, try using the words *if* or *when* to introduce the idea. Then show readers the good that can happen.

ENCOURAGING, using the indicative mood and "can" language: **When we read the Bible every day, we can refocus our hearts and, in essence, give the Lord permission to speak to us.**

Notice that in this version we also offer more specific "possibilities" of following the Bible-every-day principle.

For more help with avoiding the dreaded preachiness that dooms many manuscripts to rejection, read chapter 35.

It's Subjunctive

When we're writing or talking about something conditional—a wish, desire, something doubtful or unlikely—we've wandered into the subjunctive mood. The word *subjunctive* is from the Latin *subjunctivus*. That word is related to *subjugate, subordinate, put under*. We're dealing with things less certain than facts, subordinate to facts.

Think: Subjunctive = subordinate, suggestions, wishes, uncertainties. When we're in this kind of mood, we use a *to-be* verb (or other verb) different from what comes naturally to most of us.

Let's look at *to-be* verbs first. With both singular and plural nouns and pronouns, we use the verb *were* when we're in the subjunctive mood.

> WITH PLURAL NOUN: **The doctor said he wished all his patients were as "patient" as Peyton.**

That sounds correct—and it is—though we might spray the person we're talking to with all those alliterative *p*'s.

Note the next example, however.

> CORRECT WITH SINGULAR PRONOUN: **In *Fiddler on the Roof*, Tevye sings, in all grammatical correctness, "If I were a rich man."**
> CORRECT WITH SINGULAR NOUN: **Tevye's wife wished her husband were less prone to singing.**

These examples may seem awkward—even incorrect. The word *was* sounds more natural. But the sentence is correct as written because of the conditional, subjunctive mood of the verb.

Mood, Tense, and Dialogue

In real life, many people habitually misuse the subjunctive or avoid it altogether. Similarly, in fiction dialogue, the correct or incorrect use of verb moods can distinguish one character from another. Here's an example:

> **If Jack were proficient in grammar, he might say, "I wish I *were* in the land of cotton."**
> **Jill, who grew up without such instruction, might say, "I wish I *was* in the land of cotton."**
> **Or Jack might say, "I would prefer that Jill *use* [not *uses*] correct grammar."**
> **And Jill might respond, "I would prefer that Jack *speaks* like ordinary people."**

As noted in the last two sentences, verbs other than *to-be* verbs can be used in the subjunctive mood. Often they will come in a *that* clause, regardless of tense.

> PRESENT TENSE: **It is imperative that the writer *follow* [not *follows*] the publisher's guidelines.**
> PAST TENSE: **Cindy's parents required that she *finish* [not *finished*] her homework before using her iPod.**

Overall, in ordinary conversation, many people don't worry about what kind of mood their verbs are in. After all, who wants to be the only one singing, "I wish I were in the land of cotton"? But when you're writing for publication, work to get your verbs in the right mood. Editors will thank you. And I'm not just whistling "Dixie."

Chapter 5 Quiz

Are you sensitive to the moods of verbs? In front of each sentence, mark *IND* for indicative, *IMP* for imperative, or *S* for subjunctive. If the wrong verb is used, correct it. See answers in appendix A.

_____ 1. Do you always proofread your manuscripts carefully?

_____ 2. She wouldn't go out with him if he was the last man on earth.

_____ 3. Good writers do everything they can to make editors' lives easier.

_____ 4. My mentor wished he were able to come to my graduation.

_____ 5. Would the police respond quickly in case a burglar were to break in?

_____ 6. Don't quit now.

_____ 7. The editor asked that Christy revised her manuscript one more time.

_____ 8. Mona took time to write an encouraging note as though she weren't busy at all.

_____ 9. Remember to study the writer's guidelines thoroughly.

_____ 10. If I was you, I'd keep working on that story.

References

Indicative/Imperative/Subjunctive Mood
   The Chicago Manual of Style, Sixteenth Edition: 5.117–22, 5.141
   The Associated Press Stylebook: See Subjunctive Mood
   Publication Manual of the American Psychological Association, Sixth Edition: 3.18

Get Your Adverbs Here!

6

Imagine you're at a ball game in a large, packed stadium. The game hasn't started yet. A very sweaty guy, lugging a way-too-heavy metal crate with handles, huffs his way up the steps, calling out, "Adverbs! Adverbs! Get your adverbs here!"

You do a double take. Did he really say what you think he said?

"Icily cold adverbs! Really red-hot adverbs!" he yells loudly. "Get them all here! They're free!"

You frown. Did you inadvertently stumble into a gaggle of grammarians?

No, you just landed softly in the fantasy world of your humble grammar geek. This image came to mind as I nostalgically remembered *Schoolhouse Rock!*, the '70s and '80s kids' TV show, and its song "Lolly, Lolly, Lolly, Get Your Adverbs Here."

Online, I found the entertaining lyrics. Filled with illustrative adverbs, Bob Dorough's song even created characters to illustrate uses of this part of speech. Try Googling "Get Your Adverbs Here" for a meander down memory lane or your first experience with this delightfully helpful song. The song's very catchy tune and highly memorable rhythm somehow lodge the grammatical principles more tightly in our brains.

To follow the song's lead, I intentionally overuse adverbs in this chapter to illustrate many ways they can be used—both correctly and incorrectly. However, be sure to read the last section on avoiding such overuse. It will surely keep your writing clean and lean.

Identifying Adverbs

You may have learned (but perhaps since forgotten) that adverbs modify—tell us something about—verbs, adjectives, and other adverbs. See the following examples.

MODIFYING A VERB: **Even bestselling authors often need significant editing.** The word *often* (adverb) modifies *need* (verb).

MODIFYING AN ADJECTIVE: **The completely clueless writer was infatuated with adverbs.** *Completely* (adverb) modifies *clueless* (adjective modifying the noun *writer*).

MODIFYING ANOTHER ADVERB: **The unpublished writer almost never proofreads her work.** *Almost* (adverb) modifies *never* (adverb modifying the verb *proofreads*).

Adverbs may answer questions about when, where, and how; and they sometimes describe a condition (what) or reason (why).

WHEN: **The stadium vendor was selling adverbs yesterday.** *Yesterday* (adverb) modifies *was selling* (verb).

WHERE: **The vendor stumbled and many adverbs fell out.** *Out* (an adverb here) modifies *fell* (verb).

How: **The vendor scrambled to corral them quickly.** *Quickly* (adverb) modifies *corral* (verb).

CONDITION: **Those potentially overused words can wear out readers.** *Potentially* (adverb) modifies *overused* (adjective modifying the noun *words*).

REASON: **Why on earth do we overuse adverbs?** Turn the question around: We overuse adverbs why . . . ? *Why* (adverb) modifies *overuse* (verb).

Differentiating Adverbs and Adjectives

The above reminders may help you spot common errors in the following sentences.

JARRING ERROR: **Christians need to live different, talk different, act different.**

CORRECTLY EXPRESSED: **Christians need to live differently, talk differently, act differently.**

MISTAKEN USAGE: **Andy felt badly about the mistake.** As written, this means that Andy's nerve endings aren't functioning properly, so his ability to "feel" is impaired.

FIXED: **He felt bad.**

As I mention in other chapters, fiction writers may use incorrect grammar quirks to characterize story people. If one character consistently substitutes adjectives for the proper adverbs, as above, readers can tell who's talking even if you don't include a dialogue tag (such as *Engelbert said*).

Differentiating adjectives and adverbs often dictates when to use commas too. Will your intended word modify a noun, an adjective, or an adverb? Consider the phrase *ridiculously careless*:

WRITER NOT PAYING ATTENTION: **ridiculously, careless mistakes.**

CONSCIENTIOUS WRITER: **ridiculously careless mistakes.** No need for a comma between an adverb and the adjective (or adverb or verb) it modifies.

But use a comma between two consecutive adjectives describing the same noun.

WRITER NOT PAYING ATTENTION: **ridiculous careless mistakes.**

CONSCIENTIOUS WRITER: **ridiculous, careless mistakes.**

Avoiding Other Errors

Because we tend to misuse them in everyday, casual conversation, adverbs such as *hopefully*, *thankfully*, and *gratefully* can often muddle our writing. Most often they become misplaced or dangling modifiers. (See chapter 11.) Consider the following examples.

> CLUELESS WRITER: My manuscript-revision efforts were hopefully sufficient to earn a publishing contract. (My efforts weren't exhibiting hopefulness. I was.)
> CAREFUL WRITER: My manuscript-revision efforts were, I hoped, sufficient.
>   Or: I hoped my manuscript-revision efforts were sufficient.

Consider this example as well.

> SLOPPY WRITER: Thankfully, our forefathers included a separation of powers in the Constitution. Who is being thankful here? Although our founding fathers may have made that monumental decision with thankful hearts, this isn't generally what's meant when writers use this kind of construction.
> WHAT THE WRITER PROBABLY MEANT: We can be thankful our forefathers included . . .

Some style manuals and dictionaries now allow the casual use of such adverbs, but you can avoid miscommunication by being one of the conscientious writers.

Putting an Adverb in Its Place

Adverbs—potentially helpful little parts of speech—can come before or after the words they modify. Placement often depends on emphasis, readability, or simply your style.

> BEFORE: He grudgingly gave in.
> AFTER: He gave in grudgingly.

But beware of possibly confusing the reader. For instance, in the "before" example— *He grudgingly gave in*—the placement before the word *in* makes the sentence read awkwardly. We're ready for an object of that preposition. He gave in lieu of going? He gave in embarrassment?

See the possibility for confusion?

Avoiding Overuse of Adverbs

As helpful and effective as adverbs can be, using too many can be like spilling the whole salt shaker into your soup. Ruthlessly eliminate any unnecessary adverbs.

You probably know that many adverbs end in the suffix *-ly*: *gracefully, softly, easily, lovingly, privately, roughly, sincerely, usually, secretly, angrily, visually, gratefully*. Start with those. Examine each to determine whether you need it.

Others hide more easily, requiring extra diligence to uproot them. Watch particularly for qualifiers and intensifiers.

Using Qualifiers/Intensifiers Sparingly

Very and *really* are the two intensifiers (words that emphasize and, well, intensify) that I use far too often, especially in my first drafts. I know from my many years of editing both books and magazine articles that I'm not alone.

If I write that the person I'm featuring in a profile or a fiction story was "really sad," I'm being lazy. I should find a stronger adverb to describe his sadness. Did he feel depressed, dejected, or despondent—maybe even suicidal? Readers care. They want to really feel those emotions with that person.

Sometimes we need more than a one-word substitution. For me to write simply that my character (a father) was *very* late to his son's first varsity football game means little. But readers learn much more if I say the dad didn't arrive until the end of the third quarter—with a flask of Scotch in his sport-coat pocket.

Similarly, the adverb *just* is another nemesis in my writing. (See more about qualifiers in chapter 13.)

So, as we try to write with excellence, let's end this chapter by referring back to the opening illustration—as all conscientiously inclined writers try to do with the conclusions of their articles and book chapters. Go to the stadium, my writer friends. Find the adverbs you need—but only those you *need*, not every single one that looks attractive to you. To paraphrase the *Schoolhouse Rock!* song, we need to learn 'em and use 'em judiciously; they're free—indubitably.

Chapter 6 Exercise

Do the following exercises to hone your use—and misuse—of adverbs. If you are in a critique group, compare and discuss your answers.

1. Read through this chapter again; and circle, highlight, or write on another piece of paper all the adverbs you find. (Don't try to figure out adverbial phrases at this point, only single words.) Which ones are unnecessary? Find stronger verbs or more precise adjectives or adverbs to replace the unnecessary ones.

2. Note whether the adverbs appeared before or after the words they modify. The next time you're revising a manuscript, notice which position you tend to use more often. When would rewriting change the emphasis?

3. Question to ponder on your own or discuss with your writers group: Are adverbs truly free? Or what might they cost if used inappropriately?

References

Adverbs
>The Chicago Manual of Style, Sixteenth Edition: 5.153–68
>The Associated Press Stylebook: See Adverbs
>Publication Manual of the American Psychological Association, Sixth Edition: 3.21

Are Your Adjectives on Steroids— or Just Obnoxious?

In a Charles M. Schultz *Peanuts* cartoon strip, Sally's working on her homework, and she describes the sun setting "as red as a banana." Funny! But probably not a delight to her teacher.

Then there's the classic English novelist G. K. Chesterton's description of a "strange sunset" in the first chapter of his novel *The Man Who Was Thursday*:

> All the heaven seemed covered with a quite vivid and palpable plumage; you could only say that the sky was full of feathers, and of feathers that almost brushed the face. Across the great part of the dome they were grey, with the strangest tints of violet and mauve and an unnatural pink or pale green; but towards the west the whole grew *past description* . . ."[1] (emphasis added).

Past description? Chesterton cranks out another eight or nine lines of description that many of *today's* readers wouldn't slog through!

In chapter 40 I talk about ways good writing can help readers "experience" the scene. And I caution against purple prose—overwriting. Maybe purple is in the eye of the beholder. Some readers may find Chesterton quite visual and charming. I respect his writing, but for me this description registers as deep purple. The long descriptions and long sentences make it difficult to read. Some readers may quit reading.

Whether your adjectives are on dangerous steroids or just plain obnoxious, you'll keep readers engaged if you purposefully rein them in. Often less is more. In describing a sunset, writer Bill Barker turns an adjective (*copperplated*) into a verb (giving the sun something to do) and writes of "an evening sun copperplating the scenery."[2] Less is more!

Defining Moments

What's the difference between adjectives and adverbs?

Adjectives modify nouns. See the adjectives italicized in the following sentence:

The *arrogant* writer filled *his* manuscript with *obnoxious* adjectives.

Adverbs modify verbs, adjectives, and other adverbs. Often they end in *-ly*, but sometimes they don't. See them underlined in this sentence:

The <u>exceedingly</u> *arrogant* writer filled *his* <u>ponderously</u> *long* manuscript with <u>very</u> *obnoxious* adjectives.

For more on adverbs, see chapter 6, but I'll focus on adjectives here—and a more precise, judicious use of them.

Over the Top

Adjectives play an important descriptive role. But, as I discussed in chapter 2, it's better to use a more precise noun than to bog down a weaker one with unnecessary adjectives and adverbs—e.g., a *Lamborghini*, not *a very expensive car*.

Likewise, it's even more effective to use the most precise adjective possible than to pile one on top of another. Instead of telling us Lois made a sandwich of ham and cheese dipped in egg and then fried and topped with currant jelly, tell us she made a Monte Cristo. Greater economy of words. Here's another example:

BOGGED DOWN: the deep-bluish-purple blanket

MORE PRECISE: the indigo blanket

Take that a step further. Was the blanket a quilt, a comforter, a throw, a coverlet, or a duvet?

Reining in your adjectives can save many words in your editor-assigned word count—words you can use to develop your point better. Stringing together a lot of adjectives can actually weaken their impact.

Commas and Hyphens

If you truly need a string of adjectives, use no more than necessary. Then use commas to separate them: the *lush, shaded* lawn.

In a series of three or more elements sporting a conjunction (*and / or / nor*), many book and magazine editors follow *CMoS 16*'s recommendation to use what's called a "serial comma":

Viola's grandbaby looked so cute, soft, and cuddly.

Note the comma placement after *soft*.

Some book and magazine editors omit the last comma. So study your target publication so well that you notice these nuances.

If we use a conjunction with each item in the list, we don't need commas:

INCORRECT: **Bodie didn't know whether to laugh, or cry, or shout "Amen!"**
CORRECT: **Bodie didn't know whether to laugh or cry or shout "Amen!"**

On the other hand, we use hyphens to join together two or more adjectives (not adverbs) that no man should put asunder.

In an example above, I used the term *deep-bluish-purple* as an adjective to modify the noun *blanket*. Not highly literary writing. *Indigo* communicates better. But hyphenation alerts readers that all those words are part of the color.

Note the difference between a *deep, red box*, for instance, and a *deep-red box*: deep [size], red [color] box; deep-red [darker color] box.

See more on this topic in chapter 20.

Funny but Wrong

On June 6, 2015, the East Oregonian newspaper ran the following headline about Oakland Athletics relief pitcher Pat Venditte: "Amphibious Pitcher Makes Debut." *Amphibious* is a perfectly good adjective. But it's the wrong one. We can assume Venditte is *ambidextrous* rather than capable of pitching both underwater and on the baseball diamond.

We want to avoid a similar misuse or distortion of words called *malapropisms*. We raid French vocabulary for *malapropism* (*mal à propos*—inappropriate, the opposite of *à propos*—appropriate). Eighteenth-century playwright Richard Brinsley Sheridan created a comedic character called Mrs. Malaprop, who frequently used words sounding similar to her intent but meaning something quite different: *reprehend* instead of *apprehend*, *oracular* instead of *vernacular*, and *illiterate him quite from your memory* instead of *obliterate him*.

Bottom line: Watch for malapropisms and other misused words. And never submit anything to an editor that hasn't been critiqued or reviewed by at least one other person. We all need others' objective eyes to prevent literary embarrassment.

The Teeniest Adjectives

In English we call the words *the*, *a*, and *an* "articles." We might call them *specialized* adjectives. They, too, modify nouns.

1. Definite versus indefinite:

DEFINITE ARTICLE: *the*
INDEFINITE ARTICLES: *a, an*

Most writers don't have trouble choosing between the two categories, but sometimes we get careless. Is Rita *the* best pickleball player in the world? *One of the* best pickleball players in the world? Or simply *a* good pickleball player?

Be precise. Don't overstate the truth. Preserve important differences.

2. *A* versus *an*. Generally, stick a solitary *a* before words beginning with a consonant sound, including *y* and *w* (*a* youngster, *a* pineapple). Use *an* before words beginning with a vowel sound (*an* icy igloo).

A word beginning with *h* can be a problem child, though. Many of us would correctly write about "*an* honorary degree" because the *h* is silent, giving us a vowel sound at the beginning. But we may have heard that other *h* words require the article *an*:

> PROBLEM CHILD: We had an horrific ordeal staying at a hotel—an historic hotel— because we learned the manager was an habitual liar.

Grammar guru Bryan A. Garner writes, "Such wordings . . . strike readers and listeners as affectations in need of editing."[3]

Exceptions: In cockney dialect (remember, a little goes a long way), your character may say he's staying at *an* 'otel managed by *an* 'abitual liar. Or a character putting on airs may embrace that hoity-toity affectation.

Otherwise, feel free to stay at *a* historic hotel and pray for *an* honest manager.

Comparative Cautions

With descriptive adjectives of comparison, beware of accidental "spillage." If you're using more than one adjective to describe something, the comparative and superlative words (*more/most, less/least*) "spill over" to the other descriptions.

> CAUTIONARY: Janae was more exciting and funnier than the other comics at the competition.

Teach your brain to raise a red flag when you write words such as *more*. In the above sentence, *more*, the first adjective, spills over onto the ones following it. In essence, you're saying Janae was more exciting and *more funnier* . . .

But since *funnier* is already a comparative word, we don't want to pile another on top. So simply reverse the order of the adjectives:

> LOWER THE RED FLAG: Janae was funnier and more exciting than the other comics at the competition.

Problem solved.

Adjectives with *As* and *Than*

While the content below is truthful, which of the sentences is grammatically correct?

> CORRECT? My husband is not as competitive as I.
> CORRECT? He's not as competitive as me.

And what if we put similar comparisons in third person?

> CORRECT? The other team was not as whiny as us [Or should it be *we*?].

Here's a quick fix: Add a verb afterward.

CORRECT: **My husband is not as competitive as I [am].**
CORRECT: **The other team was not as whiny as we [were].**

Retrain your brain to write *as* comparisons correctly by at least mentally tacking the appropriate verb on afterward. Your editors will be *as pleased as I*.

I should note here that *The Chicago Manual of Style* says that traditional grammarians, in regard to formal writing, prefer ending such phrases in the nominative case (*I, we, they*), while the objective case (*me, us, them*) "represents common usage."

In the end, we can communicate so much with adjectives if we use them judiciously and correctly. In the last frame of the *Peanuts* cartoon, after Sally's red-banana fiasco, she gives us a great kicker: "Makes you appreciate the beauty of the written word, doesn't it?"

Chapter 7 Quiz

Correct any errors you find in the sentences below based on the principles in this chapter, and substitute more precise words where necessary. Put a C beside any sentences that are correct.

_____ 1. Phillippa is having a humongous-kids sale.

_____ 2. My grandkids say I'm goofier than them.

_____ 3. "Now let us precede," Madeline said.

_____ 4. The Civil War reenactors commemorated an historic battle.

_____ 5. Because Steve himself was left handed, he often joked about left-handed compliments.

_____ 6. When Kirk walked in, sporting a row of stiff, red hair down the middle of his head with everything else shaved away, I almost swallowed my bubblegum.

_____ 7. The sequel was less impressive and shorter than the original novel.

_____ 8. Nathan couldn't wait to get to the fair to chow down on cotton candy, and mini donuts, and fried cheese curds, and deep-fried pickles on a stick.

_____ 9. Hecklers shouted down the mousy well intentioned political candidate.

_____ 10. If only Tony had paid more attention to grammar, punctuation and style!

Additional Exercise

Find a descriptive passive in your writing (or in a book you're reading) that you now identify as "over-the-top," or "purple," prose. Rewrite to follow the advice you've received in this chapter: write to communicate, not to impress.

References

Adjectives versus Adverbs
   The Chicago Manual of Style, Sixteenth Edition: 5.156
   Publication Manual of the American Psychological Association, Sixth Edition: 3.21

Serial Commas and Hyphens
   The Chicago Manual of Style, Sixteenth Edition: 6.18, 7.77, 7.85
   The Christian Writer's Manual of Style, Fourth Edition: pp. 132–33; 201
   MLA Handbook for Writers of Research Papers, Seventh Edition: 3.2.2b
   Publication Manual of the American Psychological Association, Sixth Edition: 3.04,
      4.03, 4.13

Malapropisms
   The Chicago Manual of Style, Sixteenth Edition: 5.216, 5.220

Definite and Indefinite Articles
   The Chicago Manual of Style, Sixteenth Edition: 5.68–70, 7.44

Comparative Words
   The Chicago Manual of Style, Sixteenth Edition: 5.84, 5.86–87, 5.160, 6.42

Phrases Using "as" and "than"
   The Chicago Manual of Style, Sixteenth Edition: 5.79–81, 5.201

> [God] is the one who has helped us tell others about
> his new agreement to save them. We do not tell them
> that they must obey every law of God or die; but we tell
> them there is life for them from the Holy Spirit.
> —2 CORINTHIANS 3:6 (TLB)

Wrangling Pronouns
Matching Subjects and Pronouns

8

A cowboy walks into a saloon and says, "The varmint what tied their horse out front of Miller's Store best be moseyin' along. That fool horse jes' kicked Miller in the head."

Okay, I'll never make it as a joke-book author, and I'm no competition for Louis L'Amour. But the opening sentence illustrates another common grammar battleground: pronoun-antecedent disagreement. As they say in Westerns, "Them's fightin' words!"

Pronouns and Antecedents

In chapter 3, I highlighted the importance of subject-verb agreement. Here I'm emphasizing the importance of pronoun-antecedent agreement. Careful writers ensure their pronouns and antecedents agree with one another in number (singular/plural), gender (male/female/neutral), and person (first/second/third).

Liberating some terminology from the cobwebs of our "little grey cells," we recall that a pronoun (such as *I, me, he, him, she, her, it, they, them*) stands in for a noun (person, place, thing). The noun the pronoun refers to is called the antecedent.

The word *antecedent* comes from *antecede*, synonymous with *precede*. So look for the nearest noun preceding the pronoun. The pronoun should agree with that noun.

Because careless speech patterns easily sneak into writing, even experienced writers sometimes don't see the wrangling pronouns and antecedents in their work. So watch for the following agreements.

Agreeing in Number

In the cowboy's warning above, *their* (plural pronoun) points back to *varmint* (singular noun). That makes *varmint* the antecedent.

If you put a singular antecedent and plural pronoun together in a sentence, you get a couple of gunslingers squaring off for a showdown. So choose the right pronoun to avoid bloodshed in the streets.

Note that recent changes allow this conflict to exist in informal writing. Unfortunately, even the widely used 2011 NIV Bible has accommodated this usage (e.g., "Each person [singular] is tempted when they [plural] are dragged away by their [plural] own evil desire and enticed" (James 1:14).

To be clear, *CMoS 16* still encourages agreement in formal writing—our kind of writing—writing for publication. And once again I encourage writers to uphold this standard.

Dialogue may occasionally employ grammatical errors for characterization, but otherwise we promote peace between pronouns and antecedents.

> CORRECT: **The varmint that tethered his horse....** (We'll assume that in the old Wild West the cowboy didn't find any ladies in the saloon, so the masculine pronoun *his* should work.)

In each of the following three examples, identify the pronoun and antecedent. Then decide whether we have agreement or a potential gunfight at the O.K. Corral.

> 1. **A person who wants to make a good impression in a job interview should teach the butterflies in their stomach an elegant waltz.**
> 2. **Peter and Paul preached their gospel message with power.**
> 3. **When a writer has been in the business a long time, they may get careless with grammar, punctuation, and style.**

Example #1: This sentence is straightforward.
  Pronoun: *their* (plural)
  Antecedent: *person* (singular)
  AGREEMENT? No.
  CONFLICT RESOLUTION: Change *A person who wants* to *People who want.*

Example #2: A little trickier. For this exercise, we assume Peter and Paul were preaching the same gospel message.
  Pronoun: *their* (plural)
  Antecedent: *Peter and Paul* (compound subject). Using *and* designates plural.
    AGREEMENT? Yes. But if we want to emphasize the differences in their messages, we could write the sentence like this: *Peter and Paul each tailored his message to a particular audience.*

Example #3:
  Pronoun: *they*
  Antecedent: *writer*
    AGREEMENT? No. The noun *writer* (singular) conflicts with the pronoun *they* (plural).
    CONFLICT RESOLUTION: We have options. See the following:

In the days before the PC Language Police landed from some galaxy far, far away, we could change *they* to *he*: *he may get careless.* That gives us a singular noun (*writer*) and a singular pronoun (*he*).

But today's publishers want to make sure we always give equal blame or credit to both sexes. (See chapter 43.) Put more sensitively, excellent writers aim for gender inclusivity to avoid offense—a good scriptural principle. Here's one option:

> CORRECT: **When a writer has been in the business a long time, he or she may get careless.**

But that's cumbersome. So, whenever possible, switch to a plural noun.

> BETTER: **When writers have been in the business a long time, they may get careless.**

What about those pesky collective nouns? When a noun refers collectively to a group, such as an organization, band, or team (collective noun), the appropriate pronoun depends on the sense in which we're using the noun. If the group is acting as one, use a singular pronoun. If acting as individual members, use a plural pronoun.

> EXAMPLE: The word *jury* is a collective noun. Which of the pronouns referring to that antecedent in the following two sentences is correct?

> **The jury announced *its/their* unanimous verdict.**
> **The jury berated *itself/themselves* for missing the deceit beneath the defendant's charm.**

In the first sentence, the word *unanimous* means the jury members are acting as one, so we need the singular *its.* In the second sentence, we may assume all the jury members, individually, felt stupid for letting the defendant slip wool blinders on their eyes. Use the plural *themselves.*

Agreeing in Gender

Confusion in pronoun gender occurs less often. Even if we read *Sammy threw a fit that her editor dared to change a word in her manuscript,* our minds quickly switch gears. We understand that Sammy's parents may have named their daughter Samantha, never suspecting a nickname could land her in a boys' gym class.

But potential pitfalls still exist. The following sentence creates conflict in both number and gender:

> INCORRECT: **As soon as anyone has finished their exam, they may leave.**
> CORRECT: If the students involved attend an all-girls school, we could write it this way: **As soon as anyone** [singular] **has finished her** [singular] **exam, she** [singular] **may leave.**
> BETTER: **As soon as students finish their exams, they may leave.**

Beware of switching gender too. Sometimes, especially when referring to animals or inanimate objects treated like humans, writers switch back and forth from a gender-neutral *it* to a masculine *he* or feminine *she.*

INCORRECT: **Nick maintained his yacht** [antecedent] **in pristine condition, polishing her** [feminine pronoun] **brass railings and waxing its** [neutral pronoun] **newly painted deck.**

How to correct it: Use *her* or *its* in both instances.

Another potential problem:

The lion stood on his hind legs and let out its fiercest roar.

How to correct it: Use *his* or *its* in both places.

Agreeing in Person

Unfortunately, we might occasionally hear something like this from a supposedly college-educated, native English-speaking teacher:

As soon as anyone has finished their exam, you may leave.

Ouch! Arrest those fightin' words: *their*, third person; and *you*, second person. Both refer to *anyone*, third person. The caveats above notwithstanding, please be a good role model. Don't leave errors like these in a manuscript you want to sell!

CORRECT: **When you have finished your exam, you may leave** [consistent second person].

ALSO CORRECT: **The teacher told the students that as soon as they finished their exam, they could leave** [consistent third person].

Compound subjects (connected by *and, or,* or *nor*) may compound the likelihood of errors.

INCORRECT: **Neither Jeanette nor Debbie found suitable submissions from their writers.**

The antecedent for the pronoun *their* is *neither*. And *neither/nor* and *either/or* call for a singular pronoun—in this case, the feminine *her*.

CORRECT: **Neither Jeanette nor Debbie found suitable submissions from her writers.**

But what if we're discussing a male editor and a female editor? Though it might sound right to use the plural to accommodate the masculine and feminine antecedents, don't do it.

INCORRECT: **Neither Jim nor Jeanette found suitable submissions from their writers.**

CORRECT BUT AWKWARD: **Neither Jim nor Jeanette found suitable submissions from his or her writers.**

How to correct it: Rewrite the sentence completely: **Jim and Jeanette grew frustrated that they couldn't find suitable submissions from their writers.**

Now the antecedent (*Jim and Jeanette*) is a compound subject connected with *and*. So we can use the plural pronoun *they*.

Mistaken Identities

Sometimes we create a potential mistaken identity by not clarifying a pronoun's antecedent.

> AMBIGUOUS: **Lin told Joyce that if she went past *her* deadline, *she* was dead.**

To whom do each of the italicized pronouns refer? Is Lin worried about her own deadline or Joyce's?

> CLARIFIED: **Though a gracious, magnanimous, benevolent editor, Lin warned Joyce to submit her manuscript on time.**

MIAs

In some cases, antecedents are missing in action.

> MIA: **At the writer's conference, they tore my manuscript to shreds. But they taught me a lot.**

To whom does the word *they* refer? We don't know.

> CLARIFIED: **At the writer's conference, the editors who critiqued my manuscript tore it to shreds. But they taught me a lot.**

Writers who want to produce professional-quality material would do well to scrutinize their longer sentences, in particular, for conflicts in number, gender, and person. The greater the distance between a pronoun and its antecedent, the greater the possibility of error. So strip away the intervening words, and make sure your pronouns and antecedents don't become "fightin' words."

Chapter 8 Quiz

Remember: Excellent writers ensure that their pronouns and antecedents agree with one another in number (singular/plural), gender (male/female/neutral), and person (first/second/third). Revise to bring "agreement" in the following sentences. Mark any correct sentences with a C.

_____ 1. Would everyone who has not passed driver's ed please get out of their cars right now and stay off the roads?

_____ 2. After I spent seven hours in the maternity ward, they told me my contractions weren't strong enough to bring a peanut, much less a baby, into this world.

_____ 3. Mr. Birchfield actually said that if one of his students wanted a brown-noser, extra-credit assignment, he or she should ask him.

_____ 4. Reluctantly, Cherise and her best friend told their parents about their bad grades.

_____ 5. The drake came at us as if it thought we were threatening its ducklings.

_____ 6. The audience took their cues to laugh and applaud from the cards the stage manager held up.

_____ 7. None of the magicians at the guys-only party, no matter how talented they were, could produce a rabbit out of their shoe.

_____ 8. A person who wants to stand out in a crowd of experienced writers should make sure their manuscripts are as lean and clean as possible before submitting.

_____ 9. Tinkerbell and Clarabell each had their own widely differing rise-to-stardom stories.

_____ 10. Each of the skydivers had a backpack, but only one of them had a parachute.

References

Pronouns and Antecedents
> The Chicago Manual of Style, Sixteenth Edition: 5.26–29
> Publication Manual of the American Psychological Association, Sixth Edition: 3.20

Pronoun Agreement
> The Chicago Manual of Style, Sixteenth Edition: 5.30–34

The "Case" of the Questionable Pronoun

Pronoun Case

9

One of my all-time favorite movies is *The Private Eyes*, in which two bumbling detectives, played by Don Knotts and Tim Conway, investigate a double homicide at a gigantic English estate, Morley Manor. The murders of Lord and Lady Morley seem only the beginning, however.

One by one, the manor's staff meet their demise. Every time Knotts and Conway find a body, they also find a four-line clue in rhyming couplets. But the last line uses a limping rhythm and a synonym for the obvious rhyme. For example, a line that should complete the rhyme with the words *keep in touch* ends with *keep in constant contact with each other*. It's a delightful comedic device.

The last clue the detectives find, purportedly from the murderous ghost of Lord Morley, ends with this ungrammatical construction:

"I want Phyllis to come to my chamber and see
Who was the one who murdered Lady Morley and myself."

Careful writers, too, must solve a mystery: when to use such pronouns as *me*, *myself*, and *I*, as well as less self-centered ones.

Pronounicide

Many of us write "by ear," not necessarily what's grammatically correct. But if we don't pay attention to proper grammar, we're giving editors an easy excuse to reject our work.

One mom entered into a sparring match with her daughters over "pronounicide." Teenybopper Seventh-Grader said, "Chloe invited Megan and I to her party."

Stepping into her role of at-home-fortifier-of-school-grammar-lessons, Mom said, "Megan and *me*."

A younger sister, Little Miss Third-Grader, who'd been daydreaming during that grammar unit, piped up: "No, Megan and *I*."

At this point, Mom told her to imagine that Megan disappeared from the sentence. "Would you say, 'Chloe invited *I* to her party'?"

"Oh," replied Little Miss.

Pronouns can be tricky—especially when incorrect usage assaults us everywhere. Aside from *The Private Eyes'* humor value, what's the proper use of *myself* and other personal pronouns?

A "Case" Study

A little instruction and review can give us more confidence in both conversation and the manuscripts we submit. The key to the mother-daughter teachable moment above is the "case" of the pronoun.

Again, old-fashioned sentence diagramming can help. Those fortunate enough to learn diagramming in school and readers paying attention in an earlier chapter may remember we can draw a horizontal line as the spine for the bare bones of a sentence. To the left is the subject, generally the doer.

Drawing a short perpendicular line through the horizontal line, we place the verb to the right of that. A shorter vertical line above the horizontal line creates a little gate beyond which lies the direct object (the thing or person who answers questions about *what* or *whom*):

| subject | verb | direct object |

The bare bones of what the daughter should have said looks like this:

| Chloe (or she) | invited | me |

The correct pronoun for any given situation depends on its place and function in the sentence.

- Subjective[1] case is for subjects of sentences. If we substitute a pronoun for *Chloe*, we would use *she*, a subjective-case pronoun because *Chloe* is the subject (the star or doer) of the sentence.
- Objective case is for direct objects, indirect objects, and objects of prepositions.

Direct objects: Because we have a pronoun in the place of the direct object, it needs to be an objective-case pronoun. The word *me* is the object of the verb *invite*.

Objects of prepositions: The prepositional phrase *to* [preposition] *the party* [object of the preposition] dangles beneath *invited*, like a Christmas stocking from a mantle, because it refers to, or modifies, that verb:

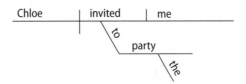

Indirect objects: What if the sentence reads like this? *Chloe gave me an invitation.*

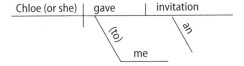

An indirect object often substitutes for a prepositional phrase using the preposition *to: Chloe gave to me an invitation.* In both instances we use the objective-case pronoun, *me.*

This may seem "elementary, my dear Watson." But reminding ourselves of the basics can help when we get into more complicated situations.

A Case of Whom

When enough people speak and write ungrammatically, those who follow older grammar styles can sound uppity.

> EXAMPLE, GRAMMATICALLY CORRECT: **"This gift is for whom?"**

Because that sentence sounds stilted to our modern ears, we might say, colloquially, *"Who's this gift for?"* Unless we're writing dialogue for a stuffed-shirt character, such as a stereotypical butler named Jeeves, we'll generally use the colloquial form.

In nonfiction we follow grammar rules more closely. So how can we solve the who/whom mystery? It depends on the case.

One mnemonic device I've used is Hemingway's title *For Whom the Bell Tolls*—not *For Who the Bell Tolls. For whom* is a prepositional phrase. *Whom* is the object of the preposition and, therefore, is in the objective case.

In contrast, we use *who* for the subjective case (e.g., *Who* [subject] *let the dogs out?*).

Here's another device, one I thought I invented until I found it in a grammar book: *whom* ends with *m*—like *him* or *them.* All of those pronouns are in the objective case. So consider these examples.

> INCORRECT: **John gave the secret documents to they.**
> CORRECT: **John gave the secret documents to him/them/whom.**

Who is like *he, she,* and *they*—no *m.* All subjective case.

> INCORRECT: **Whom/Him/Them has/have the most rejection slips?**
> CORRECT: **Who/He/They has/have the most rejection slips?**
> The word *who* is the subject [subjective case].

But here come some complications:

1. **C. S. Lewis,** [who/whom] **James tried to emulate, invented the extraordinary world of Narnia.**
2. **James tried to emulate C. S. Lewis,** [who/whom] **gave us Narnia.**

Investigate these cases:

1. Isolate the words between the commas. Then turn them around: *James tried to emulate whom?* Substitute *him* for *whom,* and you confirm we need the objective case pronoun *whom.*
2. The pronoun *who* is correct here because the clause between the comma and the period functions like a separate sentence. We could substitute *he* (a subjective pronoun): *he gave us Narnia.*

A Case of Self

In grammar, as in our spiritual lives, *self* can cause many problems. Words ending with *self* or *selves* are called compound personal pronouns (*myself, ourselves, yourself, himself, herself, itself, themselves*). We use them two ways:

- Intensive use for emphasis. (No surrounding commas needed.)

  CORRECT: **I myself handed my manuscript to the editor.**

- Reflexive use for the objective case. (For more about these, see chapter 10.)

  CORRECT: **The critique group members berated themselves** [direct object] **for missing the contest deadline.**

  CORRECT: **Amber polished her manuscript but gave herself** [indirect object] **permission** [direct object] **to fail.**

  CORRECT: **Patty studied by** [preposition] **herself.**

  CORRECT: **God drew us to** [preposition] **himself.**

A Case of Possession

Another common error surfaces when a pronoun appears before an *-ing* verb.

INCORRECT: **The editors became frustrated with us turning in manuscripts with so many grammatical errors.**

CLUE: The *-ing* verb functions as a noun—in this instance the object of a preposition: *with.* In grammatical terms, the editors weren't frustrated with *us.* They were frustrated with the submission of *our* shoddy work. So we use a possessive pronoun (*his, her, their, my, our, its*).

CORRECT: **The editors became frustrated with our turning in manuscripts with so many grammatical errors.**

A Case of Mirrors

Sometimes a pronoun mirrors—side by side—the noun it represents. In the following sentences, which pronoun choice in brackets is grammatically correct?

1. [Us/We] **Minnesotans are people of the tundra.**

Because the pronoun *we* mirrors *Minnesotans* (called an appositive), with *Minnesotans* the subject of the sentence, *we* [subjective case] is correct here. (For more about appositives, see chapter 15.)

    2. **The wacky teacher gave [us/we] hooligans a standing ovation.**

Delete the word *hooligans*, and you'll see the word *us* is correct. It's an indirect object.

    Other times, a *to-be* verb links the pronoun to the noun, as if the verb is an equal sign:

    3. **When asked who committed the cherry-tree assassination, George Washington supposedly said, "It was [me/I]."**

Turning the sentence around gives the right answer: *I* was it. Not *me* was it.

A Case of Dialogue

In fiction we can characterize story people with differing speech patterns, using word choice and grammar to distinguish one character from another. For example, there is no such word as *theirselves*—except perhaps in the vocabulary of a redneck.

Case Solved

Using the correct pronoun doesn't have to be a mystery if you think about what "case" you're working with. In the style of *The Private Eyes'* clues, I offer the following:

> Using the right pronoun
> need be a mystery no more;
> if you consider the "case,"
> it's no longer a task that's a burden.

Chapter 9 Quiz

Make corrections wherever necessary. Put a *C* beside any grammatically correct sentences. See answers in appendix A.

_____ 1. The actor, who we all love, disappointed us in that film.

_____ 2. Gratitude motivates we Christian writers to serve God faithfully.

_____ 3. The cosmetology student gave herself a pedicure.

_____ 4. The editor sent form rejection letters to my coauthor and myself.

_____ 5. Debbi, Tammie, and myself met for dinner after the conference.

_____ 6. "This is her," Lily replied into the phone.

_____ 7. Between you and I, I think many writers quit polishing their manuscripts too soon.

_____ 8. Brianna didn't appreciate him teasing her.

_____ 9. The editor, herself, took time to write an encouraging note on the manuscript—very rare!

_____ 10. We know that us parents need to pray fervently for our children.

References

Pronouns
> The Chicago Manual of Style, Sixteenth Edition: 5.26–29

Subjective/Nominative-Case Pronouns
> The Chicago Manual of Style, Sixteenth Edition: 5.48–49

Who/Whom
> The Chicago Manual of Style, Sixteenth Edition: 5.28, 5.52–55, 5.60–63, 5.220
> The Associated Press Stylebook: See Who/Whom
> MLA Handbook for Writers of Research Papers, Seventh Edition: 3.2.2e
> Publication Manual of the American Psychological Association, Sixth Edition: 3.20

Make every effort to add to your faith goodness;
and to goodness, knowledge; and to knowledge, self-control; and
to self-control, *perseverance*; and to *perseverance*, godliness.
—2 PETER 1:5–6 (emphasis added)

The Reflexology of Pronouns
Reflexive Pronouns

10

Have you ever wondered what twisted logic assaults this slightly goofy grammar geek to come up with introductions to any given topic? If you answered yes, the following road map will demonstrate the actual route my mind traveled for this chapter. (If you answered no, bless you for hanging in there with me anyway. Maybe you'll find entertainment value along with pointers for your writing.)

1. Note to self: I see and hear much misuse of what we call reflexive pronouns: *himself, herself, themselves, ourselves, itself, myself.* Need to do a chapter about it.

2. Look for a way to introduce this potential yawner of a topic in such a way that, though it may not make the editor fall off the chair, laughing, it may at least bring a smile. If I can amuse an editor, perhaps my readers will find this entertaining too—or at least keep reading.

3. Try word association for *reflex* and *reflexive*: (a) Acid reflex? No, that's *reflux.* And definitely not funny. (b) The doctor's little hammer designed to see if your knee nerves work? No, slapstick doesn't work well on paper. (c) Reflexology? Well, what is that—exactly?

4. Check the dictionary: "**noun:** (1) the study and interpretation of behavior in terms of simple and complex reflexes. (2) massage of the hands or feet based on the belief that pressure applied to specific points on these extremities benefits other parts of the body."

5. Go for it! Coin new terminology: The reflexology of pronouns is the study of reflexive pronouns, learning how to massage them skillfully so they can benefit other parts of your writing (and avoid driving editors crazy).

Though some of the material here is a review of points covered in chapter 8, review can't hurt us, right? Then we'll go into more detail regarding reflexive pronouns.

Getting Past Problematic Use

One way of looking at reflexive pronouns is that they indicate a reflexive (knee-jerk) reaction, reflecting back to something else.

A common error surfaces when a writer or speaker substitutes the reflexive pronoun *myself* for the simple personal pronoun *me*.

> OOPS: **John said, "The editor chided my coauthor and myself for misusing reflexive pronouns all over the place."**
>
> OOPS AVERTED: **John said, "The editor chided my coauthor and me for misusing reflexive pronouns all over the place."**

Some people grow up hearing poor grammar examples such as this and may not identify them as incorrect. Others may think using the word *myself* in this situation sounds more humble—perhaps—wink, wink—because it puts *self* last. But using *myself* here actually makes such people sound less fluent in the English language.

The editor was not chiding only some disembodied "self" of John or his co-author. Let's face it: the editor was chiding every part of these fellows—in total—for committing that error.

So how do we know when to use reflexive pronouns?

To be precise, some grammarians create a broad category called "compound pronouns" (a personal pronoun + *self* [*yourself*, *himself*, et al.]), then divide that into two subcategories:

- *reflexive pronouns*
- *intensive pronouns*

Other grammarians lump all these together, giving special attention to what are called *intensives*. That's what I'll do here.

Getting Reflexives Right

Most of the legitimate uses of reflexive pronouns come naturally. They sound right if our ears are tuned correctly. Here are some examples:

1. We use a reflexive pronoun when the subject of a sentence and its direct or indirect object are the same thing. (See chapter 9.)

Consider these examples:

> **Betsey gave herself a pat on the back.**
> **She gave herself a pat on the back.**

The pronoun (*her/herself*) refers to the subject of the sentence, Betsey—the same person/thing. And *She* and *herself* refer to the same person. That construction sounds natural to most people.

Few people would (incorrectly) write this: *Betsey gave her a pat on the back.* That wording implies that Betsey was congratulating some other *her*, another female. But if that were the case, the writer would need to substitute the other person's name to avoid confusion:

Betsey gave Karen a pat on the back.

Notice the difference in this example:

CORRECT: **Betsey's colleague played a practical joke on** *her* [meaning *Betsey*].

In this instance, the colleague, not Betsey, is the subject of the sentence. And *her* refers to Betsey, so they are not the same entity. The use of a reflexive pronoun, as follows, would create a physical impossibility, I believe: *Betsey's colleague played a practical joke on herself.*

Here's another example:

ADMIRABLE BUT GRAMMATICALLY INFERIOR: **We prayed that, through the tragedy, God would bring people to him.**

GOD-HONORING AND GRAMMATICAL: **We prayed that, through the tragedy, God would bring people to himself.**

2. We use a reflexive pronoun to indicate that the subject of the sentence accomplished something without assistance. It's natural (though somewhat unlikely, to be truthful, these days) to write this: *The celebrity wrote the book by himself.* It's unnatural (and ungrammatical) to write this: *The celebrity wrote the book by him.*

On another note, *The Writer's Digest Grammar Desk Reference* makes one notable, broader application, stating that both of the following sentences are correct:

I ended up with red paint all over myself.

I ended up with red paint all over me.[1]

I hope that doesn't confuse the matter but rather shows there's some wiggle room with these guidelines.

Once again, we should note that, in fiction, grammatical quirks can provide great character traits, making dialogue more distinctive. Let one character consistently misuse reflexive pronouns, and if you throw in the always improper use of a *his-self* now and then, your character might be uneducated.

Getting Intensives Right

As the term suggests, an intensive pronoun is a compound pronoun (pronoun + *self*) that intensifies the emphasis.

CORRECT: **I myself saw the accident.**

SIMILAR, ALSO CORRECT: **I saw the accident myself.**

The use of *myself* here not only provides emphasis but also eliminates any potential misunderstanding that I only heard about the crash instead of witnessing it in person. So an intensive pronoun emphasizes and intensifies as it modifies the subject.

Here's another way of thinking about intensive pronouns. Try inserting the word *by* in front of the intensive—e.g., *The clowns* [by] *themselves ran the show*. As you read the correct examples below, insert—in your mind—the word *by* in front of the italicized intensive pronoun:

> CORRECT: **The data *itself* proves the point.**
> CORRECT: **The woman *herself* admitted she was a lousy cook.**
> CORRECT: **Even a judge *himself* isn't above the law.**

As with many other elements in grammar (e.g., exclamation points and italics for emphasis), overuse weakens impact. So beware of using so many intensive pronouns that readers lose confidence in what you imply needs to be emphasized.

Getting the Punctuation Right

Regardless of how many times you may have seen otherwise, we don't need commas around intensives to set them apart.

> INCORRECT: **I, myself, am technoignorant.** (I made up that word.)
> CORRECT: **I myself am technoignorant.**

It's true we often pause briefly before and after reading the intensive pronoun, and that action can indicate the need for a comma. But in this case, resist the temptation. Put the commas back in your toolbox, and save them for a more appropriate time.

So, now, though you're probably tired of *self*-centered talk while romping through this treatise on the reflexology of pronouns, I hope you yourself will use reflexive pronouns and intensive pronouns more confidently to help editors themselves better fulfill their callings.

Chapter 10 Quiz

Correct any errors in the sentences below. Put a C in front of any that are correct. If you belong to a critique group, discuss these exercises, explaining why you answered as you did. See answers in appendix A.

_____ 1. Sally divided the work between Melanie and she.

_____ 2. Jesus, himself, promised that he would be with his followers forever.

_____ 3. The books of the Bible will never contradict itself.

_____ 4. The people of Israel themselves saw God do miraculous things during their wilderness wanderings.

_____ 5. The children cleaned their rooms by themselves without being asked.

_____ 6. The engine of the futuristic car started itself.

_____ 7. My mom divided her vintage baseball cards between my brother and myself.

_____ 8. Allyson's carpentry project left her with sawdust all over her.

_____ 9. The pastor didn't want to call attention to him.

_____ 10. After her bike-a-thon Ann-Margret treated herself to a spa retreat.

References

Intensive/Reflexive Pronouns
   The Chicago Manual of Style, Sixteenth Edition: 5.49

Where'd I Misplace That Modifier?   11

"You know you're old when . . ." Those jokes used to make me laugh. Now they contribute to my self-diagnosis of premature senility.

For instance, one day I raided my filing cabinet for the red folder that contained my notes for a four-part writing class I was scheduled to teach. I started reviewing the file, but interruptions caused me to set it aside next to the recliner in the living room. Then company came, and I put the red folder somewhere in my office. Then other deadlines crowded in. Then the tyranny of the urgent hit hard. And the red folder burrowed deep.

About a week before the conference, I went on safari in the jungle that is my office. A red folder shouldn't be hard to find even in a jungle.

I explored the mountains of papers and folders on my desk. Hacked a trail through the stacks on the floor. Rechecked my filing cabinet in case I had, in an uncharacteristic moment of neatness, put it away. But the folder was winning this game of hide-and-seek.

Having originally created those notes two computers and a different word-processing program ago, I had to recreate them from scratch.

Expeditions to find misplaced items waste time and produce frustration. And, to bring us to the topic of this chapter, we inflict the same maladies on our readers when we misplace modifiers in our writing—or otherwise treat modifiers unfairly.

Modifiers' Roles

Think of modifiers in architectural terms: A traditional A-frame house looks like the capital letter *A*, usually with loft bedrooms. A modified A-frame adds onto the *A* shape various things such as main-level rooms, decks, and garages. Architects change and/or enhance the original form. That's what modifiers do in our writing. They change or enhance other words.

Types of Modifiers

The most common modifiers are adjectives and adverbs. Adjectives modify nouns. They alter or add specificity—*semisweet* chocolate, *inappropriate* behavior, or *sleep-inducing* manuscripts. Adverbs modify verbs, adjectives, and other adverbs, changing them or making them more specific. Adverbs often end in the letters *ly*. (See chapters 6 and 7.)

Here are some examples:

ADVERB MODIFYING A VERB: **The absentminded writing instructor painstakingly** [adverb] **recreated** [verb] **her notes.**

ADVERB MODIFYING AN ADVERB: **The absentminded writing instructor very** [adverb] **painstakingly** [adverb] **recreated** [verb] **her notes.**

ADVERB MODIFYING AN ADJECTIVE: **The absentminded writing instructor painstakingly recreated her inexplicably** [adverb] **misplaced** [adjective] **notes.**

When entire phrases function in the roles of adjectives or adverbs, we run the risk of confusing and frustrating readers.

Misplaced Modifiers

Think of modifiers as magnets. They must stick close to the words and phrases they modify—the nearest reference point.

But a misplaced modifier, as the name suggests, attaches itself in the wrong place in the sentence. This problem confuses readers, evokes laughter, and/or creates an entirely different meaning than we intended. Several constructions can trip us up.

Prepositional Phrases

MISPLACED: **We asked volunteers to bring cookies for the bake sale at last week's meeting.**

The prepositional phrase *at last week's meeting* is stuck in the wrong place. It's ludicrous to ask people to bring cookies for an event that took place the week before, so move the time designation to the front of the sentence next to what it modifies.

PROPERLY PLACED: **At last week's meeting we asked volunteers to bring cookies for the bake sale.**

Here's another comical example:

MISPLACED: **The building's entrances invited everyone to enter with their tall white columns and double-glass doors.**

It tickles me to envision people who look like (or are carrying) tall white columns and double-glass doors. Let's stick that description where it belongs, modifying *entrances*:

> PROPERLY PLACED: **The building's entrances, with their tall white columns and double-glass doors, invited everyone to enter.**

Participles

A past participle is a past-tense verb that adds additional information to an independent clause. But make sure you keep together the modifier and what it modifies.

> MISPLACED: **Stanley almost gave up writing, frustrated by a string of rejection slips.**
> PROPERLY PLACED: **Stanley, frustrated by a string of rejection slips, almost gave up writing.**

A present participle is a present-tense *-ing* verb that adds additional information to an independent clause.

> PROPERLY PLACED: **Glancing over her shoulder, Stacy mounted the horse.**

The sentence below is grammatically correct because it's Stacy who's glancing over her shoulder.

> MISPLACED: **Stacy mounted the horse glancing over her shoulder.**

What a comical image, not to mention a near physical impossibility.

Appositives

An appositive is a word that mirrors another word or phrase.

> EXAMPLE: **Jesse, the editor at Clubhouse magazine, told conferees what types of articles he wants to see.**

Jesse is the editor (at least at this writing), so those two words mirror each other. In this sentence, as long as *Jesse* sticks close to his occupation (editor at *Clubhouse*), there's no cause for confusion.

But what about a sentence like this one?

> MISPLACED: **No matter how small, most of us will never forget the first check we received for our writing.**

As written, *no matter how small* modifies *most*.

> STILL MISPLACED: **Most of us, no matter how small, will never forget the first check we received for our writing.**

But the size of the writer isn't at issue. The size (amount) of the check is. So let's rearrange the sentence:

> **Most of us will never forget the first check we received for our writing, no matter how small.**

Oops! Now we could be talking about the tininess of our handwriting, the font, or even the piece of writing itself.

PROPERLY PLACED: **Most of us will never forget our first writing-income check, no matter how small the amount.**

To fix misplaced modifiers, either move the phrase close to what it modifies or recast the sentence entirely.

Ambiguous Modifiers

An ambiguous modifier always appears somewhere in the middle of a sentence. Whereas the *misplaced* modifier sticks to something it does not refer to, the *ambiguous* modifier lies between two reference points, so the reader isn't sure how to interpret it. Common words that create ambiguous modifiers include *frequently*, *repeatedly*, and *regularly*. We can clarify by repositioning, creating a dependent clause, or completely rewriting—even making two sentences.

AMBIGUOUS: **The editor who said she only considered electronic submissions repeatedly threw snail-mailed manuscripts away.**

Do we mean that she *repeatedly* said she only considered submissions electronically? Or do we mean that she *repeatedly* threw snail-mailed manuscripts away? Or both?

CLEARER (repositioning): **The editor who repeatedly said she only considered electronic submissions threw snail-mailed manuscripts away.**

EVEN CLEARER (creating a dependent clause): **Because the editor repeatedly said she only considered electronic submissions, she threw away all snail-mailed manuscripts.**

CLEAREST (two sentences): **Editor Johnson repeatedly said she only considered electronic submissions. She threw away all snail-mailed manuscripts.**

Dangling Modifiers

Perhaps the most notorious of misbehaving modifiers are the ones we leave dangling. Unlike *misplaced* modifiers (placed where they modify a reference point we didn't intend) or *ambiguous* modifiers (having two possible reference points), *dangling* modifiers have no reference point at all. The word the modifier refers to doesn't exist in the sentence. The modifier is a little magnet looking in vain for the place to affix itself. Consider this example:

DANGLING: **Having laryngitis, my speaking engagement had to be postponed.**

As written, the *speaking engagement* had laryngitis. But since that's obviously not what the writer intended, this modifier is left dangling.

SAFELY ATTACHED: **Having laryngitis, I had to postpone my speaking engagement.**

Now we have a proper subject (the pronoun *I*) to connect to the modifier.

Keep the image of magnets in your mind as you're polishing your manuscripts; and you'll find it easier to hunt for—and fix—any misplaced, ambiguous, or dangling modifiers. As a result, you'll increase your manuscript sales potential and decrease editor and reader frustrations.

Speaking of frustrations, I never did find that missing red folder!

Chapter 11 Quiz

First determine whether there's a misplaced, ambiguous, or dangling modifier in each of the following sentences. Mark *M* for misplaced, *A* for ambiguous, *D* for dangling, and *N* for none. Then rewrite the sentence to eliminate any confusion for the reader. If you belong to a critique group, do this exercise separately, then compare your answers. See answers in appendix A.

_____   1. The editors at the conference seemed far more welcoming to new writers with their pleasant smiles than we thought.

_____   2. Unwilling to revise, her manuscript arrived DOA on the editor's desk.

_____   3. Not knowing the outcome, the decision was postponed.

_____   4. Even as an eight-year-old, this song spoke to my heart.

_____   5. Having studied the market guides often she got her work published.

_____   6. During every day's bumper-to-bumper commute, I began quoting Bible verses I learned in high school to pass the time.

_____   7. The crook who burglarized several convenience stores repeatedly had to make restitution.

_____   8. After misplacing the red folder, my day was shot.

_____   9. Omar was not chosen for the musical because of his looks.

_____ 10. According to one source, more than half of all Americans are on one or more prescription medications, including one in four children.

References

Misplaced/Dangling Modifiers
    The Chicago Manual of Style, Sixteenth Edition: 5.112
    MLA Handbook for Writers of Research Papers, Seventh Edition: 3.2.2e
    Publication Manual of the American Psychological Association, Sixth Edition: 3.21

Participles
    The Chicago Manual of Style, Sixteenth Edition: 5.89, 5.136, 5.139
    Publication Manual of the American Psychological Association, Sixth Edition: 3.20

Appositives
    The Chicago Manual of Style, Sixteenth Edition: 5.21, 6.23, 6.51
    Christian Writer's Manual of Style, Fourth Edition, p. 131
    MLA Handbook for Writers of Research Papers, Seventh Edition: 3.2.2e

Whatever you do, work at it with all your heart, as
working for the Lord, not for human masters.
—COLOSSIANS 3:23

That Which Is Whom?

12

Some jokes and riddles work better orally than in print, such as this one that often circulates among kids in third or fourth grade:

QUESTION: Why won't you ever go hungry at a beach?

ANSWER: Because of the sand which is [sandwiches] there.

Okay, forgive the groaner. I got my sense of humor from my dad. But that play on words reminds me of a topic I discuss in chapter 36, in which I talk about the importance of eliminating nonessentials.

If we weren't going for humor in the riddle, we could delete *which is* and simply say *Because of the sand there*. In that chapter, I advocate using your word-processing program's search feature to go on a *which* hunt (as well as hunting for *that*, *who*, and *whom*). Frequently those words can be cut.

But there's another reason for going on a *which* (*that*, *who*, *whom*) hunt. Often we use those words interchangeably—and incorrectly.

That Versus *Who/Whom*

In everyday conversation, we often hear something like this:

He's the boy that won the spelling bee.

The word *that* may sound right. But, remember, we're trying to retrain our inner grammatical ear. A person is not a *that* or an *it*. When talking about a person, a conscientious writer will use the pronoun *who*. Consider the following examples.

FULL HUMANITY ACKNOWLEDGED: **He's the boy who won the spelling bee.**

The same guideline applies when referring to people (plural).

61

INHUMANE: **Writers that make it in this business constantly study their craft.**
FULLY HUMAN: **Writers who make it . . .**

When would we use *whom?*

INHUMANE: **Our friends that we met at a conference have coauthored a book.**
FULLY HUMAN: **Our friends whom we met at a conference . . .**

The latter is an example of the objective case—a direct object. We met *whom? Them.* (See chapter 9 for further clarification of *who* versus *whom.*)

Occasionally, I've heard or seen someone substitute *which* for *who* or *whom.*

INHUMANE: **Our friends which we met . . .**
FULLY HUMAN: **Our friends whom we met . . .**

Remember, if you're referring to a person or to people (plural), use *who* or *whom*, not *that* or *which.* Note: *Who* can also be used to refer to animals treated like humans—family pets in particular.

CORRECT: **My son has a dachshund who goes by the name of Oskar Meyer Whiner.**
CORRECT: **The scaredy-cat cowboy couldn't sleep because of the wolf that howled all night.** (The wolf, we presume, is not a family pet.)

That Versus *Which*

Confusing *that* and *which* is one of the most common errors in both spoken and written English. Some people always use *that* instead of *which*, thinking it's less stuffy sounding. Others always use *which*, thinking it sounds more educated. Neither is correct.

Grammatically, the two are not always interchangeable. In order to use the correct word, we need to understand the difference between restrictive and nonrestrictive clauses.

Restrictive clauses restrict the subject of the sentence by giving specific, limiting information about it. Taking a restrictive clause out of a sentence alters its meaning.

CORRECT: **The imaginary giraffe** *that Tommy plays with* **is twelve feet tall.**

We're not talking about just any imaginary giraffe. We're talking about Tommy's. If we took out the restrictive clause (in italics), we wouldn't fully understand the sentence because not all imaginary giraffes are twelve feet tall. Restrictive clauses are essential clauses.

Punctuation note: we do not put commas around restrictive clauses.

Nonrestrictive clauses give additional information about the subject, not limiting it but defining it. These clauses can be deleted without changing the meaning of the sentence.

CORRECT: **Tommy's imaginary giraffe,** *which is twelve feet tall,* **has to sleep in the hallway.**

The italicized clause here is *nonrestrictive* because we don't lose essential information by taking it out. We may wonder why the imaginary giraffe is banished to the hallway for his forty winks, but the sentence means the same without that clause.

Here's another example.

CORRECT: **Prisms, *which refract light*, create beautiful rainbows in sunlight.**

Here the nonrestrictive clause (in italics) can be lifted out of the sentence without changing the meaning. It adds additional, defining information, telling us how prisms create beautiful rainbows. But we can understand the sentence without the technical jargon.

Punctuation note: we *do* surround nonrestrictive clauses with commas.

Now, what happens if we turn this into a sentence with a restrictive clause instead of a nonrestrictive clause?

INCORRECT: **Prisms that refract light create beautiful rainbows in sunlight.**

Why is this incorrect? By using the restrictive clause and no commas, we're implying there are some prisms that do not refract light. Therefore, only those that do refract light create rainbows in sunlight.

The word *that* is used for restrictive clauses only. Here are more examples:

INCORRECT: **The rancher told his herd, "The cow, which eats the most grass, wins."**
CORRECT: **"The cow that eats the most grass wins."**

The word *which* is generally used for nonrestrictive clauses, which need surrounding commas.

CORRECT: **Football stadiums, which hold sixty thousand fans desperately in need of exercise, host a game of twenty-two players desperately in need of rest.**
INCORRECT: **Football stadiums which hold sixty thousand fans desperately in need of exercise host . . .**

As written, the second version implies we're talking about stadiums that hold exactly sixty thousand exercise-challenged fans, and other stadiums do not qualify for this comment.

Avoid Confusion

Above all, we want to avoid confusing the reader.

CONFUSING: **All the pickles which were packed in green jars tasted like kerosene.**
NOT CONFUSING: **All the pickles that were packed in green jars tasted like kerosene.**
NOT CONFUSING: **All the pickles, which were packed in green jars, tasted like kerosene.**

The distinction here affects the reputation of all the pickle makers. In the first sentence, as written, we might wonder if the writer intended a restrictive clause, but used *which* instead of *that*. This would mean that only some of the pickles—those in green jars—tasted like kerosene. Or we might deduce that the writer forgot the commas, which, when inserted, would mean that all of the pickles were in green jars and all the entrants needed pickle-making lessons.

The second sentence uses a restrictive *that* clause, meaning that only those pickles in green jars caused the county-fair judges to spit out the vile things. The third sentence uses a nonrestrictive *which* clause, telling us that fairgoers needed to stay away from all pickles because they could be flammable.

All of these distinctions are blurring in both spoken and written English. In *CWMS 4* Robert Hudson "recommends the that/which rules be observed when it is useful, but never slavishly."[1]

Avoid Wordiness

As I alluded to in a previous chapter, to avoid wordiness we can often simplify restrictive and nonrestrictive clauses, especially those with *to-be* verbs. Here are some ways to do that:

Restrictive clauses:

WORDY: **All the pickles that were packed in green jars tasted like kerosene.**
STREAMLINED: **All the pickles packed in green jars tasted like kerosene.**
WORDY: **The cow that eats the most grass wins.**
STREAMLINED: **The cow eating the most grass wins.**

Nonrestrictive clauses:

WORDY: **Tommy's imaginary friend, who is twelve feet tall, has to sleep in the hallway.**
STREAMLINED: **Tommy's twelve-foot imaginary friend has to sleep in the hallway.**

Although you may not be able to sustain yourself on a beach with merely the sand which is there, at least you can now confidently make the right choice whenever faced with a *that/which/who/whom* decision.

Chapter 12 Quiz

Put a check mark beside any sentences using *that, which, who,* and *whom* correctly and also using correct punctuation. Otherwise, make any corrections necessary. Mark sentences containing a restrictive clause with an *R* and sentences containing a nonrestrictive clause with an *N*. Then streamline where possible. See answers in appendix A.

_____   1. He berated the senators that blocked the bill.

_____   2. The family, which prays together, stays together.

_____   3. The cake, that my grandma baked, won the contest.

_____   4. The editors which were at the conference gave helpful tips.

_____   5. The Ten Commandments that are not merely suggestions guide
              Pete's life.

_____ 6. Way across the zoo we heard the lion that roared.

_____ 7. The pirates, which plundered every ship they encountered, were pretty nice guys when you got to know them.

_____ 8. That was the straw that broke the camel's back.

_____ 9. Tanya realized the giddy couple on the tour bus was the same couple who she had met on a cruise the year before.

_____ 10. The protruding nose hairs, which tickled his upper lip, needed to be trimmed.

References

That versus Who/Whom and That versus Which
   The Chicago Manual of Style, Sixteenth Edition: 5.54, 5.58, 5.220
   Christian Writer's Manual of Style, Fourth Edition: pp. 571–72, 591
   MLA Handbook for Writers of Research Papers, Seventh Edition: 3.2.2e
   Publication Manual of the American Psychological Association, Sixth Edition: 3.20, 3.22

Restrictive and Nonrestrictive Clauses
   The Chicago Manual of Style, Sixteenth Edition: 6.22, 6.31

Wordiness
   Publication Manual of the American Psychological Association, Sixth Edition: 3.08

May these words of my mouth [and pen or computer]
and this meditation of my heart be pleasing in your
sight, Lord, my Rock and my Redeemer.

—PSALM 19:14

Quell Those Qualifiers

13

My critique group sometimes ruthlessly carves up my manuscripts. It can hurt. But, as King Solomon wrote, "Wounds from a friend can be trusted" (Prov. 27:6). Of all those who have snuggled into our group for a time, four of us have been together for decades. We know each other so well that we've learned to give and receive honest criticism—and even ignore it occasionally.

Together we've gone to writer's conferences, studied books on writing, and grown in our skills—developing a mutual trust.

We also catch recurring errors. For instance, I really overuse the words *just* and *really*. I just don't see them in my own writing. At a critique session I'll begin reading my manuscript, and as my fellow critiquers follow along on hard copy, suddenly all three of them will simultaneously circle those words. It's infuriating!

To get back at them, I've created a character for a fiction project I'm working on. His name? Justin Reali. So now I can use Justin Reali as often as I want.

However, I also try to eliminate *just* and *really* from my manuscripts whenever they're not necessary. What's wrong with them? They're qualifiers that often weaken otherwise good writing.

What's a qualifier?

As I've mentioned before, carelessness in speech patterns often spills into our writing. When we talk, we may qualify words to create emphasis or avoid dogmatic statements.

EXAMPLE: **"He's very patient with me, and I believe almost everything he says."**

We hear qualifiers in public prayer: "Father, we just pray that you will really help us." (See more qualifiers in the sidebar "Put Out an APB" on page 69.)

But excellent writing uses qualifiers sparingly.

Simply put, qualifiers modify verbs, adjectives, and adverbs in two primary ways: intensifying or hedging. Both can create grammatical errors, weaken writing, and annoy readers.

1. **Intensifying.** Words such as *very* intensify a concept: *The speaker was very late.* The word *very* lets us know the guy didn't show up a minute or two late. The emcee was going into cardiac arrest.

2. **Hedging.** Words such as *rather* hedge or back off: *The overworked editor took a rather harsh approach to editing.*

Note the way qualifiers work with verbs, adjectives, and adverbs.

MODIFYING A VERB: **Patty *really* enjoyed getting away from her computer for a day.**

The word *really* intensifies the verb *enjoyed*. (The emphasis may or may not be needed, depending on Patti's workload.)

MODIFYING AN ADJECTIVE: **On a *kind of* dark and stormy night, Snoopy ventured out.**

Kind of modifies *dark and stormy,* an adjective phrase referring to the noun *night*. Apparently, the manifestations of the tempest hadn't reached full intensity that evening. So the dire weathercast backs off with the phrase *kind of*. Aside from the humorous variation of Snoopy's usual "dark and stormy night," this description is not strong scene setting.

MODIFYING AN ADVERB: **The editor's guidelines were *fairly* easy to follow.**

Fairly modifies *easy,* an adverb referring to the verb *were*. In this case, the qualifier hints that whoever put together those particular guidelines could have expended more effort. If we use *fairly* here, we're hedging. If the guidelines *were* easy to follow, say so. Don't hedge with the word *fairly*.

Quell the Rebellion

Qualifiers have their place, so we don't want to quash them altogether. But they tend to be rebellious little creatures, popping up unnecessarily. Conscientious writers train themselves to quell the rebellion and keep qualifiers in line. Here's the training regimen:

1. **Use qualifiers only when needed.** Instead of writing *It was really snowing*, force your "little grey cells" into action. Help us experience what it felt like or describe the size of the flakes or show us your characters stumbling, unable to see more than a few inches ahead of them.

2. **Avoid oxymorons—contradictions in terms.** *He truly lied to me* is a contradiction in terms. Also, does adding a qualifier enhance or diminish its seriousness? Write simply: *He lied.*

3. *Avoid using qualifiers with unqualifiable words—e.g.,* **Sandie's book was pretty unique.** We hear sentences like this all the time, but they're illogical. If something is unique, it's unique—one of a kind. Nothing can be almost unique, very unique, or anything else but unique.

The same holds true of such words as *ecstatic, pregnant, wrong, forgiven,* and *dead.* Either a person is or isn't. No such thing as kind of ecstatic, just a little pregnant, somewhat wrong, or not-quite forgiven. And only in *The Princess Bride* movie can someone be "mostly dead."

4. *Don't overintensify.* Rarely, you might write something like this: *I felt very, very sad.* But in the wake of Lemony Snicket's *The Reptile Room,* no other author can get away with repeating the word *ever* (as in *never ever, ever, ever . . .*) more than two hundred times in a row for extreme emphasis and humor value.

If we overuse intensifiers for emphasis, it's like crying wolf. Readers won't know when to pay attention to them.

When to Use Qualifiers

Don't banish all qualifiers from your writing. First, if there were no good reason for qualifiers, they wouldn't exist in the English language. Without qualifiers, Goldilocks, for example, wouldn't have found a chair, a bed, and a bowl of porridge "just right."

Second, excellent writers avoid making absolute statements about uncertain or disputable facts. Better to write *Statistics seem to indicate that . . .* rather than dogmatically presenting inconclusive data, trends, or outcomes as facts.

However, many writers use qualifiers due to carelessness, fear of taking a stand, lack of confidence in their facts or opinions, or laziness—not working diligently to find the precise word.

So here's to writing with confidence and precision and just really keeping our qualifiers in their place! (Wink, wink.)

Put Out an APB

Be on the alert for and delete, when appropriate, qualifiers such as these:

just	really	very	ever	somewhat	partially
seemingly	fairly	probably	maybe	seems to	appears to
appears that	basically	essentially	kind of	sort of	mostly
pretty	rather	slightly	virtually	quite	almost
pretty much	relatively	truly	actually	absolutely	

Chapter 13 Quiz

In the following sentences, identify the qualifiers and decide whether they're necessary and appropriate. If not, indicate whether the qualifiers should be cut or the sentences rewritten. Then try rewriting those sentences. If you're part of a critique group, do this exercise together, discussing various approaches. See answers in appendix A.

1. Greg learned to read when he was a very little boy.

2. It appears the man was murdered last night.

3. His relatively good looks underwhelmed her.

4. The company virtually tripled its sales.

5. Andrew actually passed the test with the highest score in the class.

6. "I'm basically ready," Joan said.

7. I accepted God's very, very, very special gift.

8. "The runner at first base kind of definitely looked like he was going to attempt to steal second," the sportscaster said.

9. I have almost forgiven the woman who introduced me to dark-chocolate-covered Dove ice cream bars.

10. Basically, what we're saying is that we need better self-control.

References

Intensifiers
   The Christian Writer's Manual of Style, Fourth Edition: pp. 206–7

Wordiness
   The Christian Writer's Manual of Style, Fourth Edition: pp. 365, 392–94

Very
   The Christian Writer's Manual of Style, Fourth Edition: p. 586

Don't become so well-adjusted to your culture that you fit into it without even thinking. Instead, fix your attention on God. You'll be changed from the inside out. Readily recognize what he wants from you, and quickly respond to it. Unlike the culture around you, always dragging you down to its level of immaturity, God brings the best out of you, develops well-formed maturity in you.

—ROMANS 12:2 (*THE MESSAGE*)

Let's Split (and Other Last Words)

14

How to Handle Infinitives and Final Prepositions

Under the influence of beatnik slang in the '50s, the expression "Like, let's split, man" invited a companion of either gender to depart.

If you're as old as I am—or a YouTube vintage-TV fan—this lingo might conjure visions of the clueless Maynard G. Krebs (played by Bob Denver). The goateed sidekick of the title character in *The Many Loves of Dobie Gillis* managed to insert the word *like* everywhere, long before Valley girls drooled it ad nauseam and Facebook allowed us to "like" everything that tickles our fancy.

Over the years I've survived, like, tons of cultural fads in our English language. And, just as I pick up accents quickly when I visit various parts of the country, I often find myself, like, picking up language fads.

I won't get into a debate about how much we should let culture change our mother tongue. But some modifications inevitably occur in a living, dynamic language. So let's look at two grammar battlegrounds: splitting infinitives and ending a sentence with a preposition.

Splitting Infinitives

In case it's been a while since you've even read the word *infinitive*, much less studied it, here's a definition: an infinitive is a verb with a *to* in front of it.

In Ecclesiastes, Solomon demonstrated that there's a time to use infinitives: "a time to be born and a time to die . . . a time to weep and a time to laugh . . . a time to keep and a time to throw away . . . a time to be silent and a time to speak" (3:2–7).

Despite changing grammar "allowables," I believe that wherever workable, excellent writers will try to prevent either the *to* or the verb from saying, "Let's split, man." In conversational English—and even in informal writing—we might say something like this:

Richard attended the reading of the will to rightfully claim his inheritance.

Notice that *rightfully* splits the infinitive, *to claim*. But let's look at some options to try to keep this family together:

Change the infinitive to a different form of the verb:

Richard attended the reading of the will, rightfully claiming his inheritance.

Turn the adverb (*rightfully*) into an adjective and position it to modify the appropriate noun:

Richard attended the reading of the will to claim his rightful inheritance.

Kick out the buttinsky adverb that's splitting the infinitive:

Richard attended the reading of the will to claim his inheritance.

Because split infinitives show up often in casual conversation, how concerned should we be about purging them from our writing? Book and magazine editors vary in their style decisions, and *CMoS 16* sanctions splitting infinitives—even stating that "sometimes it is perfectly appropriate to split an infinitive verb with an adverb to add emphasis or to produce a natural sound."[1]

Robert Hudson says sometimes a split infinitive is less awkward, "simply sounds more natural."[2] Example: *We wanted him to clearly see the consequences of his actions.*

But when we can avoid splitting an infinitive without making the sentence awkward, take the high road grammatically, avoiding offense to language purists.

Positioning Prepositions

Language purists also teach that we should not end a sentence with a preposition (e.g., *to, for, from, with, over, under, around, through, by, in, of*).

> POTENTIALLY PAINFUL EXAMPLE FOR LANGUAGE PURISTS: **What do you attribute your success to?**

Because *to* is a preposition, we can substitute different wording, often moving the preposition to where it belongs—to modify the correct word. In this case, we can move *to*, so it creates an appropriate prepositional phrase.

> EASY FIX TO AVOID UNNECESSARY PAIN: **To what do you attribute your success?**
> (*To* [preposition] + *what* [object of the preposition] = a prepositional phrase.)

That revision may sound a little stilted in modern conversation, and the following revision sounds even stuffier. But they're both correct grammatically.

> POTENTIALLY PAINFUL EXAMPLE, PART DEUX: **Who do you want to write for?**
> A FIX WITH A CHALLENGE: **For whom do you want to write?**

Here we're working with the preposition *for*, and again we can move it to the beginning of the sentence to find what it modifies and create a prepositional phrase. However, as is common in daily conversation, we've incorrectly used the word *who* as if it were the subject (subjective case) in the sentence. So we change *who* to *whom* to create the correct object for the preposition: *for whom* (objective case). (See chapter 9.)

Many people use potentially painful examples similar to the above in everyday conversation (unless they're applying for a job as an English teacher). It seems natural. But if you can, avoid prepositions at the close of a sentence—or even at the end of a clause within a sentence.

> PAINFUL EXAMPLE OF THE LATTER: **The editorial assistant didn't know what heading he should file the manuscript under, so he put it under *M* for manuscript.**
>
> REVISED: **The editorial assistant didn't know under what heading he should file the manuscript.**
>
> REVISED MORE EFFECTIVELY: **The editorial assistant didn't know where to file the manuscript.**

Less formal writing freely allows the use of prepositions at the end of a sentence, so, again, study your target publication and/or the style of the book publisher you want to sell your book to. (See what I did there?)

Sir Winston Churchill highlighted the absurdity of trying to banish *all* prepositions from the ends of sentences and clauses when he quipped that refusing to allow a sentence to end with a preposition "is something up with which I will not put."[3]

Thanks, Sir Winston. You've put this in perspective for us.

Fiction's Playground

If, therefore, you want to write fiction set in the state of Minnesota, where I live, throw in a *with* at the end of a sentence of dialogue now and then for characterization.

I'll never forget the first time I heard this language quirk when I emigrated from Missouri to my new home state. My friend, who might have said, "Let's split, man," instead said, "Do you want to come with?"

It's a common "Scandihoovian" expression. But it always leaves me hanging, waiting for the rest of the sentence. I want to say, "Could you please serve a direct object with that preposition?" With *you*? with *us*? with *whom* or *what*?

Similarly, one of your characters may habitually split infinitives when speaking. Don't overdo it. But if you sprinkle in a few here and there, readers will be able to recognize the character by idiosyncrasies such as these.

Just as Maynard G. Krebs, like, dropped in the word *like* all the time—contrasting the clean-cut Dobie Gillis's more educated-sounding dialogue—any of these peculiarities can help your characters come to life for the reader.

But, in general, know your audience, study your target publication or publisher, and follow their lead regarding split infinitives and prepositions at the end of your sentences.

The *CWMS 4* recommendation regarding split infinities applies to sentence-ending prepositions as well: "Fix them whenever they cause awkwardness or lack of clarity, and also fix them . . . when the author is likely to be accused of not knowing 'proper English.'"[4]

And, as Maynard would say, "Like, just make sure your meaning is clear, man. Like, that's what your humble grammar geek tries to do."

Chapter 14 Quiz

Revise the following sentences to avoid potentially painful reading experiences for language purists. Put a C beside any that are in their best form. If you belong to a critique group, discuss your conclusions. See answers in appendix A.

_____ 1. *Guideposts* was the magazine all the newbie writers wanted to get into.

_____ 2. Editor Kolbaba wanted to really emphasize the importance of understanding her magazine's readers.

_____ 3. Why do you think that is?

_____ 4. Ending a sentence with a preposition is something I will not put up with. [Don't use Churchill's humorous recasting of the sentence.]

_____ 5. Maynard G. Krebs managed to always get Dobie Gillis in trouble.

_____ 6. How much trouble did Maynard get Dobie Gillis get into?

_____ 7. Where are you at?

_____ 8. Who was the novel written by?

_____ 9. Craig had to remain vigilant at the party because he didn't know who his nemesis was masquerading as.

_____ 10. He tried his hardest to ultimately become a bestselling author.

References

Splitting Infinitives
   The Chicago Manual of Style, Sixteenth Edition: 5.104–7, 5.168
   The Christian Writer's Manual of Style, Fourth Edition: p. 358

Prepositions Ending Clauses/Sentences
   The Chicago Manual of Style, Sixteenth Edition: 5.169
   The Christian Writer's Manual of Style, Fourth Edition: p. 301

Are You Appositive?

(What in the World Is an Appositive?)

15

What if your blood type determined your personality and destiny? For instance, if you were an A-positive person, would that make you "A" optimist? Would you likely get an A+ on every test? Or if you were B-negative, would you be negative about everything your entire life, a gloomy Eeyore sort? And, if you were type O-negative, a relatively rare blood type, would that doom you to a life of melancholy invisibility—an absolute zero with pessimistic tendencies?

What does all this have to do with grammar? Not much, except that I love wordplay. And this chapter will explore *appositives*, a topic that could positively (or negatively) confuse some writers.

Besides, in the opening paragraph, I managed to sneak in some examples of appositives. Can you spot them?

Identification

The dictionary I've installed on my laptop (*Merriam Webster's 11th Collegiate*) defines *appositive* this way: "of, relating to, or standing in grammatical apposition."

What? Now I have to look up *apposition*: "a grammatical construction in which two usually adjacent nouns having the same referent stand in the same syntactical relation to the rest of a sentence."

Um . . . seriously? Now I have to look up *referent*: "what something refers to." And *syntactical*: "related to the way words are put together."

I find more help understanding *apposition* in the biological definition in my laptop dictionary: "the [depositing] of successive layers upon those already present (as in cell walls)."

Okay, *that* I can visualize. Appositives (usually nouns or noun phrases) add layers of meaning in the same place.

For instance, in the introduction above, I added a layer to the words *type O-negative* by saying it's relatively rare. So *a relatively rare blood type* is an appositive phrase. Likewise, to the phrase *negative about everything your entire life*, I added the appositive, *a gloomy Eeyore sort*. That's a layer of sight and sound for Winnie-the-Pooh lovers. We can see that forlorn donkey's head hung low and hear his depressed voice.

Appositives and what they refer to can be used interchangeably.

Proper Usage

Using appositives properly and wisely accomplishes four tasks:

1. Appositives provide additional information or explanation. I could say this:

    Donna's writing mentor encouraged her.

But if I know who her mentor is, I can layer that information:

    Donna's writing mentor, Gayle, encouraged her.

2. Appositives keep related information together. By identifying Gayle after the word *mentor*, I make the relationship clear. Appositives often appear in the middle of a sentence with commas surrounding them. But they can also appear at the beginning or end of a sentence.

    For illustration purposes below, consider the words *Snoopy's alter ego* the appositive:

    a. **Joe Cool, Snoopy's alter ego, sported his trademark sunglasses.**
    b. **Snoopy's alter ego, Joe Cool, sported his trademark sunglasses.**
    c. **When we saw the trademark sunglasses, we immediately recognized Joe Cool, Snoopy's alter ego.**

3. Appositives help combine sentences. Consider these examples:

    THREE SENTENCES: **Fiona named her goat Jack-in-the-Box because he was spunky. Fiona's goat won several ribbons at the fair. Fiona had been raising that goat for three years.**

    ONE SENTENCE: **After three years of raising her spunky goat, Jack-in-the-Box, Fiona won several ribbons at the fair.**

4. Appositives cut unnecessary words. If you're like me and often have to cut ruthlessly to stay under your assigned word count, remember, "Appositives are our friends." Notice the way the example above streamlined potentially cumbersome writing.

Punctuation Notes

Appositives may be punctuated in a variety of ways.

1. Commas. My brother-in-law often jokingly introduced my sister as his first wife, Jeanne, though she was his current and only wife. In print we use commas to indicate that kind of exclusivity.

> EXCLUSIVE: **Joyce's husband, Steve, supports his writing-addicted wife.**

If I were to omit the commas, I would make myself a polygamist. But because Steve is my one and only husband, I surround him with commas in the sentence to indicate that relationship.

> NOT EXCLUSIVE: **Joyce's book *The 500 Hats of a Modern-Day Woman* helps women balance their many roles.**

Because I have published more than one book, I don't fence in the title of this book with commas. Grammatically, the lack of commas indicates this isn't my one and only book.

Now, what if I'm writing about Henry VIII, who had a wife named Anne Boleyn? That scoundrel of a king actually had six wives: three Catherines, two Annes, and a Jane. So I could write this:

> **Henry VIII's wife Anne Boleyn literally lost her head over her husband, the king of England.**

No commas around *Anne Boleyn* because she was not his one and only wife. But we do need a comma between *husband* and *the king of England* because those are two "layers" of the same person. I could have written that Anne *lost her head over her husband, who was the king of England*. But making *the king of England* an appositive "cuts" two words.

2. Dashes. Used sparingly, dashes can replace commas to draw attention to the appositive or to clarify a sentence already containing several commas:

> **Because of her three aptly named children, actually her stepchildren—Scout, Moose, and Hoppi—Mindy always felt exhausted.**

3. Italics versus quotation marks in appositive titles. In appositives, as in other writing, remember this basic distinction:

We use italics for titles of works, such as books, magazines, TV shows, movies, musicals, art (e.g., Rodin's sculpture *The Thinker*), and ships (e.g., Gilligan's boat, the *SS Minnow*).

In contrast, we use quotation marks around titles of chapters, articles, short stories, TV episodes, and songs.

Think of it this way: italics for the larger production and quotation marks for works within the work. Note the appositives here:

> Cassie wrote the article, "Where Does a Novelist Go to Resign?" for *Footloose Writers* magazine.
>
> One of my favorite episodes of a sitcom from the '60s, *The Dick Van Dyke Show*, was "That's My Boy??"

4. Capitalization in people's titles as appositives. In general, when a person's position title comes as an appositive *before* that person's name, we capitalize it and don't use a comma:

> Chairman of the Board Howard Doofus deserves his coworkers' moniker, chairman of the bored.
>
> Senior Pastor Daniel Gladsum gave the invocation.

When such a title, as an appositive, comes *after* the person's name, we do not capitalize it but we do use commas:

> Howard Doofus, chairman of the board, deserves his coworkers' moniker, chairman of the bored.
>
> Daniel Gladsum, senior pastor of Sinners Anonymous Church, gave the invocation.

Caution

Avoid littering your manuscript with appositives unnecessarily. As with many writing tools, too many appositives can become tiresome and distracting. Use them when helpful, but don't overuse them.

By now, are you "A-positive" you have a handle on appositives? They can be positively handy "tools" for writers who want to "craft" their writing carefully instead of submitting the first things that come into their heads—leaving negative impressions on editors.

Chapter 15 Quiz

In sentences 1–3, below, identify the appositive. In 4–7, combine the sentences to create a well-placed appositive and cut unnecessary words. In 8–10, correct any punctuation mistakes. See answers in appendix A.

1. The Bible, a library of sixty-six volumes, is still the bestselling book of all time.

2. Ebenezer and Florence sailed their yacht, *Eb & Flo*, from Florida to Maine.

3. True joy—one aspect of the fruit of the Spirit—comes from full surrender to God.

4. Ted had an annoying habit. He cracked his knuckles loudly in public. It made Delia cringe.

5. We appreciate the teaching of Ronald Godlyman, who is pastor of Hopeville Church. He delves deep.

6. Holley's greatest weakness is chocolate fudge. She tried to resist the package in the fridge, but she finally succumbed to the temptation.

7. There's a scene in the Disney movie called *The Little Mermaid*, where the seagull named Scuttle finds something shiny in the sea and gives it to Ariel. Ariel is a mermaid princess. He doesn't know the thing is a fork or what it's used for, so he calls it a dinglehopper. Ariel uses it for a comb.

8. Henry VIII's wife Jane Seymour is not the woman who starred in TV's *Dr. Quinn, Medicine Woman*.

9. The trip from Minneapolis to my hometown of St. Louis—a painful challenge for arthritic knees—seems longer every year.

10. Dan's favorite song from Lerner and Loewe's musical "My Fair Lady" is *A Hymn to Him*, especially its catch phrase, *Why can't a woman be more like a man?*

References

Appositives
The Chicago Manual of Style, Sixteenth Edition: 5.21, 6.23, 6.51
The Christian Writer's Manual of Style, Fourth Edition: p. 131
MLA Handbook for Writers of Research Papers, Seventh Edition: 3.2.2e

What Could Be Worst?

Comparatives and Superlatives

16

Few of us would have written Charles Dickens's opening line from *A Tale of Two Cities* this way: "It was the *better* of times, it was the *worse* of times." Yet sometimes we get tangled up in comparisons and don't make the best word choices, which ultimately has the worst effect possible on the editors we're trying to woo (I love that word!), so to speak.

The above paragraph references two kinds of adjectives—comparative and superlative. As a skilled, approved worker, not ashamed (2 Tim. 2:15), aiming for excellence, we want to learn the names of our tools, right? Yet sometimes writers get these two kinds of adjectives—*comparatives* and *superlatives*—confused. What's the difference?

Remember, an adjective modifies (or tells us something about) a noun (a person, place, or thing). Now let's look at some special adjectives. Most of these principles also apply to adverbs (words modifying verbs or adjectives).

Adjectives of comparison, such as the following, can invite confusion:

good → better → best
bad → worse → worst

Such words address degrees of comparison in two ways.

1. *Comparatives.* We use the comparative *better*, for example, when comparing two things:

   CORRECT: **"I don't know who was the better writer—Shakespeare or Milton," the literature prof said.**

Unfortunately, some writers use the word *best* in similar sentences. So pay attention to how many things are being compared.

> TWO ITEMS COMPARED: **good → better**

2. *Superlatives.* Save superlatives, such as *best*, for comparisons of three or more items. Consider the following:

> CORRECT: **"But," the prof continued, "you're certainly not going to get me to choose who was the best writer of all time."**
> THREE OR MORE ITEMS COMPARED: **good → best**

Counting Syllables

When I was in high school, a male friend of mine jokingly said things like "I'll be gladder when my bladder gets flatter." (Sheesh!)

Most of us would never say anything like that, regardless of whether it's grammatically correct or not. (The guy seemed to have no filters—at least back then.) So how do we know how to express comparative degrees? Many times, if we've grown up listening to people with good grammar, we can "play it by ear."

But that's not always reliable. So here are some rules of thumb:

1. *Adjectives of one syllable.* With most adjectives of one syllable, we use an *-er* (indicating more) or *-est* (indicating most) ending. These are called inflected forms. Note these examples of an adjective, its comparative form, and its superlative form:

> **fine** [adjective] → **finer** [inflected, comparative form] → **finest** [inflected, superlative form]
> **black → blacker → blackest**

According to this guideline, *gladder* and *gladdest* are correct. You can find them in dictionaries as such. However, for some reason, it sounds odd to our ears. So some grammar gurus suggest using *more glad* and *most glad*. Or you can solve the problem entirely by using *happier* and *happiest*, despite the slight difference in nuance.

2. *Adjectives of two syllables.* Some two-syllable words also use *-er* and *-est* endings, such as these:

> **subtle → subtler → subtlest**
> **hollow → hollower → hollowest**

If the base word ends in a *y*, however, be sure to change the *y* to *i* before adding *er* or *est*:

> **funky → funkier → funkiest**
> **ugly → uglier → ugliest**

Some two-syllable words, however, use *more* or *most* (or *less/least*) for their inflected forms:

hyper → more hyper → most hyper
fragrant → less fragrant → least fragrant

3. *Adjectives of three or more syllables.* You're safe using *more/most, less/least* for words of three or more syllables, such as these:

disgusting → more disgusting → most disgusting
intelligent → less intelligent → least intelligent

Some modifiers should never be linked with a comparative, however. As I've said before, only in *The Princess Bride* movie or other humor attempts can you get away with saying someone is *mostly dead.*

In the same way, we don't use comparatives or superlatives with other absolute terms.

INCORRECT: **emptier/emptiest**
INCORRECT: **more/most unique**
INCORRECT: **more/most perfect**
INCORRECT: **more/most infinite**
INCORRECT: **more/most final**

Let such powerful words shine alone.

Doubling Trouble

Never use *more* or *most* with an already inflected form. I know a young man who, in a humor attempt, often says, "That's way more better."

Let the comparative or superlative exhibit its own innate power.

1. Your toddler may be dirtier (the correct way to indicate more dirty) than someone else's. But she is not more dirtier.
2. Your uncle may be *creepier* (the correct way to indicate *more creepy*) than anyone you know. But he's not *more creepier.*

Of course, erroneous word choices can enhance characterization in fiction—but don't overdo it.

Any: An "Other" Challenge

How do we handle the word *any* in comparisons? Is this sentence grammatically correct?

I like tea better than any beverage.

Though I'm a great lover of all things tea, this sentence is not grammatically correct. I need to insert the word *other*:

CORRECT: **I like tea better than any other beverage.**

Here's why: Without the word *other*, I'm implying that tea is not a beverage. Inserting the word *other* acknowledges that tea qualifies, and I find it a superior beverage.

Two other examples:

1. **Chelsea is more fidgety than any second-grader.**

Is Chelsea in second grade, or are we comparing her to children of a different age?

2. **Bubba is dumber than any gorilla.**

We would hope that Bubba is the name of a primate and not a human. So we would use the words *any other gorilla*.

Less or *Fewer*?

Here's another potentially troublesome twosome: *less* and *fewer*. You may find this rule of thumb helpful:

Less refers to volume or substance—e.g., I may have *less patience, less knowledge,* or *less ability* than someone else.

Fewer refers to number (something countable). So, you will understand my agitation upon seeing the lighted signs over stores' express checkout stands that say Less Than 10 Items.

Because we are quite capable of counting the number of items in the cart (though some people apparently lack that mental capacity—or they just cheat), the sign should say Fewer Than 10 Items.

Another example:

If I have submitted fewer manuscripts than I used to, I probably have fewer published articles, fewer book contracts, and fewer dollars in the bank.

Here's an interesting example of the two words in context:

CORRECT: **The distinguished gentleman has *less* hair** [singular noun *hair* refers to substance] **than before, but he also has *fewer* hairs** [plural noun *hairs* is countable—but only by his Creator].

So keep this rule of thumb in mind: substance/volume versus countability. You'll be *less* insecure in your word choice, and you'll make *fewer* mistakes.

My husband likes to borrow a line from Johnny Carson, comedian and longtime host of *The Tonight Show*, who often quipped, "That's the second-biggest/stupidest/funniest _____ I've ever seen." He filled in the blank with all sorts of words, depending on the situation, leaving us laughing and wondering, of course, what the absolute biggest, stupidest, funniest "whatever" was.

Great comedic use of the superlative, Johnny.

Chapter 16 Quiz

In the first four examples, circle or highlight the adjective and mark *comparative* adjectives with a *C* and *superlatives* with an *S*. In the remaining sentences, correct any errors; and put a check mark beside any that are correct. See answers in appendix A.

_____   1. My current doctor is kinder than his predecessor.

_____   2. I am more frustrated than I have ever been.

_____   3. This is the most ridiculous book I've ever read.

_____   4. That is the second-ugliest baby I've ever seen.

_____   5. Bree makes less grammatical mistakes than she used to.

_____   6. Dustin has the winsomest smile.

_____   7. Herbert is awkwarder in large groups than in smaller ones.

_____   8. Aaron has more charisma than any editor.

_____   9. My outspoken friend had less filters than most people.

_____   10. Despite fewer capabilities and less stamina than his fellow athletes, Jack's a great team leader.

References

Degrees of Adjectives
   The Chicago Manual of Style, Sixteenth Edition: 5.83–88

Less versus Fewer
   The Associated Press Stylebook: See Fewer, Less

> Let every detail in your lives—words, actions,
> whatever—be done in the name of the Master, Jesus,
> thanking God the Father every step of the way.
> —COLOSSIANS 3:17 (*THE MESSAGE*)

Wanna Go Out for a Spell?

Spelling and Usage

17

While organizing Pandora radio "stations" on my smartphone, I started a search for the Mormon Tabernacle Choir. Inadvertently, I left out the second *m* in *Mormon*. Imagine my embarrassment if I had made that error in a manuscript and hadn't proofread carefully before submitting. No spell-checker would have caught the error. And depending on the publication, I could have started a religious war.

I first knew I had to write on the topic of spelling when, in 2012, the University of North Carolina stopped requiring spelling exams for graduating journalism majors. Today's spell-checkers make such tests obsolete, the journalism department rationalized. To be fair, the curriculum substituted a "usage" component, ensuring that budding journalists could differentiate commonly misused options—e.g., *there/their/they're, two/to/too, conscience/conscious*.

But isn't spelling a basic tool in a writer's toolbox?

Spell-Checker Pros and Cons

Spell-checkers *can* be useful—if we don't turn them off and if we pay attention. Some manuscripts I've edited on screen contained dozens of words decorated with squiggly red lines underneath.

Shocking news: Red squiggly lines are a manuscript's cry for help. They designate misspelled (or unrecognized) words. Sometimes we need to educate our spell-checkers by adding words to our software's dictionary—if we've verified we're right. That step eliminates red *squigglies* (a word I coined and added to my computer's dictionary) for legitimate words, such as *valetudinarian*.

However, a *lack* of red squigglies can lull us into a false sense of security. That's why I'm a proponent of careful proofreading and wise input from a critique group.

For an entertaining demonstration of spell-checker shortcomings, see the poem in the sidebar (page 90), "Candidate for a Pullet Surprise," by Northern Illinois University professor emeritus Jerrold H. Zar. This poem is often carelessly circulated on the Internet as an anonymous work (for shame!) titled "Owed to a Spell Checker."

Take time to be your own human spell-checker, using online, electronic, and/or old-fashioned print dictionaries.

"But if you don't know how to spell something," complain writers who struggle with spelling errors, "how do you look it up?"

Spelling-challenged writers, rejoice. With such resources as *Random House Webster's Pocket Bad Speller's Dictionary*, you can look up a word the way you guess it's spelled and find out how far off you are.

Although I could fill a book with frequent spelling and usage errors, space considerations here require highlighting only a couple of top-ten lists compiled by some of my editor friends and me. (See more examples in the accompanying quiz.) Be vigilant. Avoid getting caught in these traps.

Spelling Traps

These example sentences demonstrate correct spellings in context.

1. **foreword/forward:** Clem looked *forward* to securing a *foreword* [endorsement from a prominent person] for his book.

2. **wiz/whiz:** To say Maryanne is a *wiz* or *whiz* at spelling is a shortened way of saying she's a spelling *wizard*. *Whiz* also is a verb meaning to go fast. After the competition the spelling *wiz* might *whiz* past everyone to find her parents.

3. **faze/phase:** We try not to let it *faze* us when teenagers go through a *phase*.

4. **lightning/lightening:** A streak of *lightning* was *lightening* the dark sky but not *lightening* our heavy mood.

5. **compliment/complement:** The *compliment* from Michelle's mentor was a *complement* to the critique she received from an editor. (*Compliment* is praise; *complement* is something that completes.)

6. **prophecy/prophesy:** You can see a *prophecy* [noun] coming true, but you might sigh at what the prophet will *prophesy* [verb].

7. **alright/all right:** Although some sources accept the slangy *alright* spelling, take the high road, which is *all right*.

8. **loose/lose:** Many a kindergartner will *lose* [verb] a *loose* [adjective] tooth. The activist cried, "*Loose* [verb] all penned animals!"

9. **flounder/founder:** A wounded *flounder* [noun, fish] might *flounder* [verb, flail] in the water. So might a swimmer. But for a boat to *founder* [verb] means it will sink [fail]. Flounder = flail; founder = fail.

10. **wrack/rack/wreak/wreck:** Ed may *rack* his brain [as in "the rack," torture by stretching] for a plan to avoid *wrack* [meaning wreck or destruction] and ruin—all

nerve-*racking* experiences. To *wreak* [verb, to bring about or inflict] havoc might leave a *wreck*. But don't *wreck* your reputation with the erroneous phrase *wreck havoc*. (To make life interesting, *CWMS 4* says *wrack my brain* is also acceptable but *rack my brain* is preferred by many grammarians.)[1]

Some proper nouns, such as people's names and geographical locations, sail through spell-checkers unmarked. Others don't. So whenever red squigglies identify potential misspellings, such as *Phillipians*, look up the word. In this case doubling the *p*, not the *l*, gives us the correct spelling: *Philippians*.

Usage Traps

Some of the above words also qualify as usage errors—legitimate words spelled incorrectly for the context. The examples below all fall into the improper usage camp but are not tied to spelling.

1. **imply/infer:** My comment may *imply* that I think the painting is ugly [my responsibility], or you may *infer* that [your responsibility].

2. **over/more than:** The cow jumped *over* the moon [position]. In so doing, she broke the women's high-jump record by *more than* [not *over*] 1,261,164,953 feet [number/quantity].

3. **less than/fewer than:** I shopped with *less than* 50 percent energy [degree], so I bought *fewer* groceries [countable number].

4. **rending/wrenching:** Brenda sobbed, hearing the *heartrending, gut-wrenching* story. (Don't mix up these two expressions—INCORRECT: *heart-wrenching* and *gut-rending*.)

5. **bring/take:** You *bring* something to where I am [movement toward me]. I *take* something to you [movement away from me].

6. **like/such as:** Steven has a physique *like* [comparison meaning similar to] Atlas. Eileen enjoys needlework, *such as* [examples, not *like*] knitting, crocheting, and embroidery. (This usage lists things she enjoys. Using *like* here would mean she doesn't necessarily enjoy these particular hobbies, but similar ones.)

7. **nauseous/nauseated:** The *nauseous* [adjective: that which makes someone feel ill] smell made Cynthia feel nauseated [adverb]. It also nauseated [verb] Mark.

   To say "I'm *nauseous*" means I make other people sick. I must confess this inappropriate usage is one of my biggest pet peeves in conversation, TV shows, and ads. *CMoS 16*, our main authority for such questions, says, "Whatever is nauseous induces a feeling of nausea—it makes us feel sick to our stomachs. To feel sick is to be nauseated. The use of nauseous to mean nauseated may be too common to be called error anymore, but strictly speaking it is poor usage. Because of the ambiguity in nauseous, the wisest course may be to stick to the participial adjectives nauseated and nauseating."[2]

8. **hold/conduct:** We don't *hold* meetings. We *conduct* them.

9. **anxious/eager:** Robin was *eager* to meet her new friends. Nothing made her *anxious* [nervous, anxiety-ridden] about their visit.

10. **while/although:** Lis updated the database *while* [simultaneous occurrence] Doug wrote the newsletter. *Although* [in spite of the fact that—not *while*] many people use these words interchangeably, let an alarm, sounding like HAL in *2001: A Space Odyssey*, go off in *your* head, saying, "I'm sorry, Dave. I'm afraid I can't do that."

You'll find an excellent resource regarding potentially problematic words in Part 2 of *CWMS 4*, called "The Word List." This section devotes almost 200 pages to helping writers find the precise words intended and/or the proper way to spell them.

Take Care, Now

Careless usage irritates editors. So an excellent writer's perpetual craft-honing regimen includes learning as much as we can about our word tools. To avoid the traps, seek feedback from a critique group or at least one other person who can look at your manuscript objectively. Then proofread, proofread, proofread!

Even editors confess occasional mistakes, however. More careful proofreading would have prevented a prominent Christian magazine from publishing this title's typo: "Away in a Manger." Or this error: "Readers were encouraged to *asses* their spiritual lives." "Sometimes an extra *s* is important," the editor contributing this blooper said.

A careless writer (or ill-prepared journalist) might keyboard the kind of blurb I saw on a TV newscast. It identified Senate Chaplain Barry Black as Senate *Chaplin*. (Thanks to silent-film comic Charlie, the word *Chaplin* raises no spell-checker red flags.)

Bottom line: Proper spelling and word usage can keep writers from looking like morons.

Candidate for a Pullet Surprise
by Jerrold H. Zar

I have a spelling checker.
It came with my PC.
It plane lee marks four my revue
Miss steaks aye can knot sea.

Eye ran this poem threw it,
Your sure reel glad two no.
Its vary polished inn it's weigh.
My checker tolled me sew.

A checker is a bless sing,
It freeze yew lodes of thyme.
It helps me right awl stiles two reed,
And aides me when aye rime.

Each frays come posed up on my screen
Eye trussed too bee a joule.
The checker pours o'er every word
To cheque sum spelling rule. . . .

To rite with care is quite a feet
Of witch won should bee proud,
And wee mussed dew the best wee can,
Sew flaws are knot aloud.

Sow ewe can sea why aye dew prays
Such soft wear four pea seas,
And why eye brake in two averse
Buy righting want too pleas.[3]

Chapter 17 Quiz

Circle or highlight the right word, justifying your choice. Don't peak (I mean *peek*!) at the answers in appendix A until you've given it your best shot.

1. Cinderella regretted ordering wedding [stationary/stationery] online.

2. Pooh chose from [between/among] honey, honey, or honey.

3. Flik saved the ants from a [hoard/horde] of grasshoppers.

4. Lightning McQueen zoomed [past/passed] his friend Mater.

5. Christopher Robin [led/lead] the parade.

6. Snow White said, "I think I'll [lay/lie] down."

7. Thumper skated better [then/than] Bambi.

8. Dory kept repeating the same [antidotes/anecdotes] to Nemo.

9. Rapunzel [could of/could have] had any guy she wanted.

10. Beauty's Beast [use to/used to] be a handsome prince.

References

Spelling Usage
> The Chicago Manual of Style, Sixteenth Edition: 5.220
> The Christian Writer's Manual of Style, Fourth Edition: Part 2, "The Word List,"
> pp. 399–597
> The Associated Press Stylebook: See Spelling
> MLA Handbook for Writers of Research Papers, Seventh Edition: 3.1.1

Punctuation and Related Matters

punctuation \pənk-chə-wā-shən\ *n* — little straight, slanty, round, and/or swirly lines we use in our writing, like street signs, to guide our readers regarding when to stop, start, pause briefly, pose inquiries, reflect excitement, hear voices, expect examples, stick two thoughts together, and more.

[May your words be] only what is helpful for building others up
according to their needs, that it may benefit those who listen [or read].

—EPHESIANS 4:29

That's What *He* Said

Punctuating Dialogue

18

If you've never seen comedic pianist Victor Borge's "Phonetic Punctuation" routine, search for it on YouTube (www.youtube.com). You'll never look at punctuating dialogue the same way again. He reads a melodramatic story, assigning each punctuation mark an exaggerated sound: A period sounds like a vowelless "*P't.*" For an exclamation point, he draws a "vertical dash" and period in the air, vocalizing this with a "*Phhht! P't!*" With his offbeat humor, Borge illustrates ways dialogue punctuation can alter readers' perceptions of a scene.

Poorly punctuated dialogue can mislead or confuse readers, sometimes causing them to backtrack to understand what's happening. They hate that! Note the punctuation in the examples below. Most principles also apply to quotations in nonfiction.

Placing Punctuation

Some writers forget where to place punctuation in relation to quotation marks. Perhaps this image will help: *tuck* a period, comma, question mark, whatever it is, safely inside the quotation mark.

An exception is a question mark or exclamation point that is not part of a title.

EXAMPLE: "Have you heard Doc Hensley's dramatic recitation of 'Jabberwocky'?" DiAnn asked.

The question mark isn't in the poem's title. If it is in the title, tuck it in.

INCORRECT AND SO SAD: "I can't get anything published", the conferee whined.
CORRECT: "I can't get anything published," the conferee whined.
ALSO CORRECT: Virelle peered over her reading glasses. "Perhaps there's a reason."

Capitalizing Tags and Beats

Should you capitalize the word following what a character says? It depends on whether it's part of a dialogue tag or an action beat.

A dialogue tag is equivalent to *[someone] said*. An action beat is some description of action, such as *he shook his head*. It's like a beat of rest in music—except the characters get to do something.

For dialogue tags, lowercase the first word after the quotation mark.

> INCORRECT: **The conferee plopped beside Lin. "I'm tired of whining." She said.**
> Use a comma before the closing quotation marks. Then lowercase *she*.
> CORRECT: **"I'm tired of whining," she said.** [Aren't we glad?]

Regard action beats (also called simply beats) as separate sentences needing capitalization.

> INCORRECT: **"I'm tired of whining," she sighed.**

Although we sometimes see this in print, it is not possible to *sigh* a sentence, *laugh* a sentence, or *snicker* a sentence—to name a few. So we could write it this way:

> CORRECT BUT WORDIER: **"I'm tired of whining," she said with a sigh.**

But in the incorrect sentence above, *she sighed* is an action beat (it's something she does), not the fact that she said it—or how—which we call a dialogue tag. So we punctuate it this way:

> CORRECT: **"I'm tired of whining." She sighed.**
> ALSO CORRECT: **"We have a secret." The little girl snickered. "You'll never guess it."**
> ALSO CORRECT BUT WORDIER: **"We have a secret," the little girl said with a snicker.**

Here's another important tip. Placing action *before* speech quickly alerts readers to who's speaking and how it's said. People reading aloud to children may use a different voice for Aslan than they do for Lucy, for instance. And they'll thank you for clues.

> FRUSTRATING: **"You can do this," Nancy whispered.**
> MORE HELPFUL: **Nancy whispered, "You can do this."**

Modifying Tags

Be careful with verbs and adverbs. When do you need commas?

> CORRECT: **"It's time to submit this article," Eva said firmly.**

Firmly (an adverb) describes how Eva said it, so we don't need a comma.

> ALSO CORRECT: **"I can't stand rejection," the conferee said, trembling.**

Trembling is an additional verb, yet it describes what the conferee is doing. So insert a comma to separate the two verbs.

Breaking It Up

Exceptionally long dialogue sentences can leave even silent readers out of breath. Maybe confused. Read long dialogue sentences—with tags—aloud to ensure the character and reader can easily say it in a single breath.

> FRUSTRATING: "Thanks for the baseball cap, Coach Laube," Rob said, plopping it on his head sideways as his dad always used to do when he was a kid growing up in Philadelphia, Pennsylvania, back in the fifties.

Go ahead and laugh. But I've seen similar sentences even in published books from respected publishers (with weary, overworked editors).

Try using an action beat beforehand.

> BETTER: Rob plopped the baseball cap on his head sideways. "Thanks, Coach Laube."

Do we really need all the background detail? If so, put it elsewhere. To keep readers turning pages, be selective with which details you include.

Watch for the word *as* in your dialogue tags and beats too. The word *as* often signals trouble spots.

> FRUSTRATING: "I'm late for class," Cyle said as he stuffed his manuscripts into his backpack, grabbed a cookie, and hurried down the corridor.

He can't do all that while he says that short sentence.

> BETTER: "I'm late for class." Cyle stuffed his manuscripts into his backpack, grabbed a cookie, and hurried down the corridor.
>
> ANOTHER OPTION: Cyle stuffed his manuscripts into his backpack. "I'm late for class." Grabbing a cookie, he hurried down the corridor.

Few things in life happen simultaneously. And readers expect writers to maintain "chronologicalness." So avoid the awkward "simultaneousness" the word *as* implies.

Tags and beats—with proper punctuation—facilitate good pacing, illustrate where characters may take a breath while speaking, or indicate a pause for emphasis.

> WEAK AND CONFUSING: "If you miss a deadline, you're dead," Jerry said, taking his place behind the lectern.

As written, it sounds as if Jerry starts speaking while he's on his way to the stage. Avoid simultaneousness; maintain chronologicalness.

> BETTER: Jerry strode to the lectern. "If you miss a deadline, you're dead," he began.
>
> MORE POWERFUL: Jerry strode to the lectern. "If you miss a deadline," he began, "you're dead."

The dialogue tag creates a pause and provides emphasis. Note the punctuation and capitalization.

Tags and beats aren't fillers. They coax your readers to go where you want them to go, and they show your readers what you want them to know.

Paragraphing Properly

Readers subconsciously expect that actions and speech within a paragraph relate to the same character. And if there's a paragraph break, a different person begins speaking or acting. Honor that expectation.

> CONFUSING: **Philip crept up behind Devon.**
>
> **Devon turned and glared.**
>
> **"Mom's calling you!"**
>
> **"So?"**

The writer may have intended for the *"Mom's calling you!"* comment to come out of Devon's mouth. But readers, seeing the paragraph break, think Philip's saying it. So it should read this way:

> **Philip crept up behind Devon.**
>
> **Devon turned and glared at him. "Mom's calling you!"**
>
> **"So?"**

Now we also know that it's Philip who says, *"So?"*

What about when a character's speech spans two or more paragraphs?

Try to avoid that. Break up what the person says, if at all possible, with a re-action from someone else in the scene (new paragraph), even if only noting body language. But if a long-winded character must hog more than one paragraph, omit the closing quotation marks at the end of the first paragraph and use opening quotation marks for the next one.

Interrupting Speech

Many writers also confuse dashes and what are technically called suspension points (what we might think of as ellipses). Both indicate an interruption.

- Use a dash (—) to indicate that your character stops talking abruptly.
- Use suspension points (. . .) to indicate that your character's voice trails off. *CMoS 16* also says they "may be used to suggest faltering or fragmented speech."[1]

Each example below is correct.

1. **The journalism student gulped. "Interviewing a pro athlete is outside my comfort zone, and—"**

   "When did that phrase enter the Christian vocabulary?" Dr. Black blurted.
2. **"Well, I don't know . . ." She gazed off into space.** [Note the action beat.]
3. **"Well, I don't know . . . ," she said.** [Note the comma after the suspension points and the lowercase *she* in the dialogue tag.]
4. **"Well . . . I . . . uh . . . don't know," she said.**

Internal Dialogue

For many years most writers have italicized direct thoughts (internal dialogue) to differentiate it from indirect thought and spoken words. Readers are conditioned to interpret these distinctions:

SPOKEN DIALOGUE: "That's the last time I'll buy a manuscript from that writer," James said.

DIRECT THOUGHT: *That's the last time I'll buy a manuscript from that writer*, James thought.

INDIRECT THOUGHT: That was the last time he would buy a manuscript from that writer, James vowed [or *thought*].

A current trend sets direct thoughts in regular roman font or in quotation marks:

That's the last time, James thought.

"That's the last time," James thought.

This trend is showing up in books, magazines, and some of the major style manuals (including *CMoS 16*). However, *CWMS 4* "acknowledges the usefulness of italic type for thoughts. The convention is widely recognized by readers, and many authors prefer it."[2]

My bold recommendation: Ask *your editor* if you can buck the prevailing trend, do your readers a favor, and use italics for direct thoughts.

Above all, remember that the punctuation you use can guide your readers, making sure they understand your intentions. So be kind to them, and plug the right punctuation into the right places! *Phhht! P't!*

Chapter 18 Quiz

In the sentences below, make any corrections necessary. Put a C beside any sentences that are correct. See answers in appendix A.

_____ 1. Viola frowned. "I suppose I could try to . . ." [Indicates voice trailing off]

_____ 2. "Everything has to be perfect," Hailey said as she curled her hair, donned her dress, and headed downstairs to wait for her prom date.

_____ 3. Use proper punctuation and paragraphing for the dialogue in this politically incorrect exchange (with only two people in the scene):

Hank pulled Petunia's pigtails.
"You're a dork," he said.
"Well, you're not exactly Mr. Wonderful.
"At least I know how to throw a football."
He tossed a perfect spiral down the field.
Running after the ball, she caught it cleanly and fired it back.
"I can do that too." Her throw bonked him on the head.

_____ 4. "The pie is out of the oven," Mother stated, sniffing in the aroma.

_____ 5. "I can't take any more of this frivolity," she laughed.

_____ 6. "Are you sure you want to eat that seventeenth piece of banana cream pie?" Rick asked, warily.

_____ 7. "Let's go for a walk," Norman suggested.
"All right," Alison retorted.

_____ 8. Angie pounded her fist on the table. "You never let me finish my sen . . ."
"What do you mean I never let you finish your sentences?" T. J. cut in.

_____ 9. "The quality of mercy is not deranged. It droppeth as the gentle brain from heaven upon the place bequeathed. It is twice blest: It blesseth him that gives and him that takes. 'Tis Mighty Mouse like the throned monarch butterfly—better than his cronies," began Waldo, slaughtering Shakespeare's beautiful piece from *The Merchant of Venice*.

_____ 10. Joanna said, "I published an article in *FarmFriendly* magazine. The article is called 'Confessions of a Cowbell Player.'"

References

Paragraphing in Dialogue
>The Chicago Manual of Style, Sixteenth Edition: 13.37
>The Christian Writer's Manual of Style, Fourth Edition: pp. 260–61

Punctuation with Quotation Marks
>The Chicago Manual of Style, Sixteenth Edition: 6.9–11, 13.39
>The Christian Writer's Manual of Style, Fourth Edition: pp. 323–24
>The Associated Press Stylebook: See Quotation Marks
>MLA Handbook for Writers of Research Papers, Seventh Edition: 3.7.7
>Publication Manual of the American Psychological Association, Sixth Edition: 4.07–8

Initial Capitalization in Dialogue
>The Chicago Manual of Style, Sixteenth Edition: 13.13–16

Commas in Dialogue
>The Chicago Manual of Style, Sixteenth Edition: 6.9, 13.18
>The Associated Press Stylebook: See Commas
>MLA Handbook for Writers of Research Papers, Seventh Edition: 3.2.2

Other Punctuation in Dialogue
>The Christian Writer's Manual of Style, Fourth Edition: pp. 152–54, 157–58, 207–10

Thoughts, Internal Dialogue
>The Christian Writer's Manual of Style, Fourth Edition: pp. 367–68

God is at work within you, helping you want to obey
him, and then helping you do what he wants.
—PHILIPPIANS 2:13 (TLB)

Hyphen Hyperactivity
When to Use Hyphens

19

Hyphens, hyphens everywhere—everywhere they don't belong. And some missing from their rightful places. Have you seen them? Have you wondered whether the word you're about to type or just finished typing should have a hyphen?

I won't try to cover every rule here, and exceptions always exist. But these guidelines cover many questionable situations.

Prefixes

Words with prefixes almost never need hyphens. Most people probably wouldn't think of hyphenating *preview, unhappy,* or *recycle.* Yet over the years, as I've critiqued or edited articles and books, I've often seen prefixes unjustly alienated from the rest of the word by a *misplaced* (not *mis-placed*) hyphen.

Authors who wouldn't hyphenate *interact,* for some reason write about an *inter-faith* worship service (replace with *interfaith*). Writers who wouldn't think of typing *un-do, un-made,* or *un-read,* for some reason find it necessary to let a hyphen rudely barge in to write *re-do, re-made,* and *re-read* instead of letting *redo, remade,* and *reread* remain their hyphenless selves.

So curb your hyphen hyperactivity. Write freely (and hyphenlessly) of the *su*persensitive, *multi*talented, *mega*church pastor (of a *pre*millennial persuasion), who worried so much about the *post*modern thought of our day, *dis*seminated freely in *cyber*space—and his *in*ability to get any *co*operation from his parishioners in combating the *anti*biblical teaching in the community's *sub*par public schools—that he developed a *pre*ulcerative condition, requiring him to *inter*mittently *re*fill his *pre*scription for a *pro*biotic medication.

You won't need a single hyphen with any of those prefixes. However, you might find yourself *under*appreciated for that *ultra*long sentence!

Sometimes hyphen usage depends on the word you're attaching to the prefix. With *mid*, for example, we can usually leave our hyphens in the toolbox: *midair* collision, *midweek* meeting, and *midstream* course correction. But when we combine that prefix (and many others) with numbers or months, for example, the hyphen gets to shine: In *mid-October* we had temperatures in the *mid-50s*.

Be careful with capitalized and already hyphenated words too. Though *non-entity*, *nonexistent*, and *nonplussed* get along fine without a hyphen, *non-Christian*, *non-Hodgkin's lymphoma*, and *non-insulin-dependent diabetes* require them.

Common sense also eases the decision. It's obviously important to differentiate between *re-cover* and *recover*—equally legitimate words. To *re-cover* a tattered book means something quite different than to *recover* it from the bully who stole it from you or to *recover* from an illness.

A few exceptions pop up from time to time, such as those in the next section.

Double Vowels

When a prefix doubles a vowel in a word, such as *semi-interesting*, it might (as in this case) need a hyphen. But it might not: *reentry* and *preexisting* don't. So *reevaluate* your mental processes if you thought you should always hyphenate a word with a duplicate vowel. You rarely do.

We generally don't need hyphens when the prefix sticks together two different vowels:

> For the *biannual* medical convention, two doctors *coauthored*[1] a paper on the *socioeconomic* factors in *preoperative* tests.

Since double vowels can be tricky, whenever the slightest doubt arises, look up the word. Many dictionaries contain lengthy lists of potentially troublesome words, such as those beginning with *re*, which almost never calls for a hyphen. Follow the principles demonstrated there.

Important: Sometimes even what's correct may trigger red squigglies from your software, alerting you that you *misspelled* (not *mis-spelled*) words. But courageously charge ahead—if you've verified you're right. Then add the correct spelling to the dictionary to *reeducate* your *semi-ignorant* software.

Suffixes

Words with suffixes seldom need hyphens either. Are you hyperactive in using hyphens? Restrain yourself when writing about *catlike* eyes, *childlike* faith, or *Christlike* character.

But insert a hyphen with suffixes following proper nouns other than *Christ* (*Job-like* patience, *Enron-like* corruption, or *Chicago-like* winds). And pop in one of those hyphens between *like* and a word ending with the letter *l* (*drool-like* substance) and words with three or more syllables (*institution-like* structure).

Compound Words

At times we may be tempted to whip out a hyphen for compound words: two or more words stuck together as one. *Nevertheless* (one word, no hyphens), if we are careful *word crafters*, we'll give the hyphen a rest when writing of *earaches, cookbooks,* and *kneecaps.*

Also note that a *bookkeeper* for a store selling *knickknacks* needs no hyphens—though her inventory of *bric-a-brac* does. (See chapter 19 for more on this topic.)

Multiword Modifiers

Perhaps the hyphen performs its most important function when it acts like a link, uniting various elements of description in a chain, such as the *freckle-faced* teen or the *six-year-old* (adjective) *boy* and his sister, a *three-year-old* (noun).

Want a touch of whimsy in your writing? An occasional long, hyphenated, *multiword* description (before a noun) can evoke a chuckle:

> After one of those *I-can't-take-one-more-demand-from-a-whiny-kid* days, Marilyn locked herself in her bedroom for her own time-out.

To indicate a range of elements before a noun, we use a somewhat odd-looking construction:

> All fifth- through seventh-grade students had a *twenty- to thirty-minute* wait.

See how the first hyphen seems suspended in air with a space between it and the next word—in suspense—as if waiting breathlessly to modify that next noun in the sentence? Perhaps that's why some grammarians call this punctuation tool *suspensive hyphenation.*[2]

Consider this construction, however:

> Students in grades five through seven had a wait of twenty to thirty minutes.

This sentence doesn't rate any hyphens because the descriptions come after the nouns.

Hyphens can also prevent ambiguity or help readers visualize relationships: Are there *extra-thick* pancakes (thicker than we would expect) on the table? Or might you find the *extra* (more in quantity than needed) *thick* pancakes a great temptation? Whether or not you insert a hyphen will signal your meaning to the reader.

Descriptions with *To Be*

We usually try to strengthen and minimize *to-be* verbs (such as *am, was, were, has been, will be*). But if a multiword description follows a *to-be* verb, do not use a hyphen:

- He was *well informed* for a school dropout.
- I, on the other hand, am *ill equipped* to solve my computer problems despite my college education.

-ly Adverbs

Leave your hyphens in their toolbox when using *-ly* words too:

- **Joel and Melody were sorry they hired the significantly cheaper nanny.**
- **Order now to get this unbelievably low price!**

When in doubt, look it up.

Never be ashamed to use a dictionary. Logging on to www.m-w.com or similar sites takes only seconds. Buy (or download for free) a dictionary software program to consult when you can't access the Internet. If all else fails, pull that dictionary off the shelf. Keep in mind that the one of choice in many editorial offices is *Merriam-Webster's Collegiate Dictionary*. (Buy the most recent edition. Also available to install on your computer.)

Wise, careful writers don't guess. They look it up.

Use those hyphens when they're needed. But exercise *self-restraint* and help stamp out hyphen hyperactivity!

Chapter 19 Quiz

Correct any errors below. Mark a *C* beside any sentences that are correctly rendered. See answers in appendix A.

_____   1. All the six-year-olds should go to the left side of the gym, and those who are seven years old or older should go to the right side.

_____   2. The church dismissed the elder because he exhibited a very un-Christ-like character.

_____   3. Rowena snuggled into the extra soft pillow that, for some reason, smelled like s'mores.

_____   4. The lawyer won the anti-trust suit handily.

_____   5. The non-believers left the snake oil salesman's presentation, laughing out loud.

_____   6. Anne, the geo-political advisor to the organization, misspelled thirteen country names in her memo.

_____   7. The well traveled business exec felt exasperated when he saw that his wife planned to take two large suitcases for a five day vacation.

_____   8. Jeffrey started chowing down on the thinly-sliced corned beef.

_____   9. During military brat Cara's sixth through eighth-grade years in school, she attended seven different schools.

_____   10. My three-year-old grandson's smile makes me melt.

References

Hyphens
> The Christian Writer's Manual of Style, Fourth Edition: pp. 200–202

Prefixes
> The Chicago Manual of Style, Sixteenth Edition: 6.80, 7.35, 7.77, 7.79, 7.85
> The Christian Writer's Manual of Style, Fourth Edition: pp. 300–301
> The Associated Press Stylebook: See Prefixes
> Publication Manual of the American Psychological Association, Sixth Edition:
>> See Table 4.2

Double Vowels
> The Associated Press Stylebook: See Hyphen

Suffixes
> The Chicago Manual of Style, Sixteenth Edition: 7.35, 7.77, 7.79–80, 7.85
> The Christian Writer's Manual of Style, Fourth Edition: See Hyphenation, Word
>> Division, p. 200
> The Associated Press Stylebook: See Suffixes
> Publication Manual of the American Psychological Association, Sixth Edition:
>> See Table 4.2

Compound Words
> The Chicago Manual of Style, Sixteenth Edition: 5.91, 7.35, 7.77–85
> The Christian Writer's Manual of Style, Fourth Edition: See Hyphenation; Word
>> Division, p. 200
> The Associated Press Stylebook: See Hyphen
> Publication Manual of the American Psychological Association, Sixth Edition: 4.13

Multiword Modifiers
> The Chicago Manual of Style, Sixteenth Edition: 5.91, 7.81–83
> The Christian Writer's Manual of Style, Fourth Edition: See Hyphenation, Compound
>> Adjectives, p. 201
> The Associated Press Stylebook: See Hyphen
> Publication Manual of the American Psychological Association, Sixth Edition: 4.13

To-Be Verbs
> The Chicago Manual of Style, Sixteenth Edition: 5.98–99, 5.151–52

Are you called to help others? Do it with all the strength and energy
that God supplies so that God will be glorified through Jesus Christ.

—1 PETER 4:11 (TLB)

Compound Infractions

Compound Word? Hyphenated Word? Two Words?

20

In many ways, excellent writing is like a great marriage of words—a string of marriages, a community of marriages—each word finding its best fit in mutual, loving harmony. So, as I often say, "What the creators of our language system hath joined together, let no writer put asunder."

Yet as I'm editing manuscripts, I find myself grinding my teeth (much to my dentist's consternation) over the careless and/or inconsistent way some writers join words together or "put them asunder."

I devoted chapter 19 to hyphenation, so here I'll do a short review, then proceed to answer the following questions:

- Which words should be hyphenated?
- Which are compound words (two words "wedded in holy matrimony")?
- Which words should never get stuck together?

If you want to see fewer edits on your manuscripts—and increase the acceptability of your work—it pays to learn to present your thoughts and words in the proper way. So let's look at basic principles and tools to avoid compound infractions and haphazard hyphenation.

Compound Words

Returning to the marriage analogy, a compound word is literally two words becoming one: *Life* and *span* unite as *lifespan*—no space, no hyphen. *Man* and *made* come together as *manmade*. *Law* and *giver* bond as *lawgiver*.

One easy way to identify whether two words are "made for each other" is to try sticking them together. If no red squigglies appear on the screen, it's a marriage made in dictionary heaven—at least Microsoft's dictionary heaven, which doesn't always agree with *Webster's Collegiate,* the dictionary of choice in many editorial offices and in this book. When in doubt, check it out.

All the compound words in the following paragraph are correct:

> One terrifying night on the Sea of Galilee, our Lord's *handpicked* disciples watched awestruck as Jesus quieted a horrific storm. Their *worldview* had been turned upside down. They wanted to be calm and *Christlike,* but their terror grew *tenfold. Nonetheless,* when Jesus appeared, Peter literally walked on water to meet his Master.

Two Words

Some words best fly solo. In the following paragraph, note the italicized pairs in this paragraph I've pieced together from manuscripts I recently edited. You may be tempted to "hitch" them together with a hyphen or as a compound word. Resist! (Disclaimer: This paragraph is riddled with Christian clichés to be avoided. It's for teaching purposes only. See chapter 44 for more on clichés.)

> The world is full of *pleasure seekers,* but those who pursue pleasure above all are often disciples of *false Christs* who use *proof texts* to justify their teaching. However, as Christians, in our makeup we are Christ's *image bearers* who seek to bring God glory. Once someone addresses our *felt needs* and we hear the *good news* that Jesus canceled our *sin debt,* we can move from *head knowledge* to *heart knowledge* and learn to abide in our Savior.

Hyphenated Words

Remember that one use for hyphens is to link together compound adjectives when they *precede* the noun they modify—but not when they come afterward.

COMING BEFORE: red-hot [hyphenated] poker
COMING AFTER: a poker that was red hot [not hyphenated]
COMING BEFORE: ill-fitting stiletto heels
COMING AFTER: stiletto heels that were ill fitting

The following examples demonstrate nouns that can snuggle together using hyphens. (Note where we also need capitalization.)

> With Bucky's *mind-set,* he had *hang-ups* about getting *X-rays.* The very thought of them made his stomach play *Ping-Pong* with the butterflies there, and his *T-shirt* became soaked as he drove to the clinic in his *Rolls-Royce* V-8.

Prefix Challenges

Burn this motto into your brain: **Most prefixes don't need hyphens.**

Prefixes include *un, non, re, pre, post, omni, pseudo, trans, multi, mega, super, counter,* and *sub.*

Our *omni*present, *pre*existent God tells us in the Bible that the *pre*incarnate Christ participated in creation and loved us with an *ever*lasting love. (Excellent writers don't write a prefix-laden sentences like that, but you get the point.)

As I typed the example above, my spell-checker got nervous. It broke out in red squigglies at the sight of the word *preincarnate*, not finding it in its memory banks. But I know *preincarnate* is correct (I verified it!). So I had to educate my dictionary. Right-clicking on the word, I chose "Add to Dictionary" from the drop-down menu. From henceforth, I have allayed my dictionary's fear of that word.

Usage Considerations

When checking the dictionary, be sure to note the word's function (e.g., noun, verb, adjective, adverb) preceding each definition. In case you find abbreviations there, I've noted their meaning below.

We pick up some groceries [*vt = transitive verb*]. **We take them home in our pickup,** [n = noun] **or pickup** [adj = adjective] **truck. Then we join a game of pickup** [adj] **basketball.**

Your dictionary is your friend.

Special Situations

Here are two interesting special situations to note:

- The wizards at Apple have decreed that neither iPods nor iPhones need hyphens.
- When first coined, terms such as *e-mail*, *e-book*, and *e-zine* came with hyphens. Although *The Chicago Manual of Style* continues to use and recommend these hyphenated forms, many publishers, as well as the current *Christian Writer's Manual of Style*, eliminate a hyphen or space in the most common "e-combination" terms. We will see this trend continue. In the meantime, I advise you, once again, to study your target publication and to be consistent in usage throughout your manuscript. And we will use *email* and *ebook* in the rest of this book.

So, once again, I strongly advise all Christian writers to immerse themselves in the helpful principles detailed in *The Christian Writer's Manual of Style*. Bottom line: study your target publication, and be consistent throughout your manuscript.

Tools and Techniques

These four steps will help you use compound words correctly:

1. Use your spell-checker. Yes, I actually said that. I often caution against relying on spell-checkers because they don't catch legitimate words used incorrectly. However, spell-checkers can help us identify potential problems if we pay attention to the red squiggly lines errors generate.

Here's one of the best uses of a spell-checker: Type in a questionable word and see if the red squigglies appear. For example, if I want to use the word *homemade*, I can type it in as one word. If no red squigglies appear, I can be fairly confident it's a compound word needing no space or hyphen.

2. Look it up. Frequently consult an up-to-date print dictionary, online dictionary (such as m-w.com), or installed software dictionary (for off-line work). Use the first spelling listed that goes with the definition you're seeking.

3. Study your target publications. Select a few periodicals you want to write for, and study them well to pick up on their house styles where publications may differ (e.g., *coworker* versus *co-worker*; *website* versus *web site* or *Web site*).

4. Be consistent. If dictionaries offer conflicting rulings, take your best guess and be consistent. Then if your manuscript is accepted, note how the editor treats it. Add that to your working vocabulary.

Although occasional compound infractions and haphazard hyphenation don't automatically doom manuscripts, they also don't inspire editors' confidence.

So when in doubt, look it up!

As our words come together—whether one word, two words, or hyphenated—let's cultivate wedded bliss and happy editors.

Hyphen Exceptions

Use a hyphen when the prefix

- immediately precedes a numeral: post-9/11; mid-1800s (but midday report)
- precedes a capital letter: pre-Pentecost; anti-Christian; but antichrist (the general spirit) and Antichrist (when referring to the person)
- precedes an existing compound term: post–Civil War (Note the "en dash" instead of a hyphen. See chapter 26 for information about this unique punctuation mark.)
- duplicates letters that could cause confusion or creates a new word that could lead to a misreading: anti-intellectual; co-op; counterclockwise, but counter-counterrevolution

Chapter 20 Quiz

For the italicized words in the following sentences, mark C for correct or I for incorrect, telling why. You may have to look up some words to be sure. See answers in appendix A.

_____ 1. He writes *non-fiction*.

_____ 2. The *self-less* young woman was *self-conscious*.

_____ 3. The Russians *re-occupied* the territory.

_____ 4. The three *eye witnesses* disagreed.

_____ 5. The Holy Spirit comes *along side* us to comfort us.

_____ 6. Ginny was born in the *mid-1960s*.

_____ 7. Satan is our *archenemy*.

_____ 8. Dr. Bakke urged us to understand *post-modern* thinking.

_____ 9. The *megachurch* drew parishioners from a large area.

_____ 10. We're studying *endtime* prophecies because we're convinced we're in the *end times*.

References

Compound Words
> The Chicago Manual of Style, Sixteenth Edition: 5.91, 7.35, 7.77–85
> The Christian Writer's Manual of Style, Fourth Edition: pp. 192, 314
> The Associated Press Stylebook: See Hyphen: Compound Modifiers
> MLA Handbook for Writers of Research Papers, Seventh Edition: 3.2.6
> Publication Manual of the American Psychological Association, Sixth Edition: 4.13

God Words
> The Christian Writer's Manual of Style, Fourth Edition: p. 192

Hyphenated Words
> The Chicago Manual of Style, Sixteenth Edition: 7.77–85
> The Christian Writer's Manual of Style, Fourth Edition: pp. 200–202
> The Associated Press Stylebook: See Hyphen
> MLA Handbook for Writers of Research Papers, Seventh Edition: 3.2.6
> Publication Manual of the American Psychological Association, Sixth Edition: 4.13

Prefixes
> The Chicago Manual of Style, Sixteenth Edition: 6.80, 7.35, 7.77, 7.79, 7.85
> The Christian Writer's Manual of Style, Fourth Edition: pp. 300–301
> The Associated Press Stylebook: See Prefixes

Proofreading, Ten Commandments for
> The Christian Writer's Manual of Style, Fourth Edition: p. 314

E-compounds
> The Christian Writer's Manual of Style, Fourth Edition: pp. 159, 458–61

Whatever you do [even using proper punctuation],
do it all for the glory of God.
—1 CORINTHIANS 10:31

The Inside Scope
Colons and Semicolons

21

At the risk of grossing you out with even the mention of the word *colonoscopy*, my recent experience (at this writing) with this procedure—due to a temporary malfunction in that particular part of my anatomy—made me think about ways poorly functioning colons and semicolons foul up our writing. They serve important functions in good writing but frequently stick their noses in where they don't belong.

So let's do a little "scoping" to make these punctuation marks work for us, not against us.

The Colon

To use a colon properly, here are a few rules to follow:

1. *Use a colon as a pointer.* The Christian Writer's Manual of Style says that a colon can introduce "an amplification, an example, a question, or a quotation."[1] I demonstrate this in the accompanying sidebar, "Spacing Out" (on page 116), when I write, "I repeat: we no longer use two spaces between sentences." The colon points to the principle emphasized.

2. *Use a colon between a title and subtitle.* I titled this chapter "The Inside Scope: Colons and Semicolons" in the table of contents to illustrate this rule. When a title and subtitle are placed on two lines, as it is at the beginning of this chapter, the colon can be omitted.

3. *Use a colon to signal the beginning of a list—sometimes.*

> EXAMPLE: **Eustace took an extra suitcase to the writer's conference to bring home the career-boosting resources he needed: sample magazines, books on writing, market guides, CDs from sessions he couldn't attend, and his own copious notes.**

Note this capitalization principle from *CMoS 16*: "When a colon is used within a sentence . . . the first word following the colon is lowercased unless it is a proper name. When a colon introduces two or more sentences . . . , when it introduces a speech in dialogue or an extract . . . , or when it introduces a direct question, the first word following it is capitalized."[2]

Only capitalize the word following a colon if it's a proper noun or begins two or more sentences. So in the example above, we don't capitalize the word *sample*.

However, in the following, capitalize the word *Writing* because it's the first word in a series of two or more sentences following the colon.

> EXAMPLE: **Eustace returned with three indelible impressions: Writing is hard work. Editors are normal people (most of them anyway). And rejection slips may simply mean we haven't found the right approach or market yet.**

4. *Don't use a colon when the introduction to the list isn't a complete sentence.*

> CORRECT—AND BRAVO FOR HIM: **Eustace threw himself into such activities as studying books on writing, poring over sample magazines, listening to workshop CDs, and participating in a critique group.**

The portion before the list isn't a sentence, so no colon is needed.

Watch for introductory words that eliminate the need for a colon, such as *including, for example, for instance, namely, consisting of,* and *such as.*

> CORRECT—AND MAY HIS TRIBE INCREASE: **Eustace bought several must-have books, including** *The Christian Writer's Manual of Style, The Christian Writer's Market Guide, A Complete Guide to Writing for Publication,* **and** *An Introduction to Christian Writing.*

5. *Use a colon before a block quotation—sometimes.* Generally, avoid long quotations because readers often skip over them. But when occasionally quoting one hundred words or more—at least six to eight lines—indent the entire "block." That indent designates the quotation's beginning and end, so we don't need quotation marks around the quotation.

In the following example, what introduces the block quotation is a formal introductory phrase, so use a colon after the word *this.*

> **In his humor column, "A Journey into My Colon—and Yours," Dave Barry wrote this: The idea of having another human, even a medical human, becoming deeply involved in what is technically known as your "behindular zone" gives you the creeping willies.**[3]

When not using a complete statement before the block quotation, use a comma.

> **In his humor column, "A Journey into My Colon—and Yours," Dave Barry wrote, The idea of . . . [the rest of the block quotation follows].**

6. *Use a colon between chapter and verse designations in Scripture references.* Most Christian writers use the colon properly in references such as 1 Samuel 12:24. But always proofread to make sure you didn't inadvertently use a semicolon instead of a colon.

7. *Use a colon after the opening salutation in a query letter.* Remember, query letters are business letters and need to follow that format. (If you need to, search Google to refresh your memory on this format.) I would, for example, address an e-query proposing an article to a magazine editor this way:

> Dear Angus Ferguson:

The Semicolon

The semicolon deserves to be used for creating a winking-face emoticon in personal emails more often than for writing articles or books. In past eras, semicolons appeared frequently, but we rarely use them today. Grammarian Robert Pinckert says semicolons are "used by those who can't decide between commas and periods. Good writers . . . stay away from semicolons. Amateurs and professors use far too many of them."[4]

So, with an actual wink, I propose guidelines, rather than rules.

1. *Don't use a semicolon to combine two sentences.* In times past, writers often employed semicolons to slap together two related, independent clauses without a coordinating conjunction, such as *and*, *but*, and *or*.

> SAD COMMENTARY, CORRECT BUT NOT PREFERABLE: Grocery shoppers paid their respects at the meat counter; they couldn't afford to buy anything.

Two independent clauses, one sentence.

Today's editors accommodate readers' shorter attention spans by employing shorter sentences. Each independent clause can become a separate sentence:

> STILL A SAD COMMENTARY, CORRECT AND PREFERABLE: Grocery shoppers paid their respects at the meat counter. They couldn't afford to buy anything.

It's grammatically correct to use a semicolon, but two shorter sentences propel readers forward faster.

In some *scholarly* publications, however, long sentences riddled with semicolons seem to procreate between the covers.

If it's been a while since you thought about clauses other than Santa and his wife, remember this: An independent clause is a grouping of words, with both a subject and a verb, that could stand alone as a sentence. A dependent clause contains both subject and verb but depends on the rest of the sentence to make sense.

The following sentence contains two clauses—one independent and one dependent. Which is which?

> EXAMPLE: Editors never bought Lulu's manuscripts because she ignored writer's guidelines.

If you identified the first clause of the sentence as independent and the second as dependent, your brain's synapses are firing away well. Using the subordinating conjunction *because* makes the second clause dependent on the first one. No need for a semicolon in that sentence.

2. *Use a semicolon in a series.* Semicolons uncomplicate lists in which commas already abound.

> EXAMPLE: **We visited many state capitals: St. Paul, Minn.; Lincoln, Neb.; Denver, Colo.; Springfield, Ill.; Des Moines, Iowa; Helena, Mont.** (Check your target publications regarding whether they use state abbreviations, as above, or postal codes— the preference of *The Chicago Manual of Style*.)

3. *Use a semicolon in a list of Scripture references.* Semicolons uncomplicate lists of Scripture passages too.

> EXAMPLE: **Jesus described himself with several metaphors, as in John 6:35; 8:12; 10:7, 14, 25; 14:6; and 15:5.**

Commas separate verse numbers within a chapter, and semicolons set off new chapter numbers in the list.

Take time to ingrain these rules and guidelines in your brain's self-editing software. They ensure proper functioning of the colons and semicolons in all your manuscripts.

And because good article conclusions and good chapter conclusions tie back to the introduction, I finish with this: After all was said and done, my husband asked, "If the doctor had yielded to your pleas for mercy partway through the aforementioned procedure, would they have called it a semicolonoscopy?"

Ba-dum pum.

Spacing Out

Contrary to what you may have learned in a typing or keyboarding class, hit the space bar only once after a colon, as well as a semicolon—and after a period, a question mark, and an exclamation point, for that matter. I repeat: we no longer use two spaces between sentences.

If, for years, you (like I) habitually inserted two spaces, retraining yourself will take time. Meanwhile, try this remedy: After you've finished your manuscript, use the Find-and-Replace feature of your word-processing software to find extra spaces. Hit the space bar twice in the "Find" box and once in the "Replace" box.

Chapter 21 Quiz

In the following sentences, correct any errors you find in the use of colons and semicolons. Mark a *C* beside any that are correct. See answers in appendix A.

_____ 1. My grandfather always joked that he was going to write a book called *My Humility and How I Attained It; One Man's Exciting Journey.* The book would contain a foldout, life-size picture of him in the front.

_____ 2. In Jennie's mystery novel, her amateur sleuth always kept the following essentials in her car: a flashlight, a pair of black gloves, a card of bobby pins, a roll of transparent tape, and a box of chocolate-covered cherries.

_____ 3. The economist reported that the price of helium is rising for a number of reasons, most of which he couldn't explain; sales of balloons, therefore, and helium-canister rentals—just to make people's voices sound funny at parties—are tanking.

_____ 4. The preacher used the following verses to show us the folly of opening a Bible at random to determine God's will: Matthew 27:5; Luke 10:37b.

_____ 5. Saúl opened restaurants in three new locations last year: Roseville, Minn.; Lakeville, Minn.; and Hudson, Wisc.

_____ 6. The fruit of the Spirit include:
- love,
- joy,
- peace, and
- patience.

_____ 7. Dr. Hensley told his adult Sunday school class that all the teachings of Jesus can be summed up in two words: "Follow me."

_____ 8. The Love Finds You romance series uses unusual settings, Valentine, Nebraska, Romeo, Colorado, and Bridal Veil, Oregon.

_____ 9. The physical therapist told Farmer Brian he had to quit lifting heavy things: such as hundred-pound sacks of manure, if he wanted to quit saying, "Oh, my achin' back."

_____ 10. When I was a teenager, I inadvertently put the reference 2 Samuel 12;24 at the bottom of a letter to a male friend who became a missionary. (I meant *1* Samuel 12:24.) Embarrassing!

References

Colons
The Chicago Manual of Style, Sixteenth Edition: 6.59–65
The Christian Writer's Manual of Style, Fourth Edition: pp. 128–29
The Associated Press Stylebook: See Colon
MLA Handbook for Writers of Research Papers, Seventh Edition: 3.2.4
Publication Manual of the American Psychological Association, Sixth Edition: 4.05

Semicolons
The Chicago Manual of Style, Sixteenth Edition: 6.54–58
The Christian Writer's Manual of Style, Fourth Edition: pp. 352–53

The Associated Press Stylebook: See Semicolon
MLA Handbook for Writers of Research Papers, Seventh Edition: 3.2.3
Publication Manual of the American Psychological Association, Sixth Edition: 4.04

State and Province Abbreviations
The Christian Writer's Manual of Style, Fourth Edition: pp. 359–60

> A quiet spirit can overcome even great mistakes.
> —ECCLESIASTES 10:4 (NLT)

Stamp Out Apostrophe Abuse

22

Some people's nightmares consist of sinister psychopaths chasing them down a dark alley. My nightmares consist of facing a jury of my peers in two courtroom scenarios:

1. Charged with possession of a black marker with intent to deface public property. Never mind that I was correcting the felonious misuse of apostrophes.
2. Charged with attacking the Sunday worship graphics person. Never mind that I was correcting song lyrics that, instead of using a needed apostrophe at the beginning of a word, used a single quotation mark magnified on the Jumbotron to the size of a Mexican Chihuahua.

I'm baffled that Microsoft Word's software engineers can't create a grammar program smart enough to recognize an apostrophe at the beginning of a word. Nor can I understand how any otherwise intelligent person can't correct an apostrophe facing the wrong way.

To be honest, in my column in the *Christian Communicator* magazine called "Writing GPS: Grammar, Punctuation, and Style," I dissed Microsoft Word software engineers—in a smart-aleck humor attempt—about this apostrophe issue. Then I later had to apologize. And I conveyed my gratitude to the editor who emailed me with a quick shortcut I didn't know existed. To create an apostrophe at the beginning of a word, hold down the Ctrl key, and hit the apostrophe key twice. Ta-da!

Still a little convoluted, I think, but this tip shaves a few seconds and keystrokes off my other suggested solution in the sidebar on page 123. I understand this shortcut may not work for some Mac users. But PC users, rejoice.

Okay, here's my nightmare's backstory. The manuscript I'm critiquing at this writing addresses the wanderings of the *Israelite's* in the desert. Online weather reports today say temperatures will hover in the *70's*.

So far I'm able to keep my cool over the apostrophe abuse.

Then, as I back out of my driveway, I see my neighbors' mailbox with "The Vecino's" lettered on the side. I reach for my black marker.

The sign in the grocery store reads: Tomato's and Cantaloupe's on Sale! I uncap my marker, and rescue the sign from apostrophe exploitation.

Nearby, the neon-orange lettering on the bookstore's window reads: All CD's and DVD's 25% Off. In this nightmare, the bookstore manager snatches my arm as I'm about to commit yet another act of—in nightmarish logic—justifiable vandalism.

I know I'm not alone in this hypersensitivity. But it may qualify me, in the minds of some, for a verdict of "not guilty by reason of insanity."

Hyperbole and humor attempts aside, Christian writers who love words and want to be excellent stewards of language and punctuation will want to use even apostrophes correctly.

Correct Usage

Apostrophes play an important role in three main areas: possessives, contractions, and other omitted material. I'll hit the basics here first, then discuss them more in detail.

1. Possessives: expressions indicating that something belongs to someone or something else, using 's at the end of a word.

   CORRECT: **The rejected book proposal failed to include the author's credentials.**

2. Contractions: shortened versions of a compound word or two words, substituting an apostrophe for omitted letters.

   CORRECT: **I can't** [for *cannot*] **help my apostrophe obsession.**
   CORRECT: **He's** [for *He is*] **oblivious to correct apostrophe use.**

3. Other omitted material: omitting part of a word in dialogue, also for years or decades.

   CORRECT: **"Susie Mae is dyin' to know what happened," Pa said.**
   CORRECT: **My friends Mary, Paul, and Peter still love the music from the '50s and '60s.**

Incorrect Usage: Plurals

In general, we don't use apostrophes to indicate that something is plural. Why would we?

EXAMPLE: **The Israelites** [not *Israelite's*] **wandered.**

Using the word *Israelite's* indicates you're talking about something an Israelite (singular) possesses, such as one Israelite's garment.

EXAMPLE: **Temperatures hover in the 70s** [not *70's*].

The numeral *70* stands for the word *seventy*. Its plural is *seventies*, not *seventy's*. So we smoosh the *s* right up next to the *70*—no space, no apostrophe. We do the same thing with decades, such as the 1970s or 1850s.

> EXAMPLE: **The late-blooming writer wished he had paid more attention in college rather than squeaking by with straight Cs.**

Note these explanations of other examples:

- Names on mailboxes don't express possessives but rather identify the occupants: Mr. and Mrs. Vecino and their spunky offspring, in plural form, are *the Vecinos*.
- Grocers put *tomatoes* (not *tomato's*) and *cantaloupes* (not *cantaloupe's*) on sale. These produce items don't possess anything. We're talking plural here. No apostrophes.
- The 25 percent discount applied to all *CDs* and *DVDs* (not *CD's* and *DVD's*). *CD* stands for *compact disc*, and we wouldn't write *Mr. Courtney recorded thousands of compact disc's*.
- *ATM* stands for automatic teller machine, so the plural is *ATMs*, not *ATM's*. (Please also help us battle redundancy: the term *ATM machines* would mean *automatic teller machine machines*.)

Here are two exceptions to the no-apostrophes-for-plurals rule:

- Plurals of abbreviations with periods.

> CORRECT: **The book proposal cited the author's two Ph.D.'s in the field of study discussed.**

Note: If the style of your target publication is to omit the periods in academic degrees, which is the recommendation of *The Chicago Manual of Style*, the apostrophe should also be omitted.

> CORRECT: . . . **the author's two PhDs**

- Plurals of stand-alone lowercase letters.

> CORRECT: **There are only two *r*'s in the word *persevere*.**

Correct Possessives

When we want to indicate that something belongs to someone or something else, we usually have no problem forming a possessive of a proper noun (*Ann's article*) or a common noun (*the market guide's listings*).

When forming possessives with pronouns (such as *he, she, they, it*), however, we can get into trouble. Most writers wouldn't use *hi's* or *he's* instead of *his*, but these might trip up some of us:

- **The book is *yours*** [not *your's*].
- **The exquisite necklace is *hers*** [not *her's*].

- The critique group set down *its* [not *it's*] rules in writing.
- The decision is *theirs* [not *their's*].

When referring to something owned by two or more people or items, where do we need apostrophes? Check out these correct examples:

- The magazine's and book publisher's guidelines are in the market guide.

Here the guidelines for the magazine and the book publisher are different items, so we use an apostrophe for each of those words.

- Paul and Silas's message received mixed reviews at Philippi.

Assuming Paul and Silas were preaching the same basic message, we only need one apostrophe (after the latter) to cover them both.

Plural Possessives

Possessives get trickier with plurals. Generally, to indicate the possessive of a plural, we add only an apostrophe to the end of the plural form of the noun.

CORRECT: The panel moderator asked for the editors' pet peeves.

Irregular plurals, however, can throw us off.

INCORRECT: Mom put away the childrens' toys—again.

Children is already plural, so we don't pluralize it with an *s*. And since it doesn't naturally end in *s* as most plurals do, we slap on an *'s*.

CORRECT: One night the children's toys magically put themselves away. Nah!

Correct Contractions

We would seldom write a sentence like this:

It is clear that either he does not want to go or cannot go with you.

In dialogue, something like that might denote a stuffed-shirt character. But most of us don't talk or write that way. It sounds stilted. We use contractions:

It's clear that either he doesn't want to go or can't go.

Most writers have no trouble creating contractions, but beware of homophones (sound-alike words).

- Use *they're* (not their) when you mean they are.
- Use you're (not *your*) when you mean *you are*.

Other Omitted Material

Perhaps because the meter of "Silent Night" didn't have enough beats for the word *around*, the translator of Joseph Mohr's hymn employed poetic license to omit the beginning *a*: *'round yon virgin*.

Here are some other considerations regarding using apostrophes for omitted material:

- *In using dialect.* Beware of overusing apostrophes to drop letters in speech patterns. It becomes tiresome and difficult to read. However, *occasionally* inserting an apostrophe for a *g* in an *-ing* word can flavor dialogue and direct quotations.

  Some years ago, I wrote a profile of a professional race-car driver named Lake Speed (yes, that's his given name). Describing an exciting race, he said, "I thought I was fixin' to win the thing." Most readers will hear his drawl throughout the rest of the piece without my dropping the *g* every time he did in our interview.

- *In years.* When we write *class of '68*, we mean *1968*. The apostrophe indicates the omission of the first two digits. But now, more than a decade into a new century, we need to be careful to use all four digits whenever any confusion could exist.

- *In certain expressions.* Here are some examples. But remember: when in doubt, look it up!

  - *o'clock*: This designation originated from the archaic time expression *of the clock*. Since we're leaving out everything but the *o* and *clock*, we use an apostrophe to indicate the omission.
  - *rock 'n' roll*: Note that we're using *'n'* in place of *and*, so we're omitting two letters instead of only one. Also note the spaces around *'n'*.
  - *dos and don'ts*: Though some publications differ, *dos and don'ts* is the most commonly accepted designation.

A final word of caution: once you become adept at using apostrophes in all the right places, you, too, may find yourself inexplicably drawn to your local office-supply store to buy the biggest black marker you can find.

Right Face? Left Face?

To create an apostrophe at the beginning of a word, type two apostrophes, then delete the one that's facing the wrong way. *'Round yon virgin* becomes *''Round yon virgin*, which painlessly becomes *'Round yon virgin*, using the delete key.

Chapter 22 Quiz

Mark each sentence or phrase below with *C* for correct or *I* for incorrect. Then revise those that are incorrect for proper apostrophe usage. See answers in appendix A.

_____ 1. Writers should not try to keep up with the John Grisham's of this world.

_____ 2. When using his cash cards, Mr. Watkins can never remember his PIN's.

_____ 3. the boy's dormitory

_____ 4. Beverly and Virginia's outfits

_____ 5. There are only two *r*'s in the word *persevere*.

_____ 6. the peoples' compassion

_____ 7. Heinrich was grateful to earn mostly Bs in calculus.

_____ 8. Ms. Herlocker admired Marianne because she laughed at Charles' jokes.

_____ 9. I'm not sure how we lived through the '70's.

_____ 10. Harry withdrew money from two ATM's before heading to a store selling gigantic TV's.

References

Apostrophe Usage
> The Chicago Manual of Style, Sixteenth Edition: 6.113–15
> The Christian Writer's Manual of Style, Fourth Edition: p. 46
> The Associated Press Stylebook: See Apostrophe
> MLA Handbook for Writers of Research Papers, Seventh Edition: 3.2.7

Apostrophes with Plurals
> The Chicago Manual of Style, Sixteenth Edition: 7.8, 7.14, 7.59–61
> The Associated Press Stylebook: See Plurals
> MLA Handbook for Writers of Research Papers, Seventh Edition: 3.2.7

Apostrophes with Plurals of Single Letters and Abbreviations
> The Christian Writer's Manual of Style, Fourth Edition: p. 295

Apostrophes with Possessives
> The Chicago Manual of Style, Sixteenth Edition: 5.50, 7.15–25
> The Christian Writer's Manual of Style, Fourth Edition: pp. 297–99
> The Associated Press Stylebook: See Possessives
> MLA Handbook for Writers of Research Papers, Seventh Edition: 3.2.7
> Publication Manual of the American Psychological Association, Sixth Edition: 4.12

Contractions
> The Chicago Manual of Style, Sixteenth Edition: 5.50, 7.29
> The Christian Writer's Manual of Style, Fourth Edition: pp. 46, 136–37
> The Associated Press Stylebook: See Contractions

Apostrophes in Dialect
> The Christian Writer's Manual of Style, Fourth Edition: pp. 153–54
> The Associated Press Stylebook: See Dialect

Capital Crimes and Misdemeanors

Capitalization

23

Taking his place on the witness stand, the defendant described in a smarmy voice how the day of the alleged assaults began. "I woke up, wondering where my sweet little boys were," he said. "I just love them so much."

We, as jurors, had previously heard testimony from several witnesses that later the defendant, in a fit of anger, jumped into the car of his live-in girlfriend (the mother of those sweet little boys) and tried to run her down, then attempted to make road-kill of the neighbors who charged in like Galahads to save a Guinevere in distress.

During our deliberations, several jurors bellyached about the unfairness of the laws governing the case. But we kept coming back to police officers' photographic evidence of the torn-up lawn, the credibility of the defendant and other witnesses, the judge's instructions, and the definition of the charges against the defendant.

As foreperson, I struggled to maintain order when vitriolic arguments conjured images of the movie *12 Angry Men*. After several hours, the holdouts came to their senses and agreed with the majority that the guy was guilty.

Though not pertaining to a capital crime (one punishable by death), this case underscored the importance of knowing the "laws" of good writing as well—and working within that framework. I couldn't help but apply that situation to this chapter on *capital* letters and *capital*ization.

Know the Rules

Some writers have gotten away with murder, so to speak, in breaking capitalization rules, and some conventions have changed over the years. C. S. Lewis and other authors in previous eras capitalized any word they wanted to emphasize.

And authors such as Ann Kiemel (Anderson), who started writing in the '70s, tried to make a statement by always lowercasing the word *I*. But novelties quickly become distracting to the reader—something we always want to avoid.

Return to Basics

Here are basic capitalization rules that govern our writing:

1. Capitalize proper names (of specific people, buildings, landmarks, institutions).

    CORRECT EXAMPLES: Joe Stinkowitz, the Tower of Pisa, Mount Rushmore, the Internal Revenue Service

2. Capitalize the first word of every sentence and the first-person singular pronoun *I* wherever it appears. Don't let bad texting habits spill over into your writing for publication, even in emails to editors. Your word-processing software should self-correct, but don't get cutesy and override it.

3. Capitalize words such as *mother, father, uncle,* and *grandma* when used as proper nouns or in place of the person's name.

    CORRECT: When I was in my teens, Grandma lived with my family.
    CORRECT: I knew I was in trouble when Dad said, "Get in here, Daughter."

4. Don't capitalize those relationship nouns when immediately preceded by a possessive noun or pronoun (e.g., *Jane's, the boy's, my, his, her, our, your, their*).

    CORRECT: Beth's uncle influenced her greatly.
    CORRECT: Rod gave his mother a gift.

5. Capitalize professional and military titles only when immediately preceding a name as part of the name.

    INCORRECT: Julie queried the proper Editor.
    CORRECT: Julie queried the proper editor.
    CORRECT: Julie queried Editor Morris.
    INCORRECT: I need to write to my Congressman.
    CORRECT: Christine wrote a profile of General Ulysses S. Grant.
    INCORRECT: We met John G. Roberts, Chief Justice of the United States.
    CORRECT: Leith agreed with Chief Justice Roberts.

6. Don't use all caps for emphasis. It's the print equivalent of shouting, and it wears out the reader. Indicate emphasis with italics.

    INCORRECT: God wants our LOVE above EVERYTHING else.
    CORRECT: God wants our love above *everything* else.

    In the corrected version, we help readers focus on only one word: *everything.*

7. Capitalize *Bible(s)* and *Scripture(s)* as nouns, but lowercase the adjectives *biblical* and *scriptural*. Most writers capitalize the nouns properly, but some erroneously slap capital letters on the adjectives.

> INCORRECT: **We made sure the new pastor's teachings were Biblical.**
> CORRECT: **The pastor's deep, biblical teaching refreshed the thirsty congregation.**

Apply the same guidelines to the word *scriptural*.

Watch Titles and Subheads

The following guidelines come from the newest edition (at this writing) of *The Chicago Manual of Style* (Sixteenth) and may differ from what you've been taught.

In both titles of works and subheads, capitalize the following according to headline style: first and last words and all other major words, such as nouns, pronouns, verbs, adjectives, adverbs. (Brush up on your parts of speech if necessary.) In addition, observe these elements:

- Do not capitalize articles (*a, an, the*).
- Do not capitalize these conjunctions: *and, but, for, or, nor*.
- Do not capitalize the word *to* when used as part of an infinitive (e.g., *Driven to Succeed, Nowhere to Go*).
- Do not capitalize prepositions, regardless of length (e.g., *of, by, for, in, on, to, through, about*). Exception: If a preposition is used as an adjective or adverb, capitalize it (e.g., *Crank Up the Air Conditioner*).

We should note that some magazines use a different style, so follow their rules for titles and subheads.

Hyphenated Words in Titles

Hyphenation can be more challenging, but here's a trick: if you capitalize the title as if the hyphen or hyphens aren't there (see capitalization guidelines above), you'll likely get it right. Here are some examples—all correct:

> **Keys to Surviving Record-Breaking Heat**
> **Self-Editing for Dummies**
> **Fourth-of-July Fireworks Fizzle**
> **What Nine-Tenths of Women Most Fear**

However, many magazines don't capitalize the word after the hyphen. So if you're writing for periodicals, follow the style your target publications use. Most importantly, be consistent within your article or book.

Observe Special Considerations

Here are some other guidelines to observe:

- Capitalize the words *Internet* and *World Wide Web*. Do not capitalize *www* in an Internet address.

- Dictionaries don't all agree regarding capitalization of words such as *net* (short for *Internet*), *website (or web site), web,* and *web page.* Such decisions often depend on in-house style. You'll see them both ways in print. Make sure you're consistent within your manuscript.
- Capitalize keyboard function keys and menu items, such as *Ctrl, Alt, Option, Tools, Cut.*
- Don't capitalize words like *iPad* and *eBay* when they begin a sentence.
- Do capitalize brand names that are trademarks, such as *Eggo.* According to *The Chicago Manual of Style,* "There is no legal requirement to use [the trademark symbols ® and TM, and they should be omitted wherever possible."[1] That manual, and others, *do* encourage using generic terms, such as tissue instead of *Kleenex.* But if you're writing dialogue in fiction and have your football linebacker character say, "May I please have a tissue?" your readers might throw the book across the room in disbelief.
- Capitalize *God,* but lowercase *godly.* But when referring to a false god or gods, put them in their place by using lowercase.
- Lowercase *heaven* and *hell*—although we know they are real places.

The big question, especially for Christian writers, is: do we capitalize pronouns referring to God and Jesus?

Answer: It depends. I grew up capitalizing pronouns referring to deity. It signified reverence to us. And when you described a scene with Jesus and another male, readers knew the capped pronoun referred to Jesus.

Yet the King James Bible, also highly revered, didn't capitalize deity pronouns. So when I started writing, I felt awkward capitalizing deity pronouns in what I wrote while using lowercase in quotations from the Bible. The style wasn't consistent. Today more and more publications and publishing houses are lowercasing deity pronouns.

But if you have a strong compulsion to capitalize them, discuss this with your publisher.[2] For consistency between what you write and the Scripture you want to quote, you can use a translation such as the New American Standard Bible (NASB) or the Holman Christian Standard Bible (HCSB), which capitalize deity pronouns. At this writing, the HCSB version is not on BibleGateway.com, but it is available on Amazon.com as a free ebook. So if you download it onto your computer, you can cut and paste from there.

Consider Your Target Market

Capitalization guidelines often vary from publication to publication, so that's another reason to carefully study your target market before submitting.

The deity-pronoun question is a case in point. Check to see whether that periodical capitalizes them or not. In the book world, some publishers do not cap deity pronouns but allow authors with strong convictions to do so.

Remember, editors love careful, excellent writers—even in such a little thing as capitalization. Though a magazine or book editor won't likely reject a manuscript or proposal solely on the basis of capitalization errors, carelessness gives editors pause. Can they trust such writers to be accurate in quotations, fact-checking, and other content?

Follow the Rules

While I was on jury duty, the judge repeatedly reminded us neither to watch news broadcasts and lawyer and cop shows nor to do Internet searches related to the case. Once we began deliberations, two deputies herded us between the deliberation room and a locked lunchroom and back again to guard us from outside influences. We had to decide the case solely on facts and evidence presented in the courtroom and the judge's instructions—whether we agreed with the laws or not.

Similarly, writers may not always like grammar rulings. But we cannot make up our own or listen to other voices. We study the rules to write and revise skillfully. We submit our best work under the watchful eye of mentors, critique groups, and editors. And we dedicate ourselves to be found "not guilty" of, among other things, committing capital crimes and misdemeanors.

Chapter 23 Quiz

Capitalize on this skill-building opportunity. Use standard proofreading marks (listed in appendix B) to make corrections: Three short lines under a letter mean capitalize. A forward-slash mark through a capital letter means change to lowercase. If everything in a sentence is correct, mark it with a C. (See appendix B to learn more about proofreading marks. These, too, are important tools of the writer's trade.)

If you belong to a critique group, do this exercise together and discuss your rationale. See answers in appendix A.

_____ 1. We want to be Godly people.

_____ 2. The Professor's lectures provided the students a much-needed nap.

_____ 3. I envied my Grandfather's knowledge of the scriptures.

_____ 4. Donald, a Captain in the US navy, led the children in the pledge of allegiance.

_____ 5. I finished my Proposal for a book titled *A hitchhiker's guide to spiritual disciplines*.

_____ 6. I-Pads are being used increasingly in Public Transport and on Gym Treadmills.

_____ 7. Exercise caution with Internet research.

_____ 8. The Lord shows us his love every day.

_____ 9. I need to write to senator Dewmore.

_____ 10. We DON'T want to be careless writers.

References

Capitalization Rules

    The Chicago Manual of Style, Sixteenth Edition: 5.5–6, 7.48, chapter 8: Names and Terms

    The Christian Writer's Manual of Style, Fourth Edition: pp. 88–114

    The Associated Press Stylebook: See Capitalization

    Publication Manual of the American Psychological Association, Sixth Edition: 4.14–20

Title and Subtitle Capitalization

    The Chicago Manual of Style, Sixteenth Edition: 8.155–58

    The Christian Writer's Manual of Style, Fourth Edition: pp. 88–89

    The Associated Press Stylebook: See Capitalization

    Publication Manual of the American Psychological Association, Sixth Edition: 4.15

Commatose

All about Commas

24

I'm more of a Tilt-a-Whirl Girl than a Roller-Coaster Boaster. My taste in amusement-park rides may have something to do with my fear of heights. But I have squeezed myself under the torturous safety bar of a few coasters in my life and submitted myself to three minutes of sheer terror.

Oddly enough, the one coaster-like ride I almost enjoy is the Mad Mouse. I get a kick out of the shorter vertical drops. And when the track appears to end—flinging me out into space—sharp, ninety-degree turns produce one lawsuit-worthy whiplash after another.

"How in the world is she going to get to a grammar, punctuation, or style issue from here?" you may ask.

Roller-coaster engineers design a specific rhythm for the "enjoyment" of the riders: the anticipation of ticking up the steep incline or maneuvering the twists and turns that leave riders screaming. But some coasters also have that unnerving, herky-jerky feel. In writing, also, we aim to engineer a perfect rhythm. One vital tool in this task is the lowly comma.

Too many commas and ill-placed ones can create an unpleasant, herky-jerky reading experience. At the opposite extreme, a lack of commas can leave readers comatose. But well-placed commas create a pleasant flow in our writing.

I won't try to cover all the uses of commas, but here are some primary guidelines.

Pauses and Clauses

Though "writing by ear" doesn't always produce quality prose, sometimes we can feel where a comma belongs by noticing where we pause as we read a sentence. One example is an introductory phrase, such as the one in this sentence:

Once upon a time, a young novelist dreamed of instant fame and fortune.

More often the following basic categories show us where to use commas. To fully understand the need for commas here, we need to review clauses and sentence types.

Compound Sentences

A compound sentence contains at least two independent clauses, usually joined by a comma and then a coordinating conjunction (such as *and, but, so, or*). An independent clause will still make sense even if used as a separate sentence.

> Correct (and exciting): **Terry skimmed the manuscript quickly, and he realized this book could turn his publishing house around.**

Notice the comma before *and*, the coordinating conjunction that joins the two independent clauses. Don't leave out the comma.

Complex Sentences

A complex sentence contains at least one independent clause and one dependent clause. These are joined by a subordinating conjunction (such as *when, as, while, before, although, unless, because, until*). Even though a dependent clause has a subject and a verb, it can't survive alone. It's dependent on the rest of the sentence.

> Also correct: **Because Terry read the manuscript, he knew its potential.**

Because is the subordinating conjunction that makes that first clause dependent on the second. Note where we put the comma. Everything in front of the comma in that sentence is a dependent clause. Everything after the comma in that sentence is an independent clause.

Before-and-After Rule

Before: When the dependent clause comes *before* the independent clause, use a comma to separate the two.

> **Because Terry has been in the publishing business for decades** [dependent clause], **he recognized a great book** [independent clause].

After: When the dependent clause comes *after*ward, we don't need a comma.

> **Terry could hardly contain his excitement** [independent clause] **as he read the manuscript** [dependent clause].

Here *as* is a subordinating conjunction, and we don't need any commas in this sentence because the dependent clause comes after the independent clause.

Remember the before-and-after rule, and you'll get it right every time.

Comma Splices

Sometimes writers erroneously slam two independent clauses together with only a comma, omitting a coordinating junction. We call this error a comma splice.

COMMA SPLICE ERROR: **Terry read the riveting manuscript, he recognized a blockbuster.**

We could correct this error four ways:

1. Substitute a semicolon for the comma—though not recommended:

   Terry read the riveting manuscript; he recognized a blockbuster.

2. Insert a coordinating conjunction after the comma:

   Terry read the riveting manuscript, and he recognized a blockbuster.

3. Divide into two sentences:

   Terry read the riveting manuscript. He recognized a blockbuster.

4. Create a complex sentence by inserting a subordinating conjunction:

   As Terry read the riveting manuscript, he recognized a blockbuster.

Choose wisely. And vary what you use in various situations. The options you choose affect the rhythm and flow of your writing.

Parentheticals

If a word or phrase could be put in parentheses—but it's a slight interruption and you want a less-intrusive feel than parentheses or a dash—use commas.

CORRECT (AND FUN IDEA): **The editor, much to his surprise, received a bag of M&M's[1] from a writer he had helped at a conference.**

CORRECT (AND TOO COMMON): **Krista procrastinated all summer, unfortunately, on the article now due in two days.**

Serial Commas

When you're studying a magazine you think might be a good fit for your work, notice its use of commas in series of elements. We always use commas between words in a list, but note the following sentence. Is this correct or not?

CORRECT? **Orville proofread his manuscript for errors in spelling, grammar, and punctuation.**

Should we have inserted a comma before the last item in the list—called a serial comma—or not? The answer depends on the style manual the publication or publishing house uses.

Most book publishers and many magazines use as their standard *The Chicago*

Manual of Style, which says yes to a serial comma. Newspapers and some magazines use *The Associated Press Stylebook*, which says no to a serial comma. Don't ask editors what they use. Simply note what they do, and do the same when submitting there.

Caution: At times you will want to insert that final comma for clarity even if the publication doesn't generally use it. The following example has been floating around writing circles for years:

> Correct? **I dedicate this book to my parents, Mother Teresa and the pope.**

As written, it appears that Mother Teresa and the pope are the writer's parents. To prevent scandal, we add a comma after *Teresa*, indicating the author is dedicating this book to four people, not two.

Appositives

That example leads to appositives—words and/or phrases that generally snuggle next to each other, naming or describing the same thing. Put commas around appositives.

I cover appositives in more detail in chapter 15, but to discuss the specific role of *commas* with appositives, I'll give a few examples here.

Consider the Mother Teresa example sentence: Without the second comma, *Mother Teresa and the pope* are appositives to *my parents*. They stand for the same thing. We assume the writer isn't claiming the pope and Mother Teresa as her parents. So we need a comma after *Teresa*.

Now look at these two examples.

> Correct: **My prayer partner from church, Phyllis, encouraged me to make time for a cup of tea with her this week.**
> Correct: **My prayer partner Phyllis urged me to make time for a cup of tea.**

In the first, I'm specifically saying I have one prayer partner at church. Her name is Phyllis. In the second, I'm saying I have more than one prayer partner. But I'm talking about Phyllis here.

Similarly, the following sentence makes me a criminal:

> Throw-me-in-the-slammer example: **My husband Steve supports me a great deal in my writing.**

Here I'm accusing myself of bigamy because there are no commas indicating that *Steve* and *my husband* are the same.

> Corrected, keeping me out of jail: **My husband, Steve, supports me . . .**

The commas create an appositive, clarifying that he's my one and only.

Restrictive versus Nonrestrictive

In related fashion, words such as *who, that,* and *which* sometimes signal a need for a comma. These words may indicate either a restrictive clause or a nonrestrictive clause.

- *Restrictive clauses* can't be deleted from a sentence without altering its meaning. They don't need commas.

  EXAMPLE: **Writers who diligently work on their craft rise to the top of the slush pile.**

If we take out the words *who diligently work on their craft*, we're ridiculously saying all writers rise to the top of the slush pile.

- *Nonrestrictive clauses* can be deleted without changing the sentence meaning. They *do* need commas.

  EXAMPLE: **Conscientious writers, who diligently continue studying their craft, delight editors.**

The use of *conscientious* allows us to lift out the *who* clause without changing the meaning. Note the need for commas.

---

e.g. and i.e.

Since this is a chapter about commas, you may be watching for them throughout the chapter and noting how they are used. You may notice a comma after *e.g.* This abbreviation stands for the Latin *exempli gratia* (in case you're thinking of taking up this foundational language, which isn't a bad idea). And *exempli gratia* essentially means "for example." In English we can think of *e.g.* as standing for *example given*. So the material that follows *e.g.* can be a list—and we put a comma after the *e.g.* Notice how it's used in this chapter and sidebar.

We also use a comma after *i.e.*, which comes from the Latin *id est*. And *id est* means "that is"—essentially, "in other words." In English we can think of *i.e.* as I'll explain. So what follows *i.e.* is often a clarification of some type.

CAUTIONARY EXAMPLE: **We all know we need to polish our manuscripts (i.e., make sure we're turning in clean copy), but sometimes we hurry too much and submit our work prematurely.**

We use the comma to indicate a pause and to alert readers that the ending periods of *e.g.* and *i.e.* are not the end of the sentence.

If you have trouble remembering when to use *i.e.* and when to use *e.g.*, use the little abbreviations I used above: *i.e.* = I'll explain, and *e.g.* = example(s) given.

Geographicals

Okay, I made up the word *geographicals*. But I wanted a single word for this subhead. Writers generally know that we put a comma between city and state, but we seldom hear that we also insert one after the state name.

CORRECT: **Knockemstiff, Ohio, is an actual ghost town.**

The same principle holds true with cities and countries.

CORRECT: **The hamlet of Nobottle, England, welcomes horse enthusiasts.**

Hang On!

As we choose how to present what we're trying to say, our many options create different emphases and design a roller coaster of rhythms—all part of the manuscript-polishing process. Commas play a large part in determining whether we engineer for the reader a herky-jerky frustration or an exhilarating ride.

Chapter 24 Exercise

Edit this brief snippet of a story, inserting and deleting commas. Pretend you plan to submit it to a publication that does, indeed, use the final serial comma. If you find an example of a comma-splice sentence, choose wisely from the four solutions to correct it. See appendix A for my suggested revision.

> Once upon a time a bright young woman, Sunny Diamante, who scored extremely high on her SATs was accepted at several prestigious universities. She chose to study English at Harvard University in Cambridge, Massachusetts with an eye toward teaching at the college level.
>
> Sunny and her roommate clicked instantly, they were both bookworms from small towns. They loved the same books, music and sports. During the first semester they even fell in love with the same guy their freshman comp professor.
>
> He himself looked like he'd barely graduated college. They eventually learned he was a child prodigy who finished high school by the time he was twelve. He was actually younger than they were though he had his doctorate, he certainly didn't look old enough.
>
> Before they finished their freshman year each woman had written a romance novel about a college student and a young English professor with chiseled features, long eyelashes and curly black hair that dangled over his sky-blue eyes.

References

Commas
> The Chicago Manual of Style, Sixteenth Edition: 6.16–17
> The Christian Writer's Manual of Style, Fourth Edition: pp. 130–34

Compound Sentences
> The Chicago Manual of Style, Sixteenth Edition: 6.28
> The Christian Writer's Manual of Style, Fourth Edition: pp. 130–31

Complex Sentences
> The Chicago Manual of Style, Sixteenth Edition: 6.16–53
> The Christian Writer's Manual of Style, Fourth Edition: p. 132

Subordinating Conjunctions
> The Chicago Manual of Style, Sixteenth Edition: 5.200–201
> The Christian Writer's Manual of Style, Fourth Edition: p. 132
> Publication Manual of the American Psychological Association, Sixth Edition: 3.22

Serial Commas
>The Chicago Manual of Style, Sixteenth Edition: 6.18
>The Christian Writer's Manual of Style, Fourth Edition: pp. 132, 135
>The Associated Press Stylebook: See Comma
>Publication Manual of the American Psychological Association, Sixth Edition: 4.03

Appositives, Restrictive and Nonrestrictive Clauses
>The Chicago Manual of Style, Sixteenth Edition: 5.21, 6.22–23, 6.26
>The Christian Writer's Manual of Style, Fourth Edition: p. 131
>The Associated Press Stylebook: See Essential Clauses, Nonessential Clauses

Geographical Commas
>The Chicago Manual of Style, Sixteenth Edition: 6.46
>The Associated Press Stylebook: See Addresses
>MLA Handbook for Writers of Research Papers, Seventh Edition: 7.3

You can show others the goodness of God, for he called
you out of the darkness into his wonderful light.
—1 PETER 2:9 (NLT)

In This Corner . . .
Italics versus Quotation Marks

25

Long before World Wrestling Entertainment, back in the '40s, my husband's uncle was a big fan of professional wrestling. His wife thought it was stupid. Finally, he talked her into going to a wrestling match. So there she sat, clutching her purse, choking on cigar smoke, desperately wanting to be anywhere else.

Then the action began—grabbing, headlocks, wrestlers on the ropes, down for the count. Despite her best efforts, the lady really got into it: wincing, leaning left, leaning right, closing her eyes, holding her breath, grasping her purse tightly, twisting it back and forth. By the end of the night, she had twisted her purse so violently she totally ruined it!

We may not face a knockdown fight with punctuation in our manuscripts, but learning a few basics can keep combatants in their own corners and simplify life for editors with whom we want good working relationships.

Now, in one corner of this chapter's wrestling ring, chomping at their mouthpieces, waiting to strut their stuff, are *italics*. In the other corner is the tag team of *single and double quotation marks*. Let's watch them go at it.

Italics

Here are some ways italics can correctly "tag team" in your writing.

1. *Emphasis*
Though the problem existed before, the advent of email (especially before we could easily add bold type and italics) led to a proliferation of all caps for emphasis. But all capitals seem like shouting in print. Instead, to emphasize a word or phrase, use *italics*. Not ALL CAPS. Not **bold**. Not even <u>underlining</u>.

"Whoa," you may say, "my freshman English teacher, Mrs. Persnickettyface, insisted we underline words we wanted to emphasize."

In precomputer days, we had no italics at our disposal—unless we were typesetters. To those "heroic souls," an underlined word meant "Set in italics." But now, with a quick Ctrl+I, we transform regular roman type into italics.

Underlining is a standard proofreading mark for changing to italics, however. So when self-editing on hard copy or critiquing someone else, use this handy tool.

Be careful when using italics in quotations from Scripture or other sources. It's permissible to italicize words we want to emphasize, but alert the reader this way:

> "The Lord ... is patient ... , not wanting *anyone* to perish, but *everyone* to come to repentance" (2 Peter 3:9, emphasis added).

Caution: Overusing italics for emphasis actually weakens the emphasis. Use sparingly.

2. *Referring to a Letter, Word, or Phrase*
Using italics in these instances makes them stand out for the reader.

> CORRECT: Craig forgot to capitalize the letter *L* in *Lord*.
>
> CORRECT: When conversing, Al likes to insert the word *kumquat* for its humorous sound.
>
> CORRECT: The infinitive *to insert* is stronger than the more common *to put in*.

Note: Some periodicals may use quotation marks instead. Follow the style of your target publication.

3. *Titles*
Here's where things can get a little confusing. We may have to sound the bell to send the wrestlers back into their corners for a breather.

In general, italicize longer works, using roman (regular) type and quotation marks for related shorter works:

- Use italics for titles of books, names of magazines (in print or online), blogs, and computer games.
- Use quotation marks for titles of songs, poems, articles, and short stories (which may or may not be part of a longer work).

> CORRECT: Did you read Kathy Carlton Willis's article "Hope-Filled Words in Hopeless Times" in the *Christian Communicator*?
>
> CORRECT: In her children's novel *Escape into the Night*, Lois Walfrid Johnson grabs young readers' attention with her first chapter title, "Nighttime Surprises."
>
> CORRECT: The preschoolers drew humorous illustrations of the one-eyed, one-horned creature from "The Purple People Eater" song.

However, some book titles, such as The Holy Bible and individual books of the Bible, aren't italicized.

Other titles and names we *do* italicize:

- ships—from the *USS Merrimack* to the *Good Ship Lollipop*
- works of art—from movies to CDs, from Rodin's sculpture *The Thinker* to Andy Warhol's pop art *Stamped Lips*
- court cases, such as *Roe v. Wade*

4. *Non-English Words and Phrases*

I confess I dislike writers pretentiously showing off their knowledge of other languages, especially French for some reason. If readers are enjoying your book on an e-reader, they could touch those foreign-to-us words on the screen and get definitions. But will they take the time? And what if you've produced an old-fashioned, paper-and-ink book?

So if you need to use non-English words for the context, such as *s'il vous plaît, mon amie*, placing them in italics at least alerts the readers that there's a reason they may not understand what they just read.

Exception: A foreign word or phrase commonly used in English doesn't need italics, amigo.

5. *Italics within Italics*

When we want to italicize something within an already italicized phrase, we simply shift into reverse and use roman (regular) type. Note: for illustration purposes, I use italics for direct thoughts. Today's trend, per *CMoS 16*, is to use quotation marks—or even nothing at all—to indicate direct thought. (See my comments in chapter 18.)

> CORRECT: The mother of teens thought, *I should write a book called* Are You Going to Wear *That* Out of This House? *Yes, that's what I'll do. How hard can it be to write a book?*

The title of the book is now in roman type amid the mother's thoughts (italicized).

Double Quotation Marks

Here are some uses of double quotation marks—or what we often refer to as simply putting something "in quotes."

1. *References*

To alert readers that a word may not mean what they think it means, put it in quotation marks.

> CORRECT: Though his daughter insisted she and the ubiquitous Bill were "just friends," Sam questioned the young man's intentions.

Use this tool sparingly, however.

2. *Dialogue*

Most writers do well with dialogue quotation marks. (See chapter 18.) But here are two reminders:

- Begin a new paragraph for each new speaker. Readers expect a new paragraph to mean someone else is talking. Then remember to use both opening and closing quotation marks.
- If a character's piece of dialogue is longer than one paragraph, omit the closing quotation marks at the end of paragraphs other than the final paragraph. Use opening quotation marks for a new paragraph, and save the closing quotation marks for the end of his diatribe. I've used ellipses in the following example to shorten this long speech:

Zelda threw her napkin on the restaurant table and stood. "This is the end of our relationship, George. I can't take it anymore.... [No closing quotation marks because Zelda keeps blabbing on in the next paragraph without allowing her boyfriend to even make a peep.]

[Use opening quotation marks here.] **"You're too namby-pamby. You won't stand up for yourself.... And, by the way, you can take back all your stupid presents. I'm outta here!"** [Now you can throw those closing quotation marks in there. George is happy Zelda has shut up after her multiparagraph tirade.]

Bottom line: To avoid this awkward construction that can confuse readers, keep your characters' speeches brief (a few words, a sentence or two, or one paragraph) whenever possible.

3. *Direct versus indirect quotations*
Use double quotation marks for direct quotations. But don't use them for indirect quotations.

CORRECT *DIRECT* QUOTATION: **"If God allowed this to happen," the missionary said, "he must have a good plan."**

CORRECT *INDIRECT* QUOTATION: **The missionary said that if God allowed this to happen, he must have a good plan.**

CORRECT *DIRECT* SCRIPTURE QUOTATION: **Jesus said, "Ask, using my name, and you will receive, and you will have abundant joy" (John 16:24 NLT).**

CORRECT *INDIRECT* SCRIPTURE QUOTATION: **Jesus instructs us to use his name with our requests (John 16:24).**

(For detailed help regarding Scripture quotations, see chapter 33.)

4. *Long quotations*
See guidelines in chapter 32.

5. *Other considerations*
- We don't need quotation marks for the words *yes* and *no*, as in the following sentence:

INCORRECT: **Mom had to learn to say "no."**
CORRECT: **Mom had to learn to say no.**

- Don't use quotation marks for Q&A interviews.

- Don't use quotation marks for wording on common short signs. Capitalize as if the sign were a headline.

    CORRECT: Unfortunately, I didn't see the Do Not Enter sign.

Single Quotation Marks

To pin down a quotation within a quotation, use single quotation marks.

CORRECT: Angela told the police, "My neighbor was screaming, 'Take anything you want, but don't touch my *Mona Lisa*!'"

Note the way the ending single quotation mark cuddles up close to the double quotation marks with no space between them.

What if you have a quotation within a quotation within a quotation? You have two options:

Option 1. Alternate between double and single quotation marks.

CORRECT BUT CONFUSING: The journalist wrote, "Officer Onthespot stated, 'The witness, Angela Fiel, said, "My neighbor was screaming, 'Take anything you want, but don't touch my *Mona Lisa*!'"'"

Option 2. Rewrite.

MUCH BETTER: According to the newspaper, Officer Onthespot said a neighbor heard the victim screaming, "Take anything you want, but don't touch my Mona Lisa!"

Untwisted

Next time you're writing a passage that raises questions about italics or quotation marks, untwist the knots in your stomach, let these two wrestlers shake hands, and give a gift to your editor—less work.

Chapter 25 Quiz

Underline the phrases in sentences below that need italics. Insert quotation marks where needed—single or double. Delete any unnecessary quotation marks. If nothing is needed, mark it with a *C*. See answers in appendix A.

If you belong to a critique group, do this quiz as a joint exercise. Or work separately and talk through your answers to cement these concepts in your minds.

_____ 1. Oklahoma! features the song Oh, What a Beautiful Mornin'.

_____ 2. In his biography of Jesus, Mark tells us about a time that a teacher of the religious law asked Jesus which of the commandments was most important. [Scripture quotation begins here:] The most important one, answered Jesus, is this: Hear, O Israel: The Lord our God, the Lord is one. Love the Lord your God with all your heart and with all your soul and with all your mind and with all your strength. The second is this: Love your neighbor as yourself. There is no commandment greater than these (Mark 12:29–31). [Hint: Don't peek at your Bible. The punctuation there may confuse you.]

_____   3. My all-time favorite movie is The Princess Bride.

_____   4. Mom said I can't have any Mrs. Fields chocolate-chip cookies on this shopping trip.

_____   5. I've been reading through The One Year Chronological Bible.

_____   6. Luci Shaw, in her book The Crime of Living Cautiously, wrote, Are you feeding your fears or fueling your faith?

_____   7. Comedian Steven Wright asked, Why isn't the word phonetically spelled with an F?

_____   8. The editor said "yes" to my book proposal!

_____   9. When Mr. Bell got up from the park bench to go to his job interview in the building next door, he noticed the "wet paint" sign.

_____   10. Miranda published her first children's book, "Roni Rabbit's *Really* Ridiculous Rocket."

References

Use of Italics

The Chicago Manual of Style, Sixteenth Edition: 7.47, 7.54, 8.2, 8.161, 8.171, 13.60, 14.103
The Christian Writer's Manual of Style, Fourth Edition: pp. 214–18
The Associated Press Stylebook: See Italics
MLA Handbook for Writers of Research Papers, Seventh Edition: 3.3, 3.3.1
Publication Manual of the American Psychological Association, Sixth Edition: 4.21

Double and Single Quotation Marks

The Chicago Manual of Style, Sixteenth Edition: 6.11, 7.49, 7.50, 7.55, 8.175, 13.28–31
The Christian Writer's Manual of Style, Fourth Edition: pp. 260–61, 323–25
The Associated Press Stylebook: See Quotation Marks
Publication Manual of the American Psychological Association, Sixth Edition: 4.08

Gimme a Break!
Em Dashes? Commas? Parentheses?

26

Years ago I attended a general-market writer's conference, where bestselling adventure novelist Clive Cussler spoke. He related the way that—after accumulating many rejection slips—he finally got his big break. He made up a bogus literary agency, ordered impressive letterhead stationery, and used it to write a letter to a top agent he had in his sights. To the best of my memory, the letter went something like this:

Dear Henry,

It was good to see you at the cocktail party recently. I thought of you this morning when I received a great adventure novel proposal from an up-and-coming writer. As you know, it's not the kind of thing we handle, but I thought your agency might be interested. So I'm enclosing a copy in case you want to jump on it.

Thanks, buddy,
Morey

The trick worked, and Cussler got his big break.

Whom you know can be part of the picture. But the biggest "break" you can engineer for yourself is to become the best storyteller and writer you can be. It doesn't matter whom you know if your writing is amateurish. Be a pro.

At today's understaffed magazine and book publishers, manuscripts that need a lot of editing boomerang back to the senders. So give editors and yourself a big break. Keep studying the craft—right down to the smallest of punctuation decisions.

For instance, as you write, how do you show a break in thought or insert supplemental information? With a dash? A pair of parentheses? A comma? The choice you make creates a different nuance. Let's look at these choices.

Parentheses

When you want to break into your reader's train of thought with extra information or clarification, you might use parentheses. Parentheses enclose information of less importance or that may or may not be known to the reader—even an inside secret, of sorts. All the following examples are grammatically correct.

> FOR NONESSENTIAL INFORMATION: **The fledgling writer (age sixteen) liked to write poetry but never read any.**
>
> FOR INFORMATION THE READER MAY OR MAY NOT KNOW: **The sometimes-diligent dieter stepped on the doctor's scale and became ecstatic. Then she realized the 134.3 reading was in kilograms (296 in pounds).**

Or you might want to put the equivalents in parentheses:

> CORRECT: **The newborn weighed 8 pounds, 8 ounces—3.86 kilograms. (One pound equals approximately 1.45 kilograms.)**

In this instance, we have a complete sentence before the parentheses. We also have a complete sentence *within* the parentheses. So we need a period at the end of each.

If you use an opening parenthesis, make sure you also insert the closing parenthesis, so the reader knows where the parenthetical thought stops. (Notice spelling: *parenthesis* = singular, *parentheses* = plural.)

For Scripture references after a quotation:

> INCORRECT: **"I will sing to the Lord all my life." (Ps. 104:33)**
>
> CORRECT: **"I will sing to the Lord all my life" (Ps. 104:33).**

Don't insert the punctuation within the quotation marks. Instead, save it until after the closing parenthesis.

Brackets

What's the difference between parentheses and brackets, and when do you use each?

Parentheses are rounded. Brackets are squared.

If you have trouble remembering which are which, think of the following rhyme. According to a fictitious story, Shakespeare saw a pair of bowlegged cowboys walking down the street and said to his companion, "Behold what manner of men are these, who wear their legs in parentheses?"

Parentheses are bowlegged. Brackets are angular.

The two most common uses of brackets are these:

1. *Clarification within quotations.* Put brackets around information inserted into a direct quotation in order to clarify meaning. For example, if you're quoting from a book and you find that a word has been left out, you may supply the missing word within brackets [like this].

Or if the noun a pronoun refers to isn't in the quotation, you may supply what's missing to clarify.

AMBIGUOUS (if we don't know the Bible): "He said to them, 'Follow me, and I will make you fishers of men'" (Matthew 4:19 ESV).

CLARIFIED: "[Jesus] said to [the disciples], 'Follow me, and I will make you fishers of men'" (Matthew 4:19 ESV).

2. *Parentheses within parentheses.* Occasionally, we may need to set off a parenthetical clarification within a pair of parentheses.

CORRECT: Acting legend Elizabeth Taylor starred in scores of films but won only two Oscars (*BUtterfield 8* [1960] and *Who's Afraid of Virginia Woolf?* [1966]).

Dashes

Dashes call attention to themselves. They make a strong impact and create emphasis. So use them when you want to make sure the reader sees the information that follows a dash or lies between a pair of dashes.

Parentheses subordinate information within. Dashes act like arrows, emphasizing an important fact or phrase—or even changing direction.

1. *Single dashes.* See the way I used just one dash in the previous sentence? I veered off in a different direction, and I wanted to make sure you saw that additional use of this punctuation.

EXAMPLE: I've often said, "The elements we enjoy in others' writings can become strengths in our own—if we pay attention."

In dialogue, we use a dash to indicate abruptly ended or interrupted speech.

CORRECT: Gloria grabbed a tissue. "But Mom, I—"
"Don't 'But Mom' me," her mother yelled.

You can even interrupt in the middle of a word:

"Stop! Don't drink that wat—"

Omit other punctuation after the dash, except the closing quotation mark.

2. *A pair of dashes.* Two dashes function like a set of parentheses, but they call more attention to the material inside.

CORRECT: His decision—not easily made—impacted the entire industry.
CORRECT: Her manuscript—though she slaved over it for months and sought input from her critique group—still didn't meet the editor's needs at that time.
CORRECT: The sound of snoring—his own—woke him.

Because commas or parentheses could also work in the above examples, we make our choice based on how much emphasis we want to give the material inside.

So how do you create dashes? A standard keyboard offers no key for a dash, and a dash differs from a hyphen in length. To create a dash, type two hyphens in succession without a space between them (--). Then type the next word, creating no spaces between the dash and the words surrounding it (word--word). Microsoft Word will change the two hyphens to a dash after you type a space or punctuation.

(Although *CMoS 16* says to omit any space between the dash and surrounding words, some publications do put space between the dash and the surrounding words, so always follow your target publication's style.)

Note: In cooking, a dash is a small amount. In writing, it's also best to use dashes sparingly. Using too many dashes weakens their punch.

3. ***En dashes.*** What we've looked at so far in this section are called em dashes. In the days of typesetting with individual letters made of lead, an "em" was a measurement of width: the width of the letter *M*. And this is the width of the standard dash, which we use as described above. However, an en dash is shorter, the width of the letter *n*. We use the en dash primarily for ranges of numbers, as in the following examples.

Many writers would use hyphens in the examples below, but all these sentences correctly use an en dash. Go, thou, and do likewise, and your editor will thank you.

- Billybob's high school years (1982–92) were the best years of his life!
- The history prof told us to read chapters 2–16, pages 126–747, by tomorrow!
- When Dean became a Christian, his mentor encouraged him to memorize John 1:1–14, Psalms 23–24, and Philippians 2:1–11.

En dashes are also used instead of hyphens in some instances involving compound terms.

- post–Civil War America
- C. S. Lewis–style writing

To create an en dash, type the first number, space, hyphen, space, second number, space (or punctuation). Microsoft Word will change the hyphen to an en dash. Now delete the spaces between the en dash and the numbers.

Commas

I devoted a whole chapter to commas (chapter 24), so refer to that for more detailed information about the uses of commas. There I wrote, "If a word or phrase could be put in parentheses, but it's a slight interruption and you want a less-intrusive feel than parentheses or a dash, use commas."

Earlier in *this* chapter I used the following example for parentheses:

CORRECT: The fledgling writer (age sixteen) liked to write poetry but never read any.

ALSO CORRECT: The fledgling writer, sixteen, liked to write poetry.

Using commas, we can eliminate the word *age* and minimize the break, contributing to a smoother flow. (Dashes don't work well here.)

Need a break?

If you want to create a break in a sentence's flow, how much emphasis do you want to give that interruption?

- To subordinate it, use parentheses.
- To call attention to it, use a dash or two.
- To make it as unobtrusive as possible, use commas.

These are nuances excellent writers work hard to create. And it's surprising how many "breaks" those writers get in this business.

Chapter 26 Quiz

There are many nuances here. Revise the following sentences for the best use of parentheses, brackets, em or en dashes, and commas in your understanding. Put a C beside any that work well as they are. Compare your answers with your fellow critique group members. See answers in appendix A.

_____ 1. Carlos's new teacher, Carlos couldn't stand the old buzzard, loved to embarrass him in front of the whole class.

_____ 2. When I was twelve, my whole family walked up all the steps [897 of them!] to the top of the Washington Monument.

_____ 3. I hope the advice I repeat often—write to communicate, not to impress, will become a motto for many writers.

_____ 4. Jennie created a masterpiece - a sculpture I will never understand, but a masterpiece nonetheless.

_____ 5. Lincoln began his address at Gettysburg this way: "Four score and seven years ago—eighty-seven years ago—our fathers brought forth on this continent a new nation, conceived in liberty, and dedicated to the proposition that all men are created equal."

_____ 6. Eighty-seven years (609 in dog years) is a long time.

_____ 7. Ken tapped his fingers on the table and said, "I wish—" His voice sounded wistful.

_____ 8. The pastor of the small church, age eighty-four (though you'd never know it), led the junior high students on a tent-camping, evangelistic effort in Appalachia.

_____ 9. Paul presents the gospel in a nutshell in 1 Corinthians 15:3-4.

_____ 10. Lamar said that what he calls The War of the Bloombergs (2010—15) began when his neighbor, Mr. Bloomberg, totaled his wife's precious Cadillac Deville.

References

Parentheses

The Chicago Manual of Style, Sixteenth Edition: 6.13, 6.92–96
The Christian Writer's Manual of Style, Fourth Edition: pp. 261–62
The Associated Press Stylebook: See Parentheses
MLA Handbook for Writers of Research Papers, Seventh Edition: 3.2.5
Publication Manual of the American Psychological Association, Sixth Edition: 4.09

Brackets

The Chicago Manual of Style, Sixteenth Edition: 6.13, 6.95, 6.97–102
The Christian Writer's Manual of Style, Fourth Edition: pp. 80–81
The Associated Press Stylebook: See Brackets
MLA Handbook for Writers of Research Papers, Seventh Edition: 3.2.9
Publication Manual of the American Psychological Association, Sixth Edition: 4.10

Dashes

The Chicago Manual of Style, Sixteenth Edition: 6.75, 6.78–91
The Christian Writer's Manual of Style, Fourth Edition: pp. 143, 162–66
The Associated Press Stylebook: See Dash
MLA Handbook for Writers of Research Papers, Seventh Edition: 3.2.5
Publication Manual of the American Psychological Association, Sixth Edition: 4.06

Diagnosis Terminal

Sentence-Ending Punctuation

27

Comedians have asked it. People on websites such as Yahoo! Answers have asked it. Facebookers have asked it—with accompanying photos.

"If flying is so safe, why do they call an airport a terminal?" And people actually offered answers for this attempt at humor.

In this chapter about terminal punctuation, fear not. Thou art not dooming thy work to certain death. At the risk of evoking a "Duh!" from readers, I offer this: Terminal punctuation refers to the same concept as a bus, plane, or train terminal—a place where some mode of transportation stops. The end. In this case, the end of a sentence.

The writer's toolbox contains three common punctuation marks for ending sentences: periods, exclamation points, and question marks. Let's look at the proper use of each one.

Simple Periods

The British call a period a full stop, which we might contrast with a *rolling* stop in the American driving-scene vernacular—the comma.

Periods terminate a declarative sentence—one that declares what is, what was, what will be. You have just read, therefore, a declarative sentence.

Here are some important tips:

- Don't string punctuation marks behind a sentence. One punctuation mark is almost always enough.

  CORRECT: **The murder happened at 5:30 a.m.** [not *5:30 a.m..*]

- Exclamation points and question marks don't need a period or other punctuation mark behind them.

> CORRECT: **He yelled, "Ouch!"** [not *"Ouch!"*.]
> ALSO CORRECT: **Rene found hope in reading the article, "Facing the Impossible?"** [not *"Facing the Impossible?"*.]

Even if the article title (in quotation marks) were a book title (in italics), the reader is smart enough to figure out the question mark is part of the title, not signifying a question.

For declarative sentences ending with quotation marks, Americans *tuck the period inside* the quotation marks. (Brits and Canadians kick it outside.)

> AMERICANS: **"Her grandma's grammar is atrocious."**
> BRITS/CANADIANS: **"Her grandma's grammar is atrocious".**

On the other hand, shoo the period outside of an end-of-sentence closing parenthesis.

> INCORRECT: **He tried (barely.)**
> Correct: **He tried (barely).**

If an entire sentence is in parentheses, tuck the period inside.

> CORRECT: **Ryan boasted of persistence, sending his manuscript to 157 different publishers. (However, he neglected to study the markets first.)**

Frenetic Exclamation Points

In some writers' work, exclamation points seem to procreate like rabbits. But overuse weakens their impact, like continually jumping out from behind a tree and shouting, "Boo!" After a scare or two, the effect simply becomes annoying. Use exclamation points sparingly.

Three primary uses are exclamatory sentences, exclamatory sentence fragments, and interjections.

1. *Exclamatory sentences.* Some exclamatory sentences exclaim something astounding, as if we are injecting the phrase *Can you believe it?* after them. Others signal urgency.

> "CAN YOU BELIEVE IT?" EXAMPLE: **Jonah spent three days and three nights treading water in the digestive juices of a giant fish!**
> URGENCY EXAMPLE: **It's now or never!**

In dialogue, exclamation points often indicate hollering.

> CORRECT: **Pete saw the bully approaching. "Get off my property!" he yelled.**

2. *Exclamatory sentence fragments.* These incomplete sentences (usually missing a verb) convey emotions, such as surprise, excitement, even disgust.

What a gorgeous day!
How thrilling!
Such a filthy floor!

3. *Interjections.* These short exclamations, interjected into conversation as a reaction, are often just one word.

Yikes!
Ouch!
Drat!

Tip: Never, ever use more than one exclamation point at the end of a sentence in anything you submit to an editor. Stacked exclamation points scream, "Amateur!"

Curious Question Marks

Sentences that ask questions are called interrogatory (think *interrogate*) sentences. They usually involve words such as the following italicized ones that a query letter must address (don't you love how I threw in another teaching point?):

- *Who* is your audience?
- *What* will your article's takeaway be?
- *Where* does it fit in the target magazine?
- *When* can you complete it?
- *Why* are you the person to write it?
- *How* will you develop the piece?

Other interrogatory phrases include *do you, have they, will he, must she, is it, are you, am I,* and *can we.*

Challenges can come in placing this punctuation mark.

1. *Internal questions.* Notice where the question mark is in reference to the closing parenthesis in the following sentence:

They usually involve words . . . that a query letter must address (don't you love how I threw in another teaching point?).

The question mark hangs around with the rest of the sentence inside the parentheses.

Capitalization tip: in this instance and the example below, the question is part of a larger sentence concept, so we don't need to capitalize the sentence inside the parentheses (or between the commas).

CORRECT BUT AWKWARD: The question, why can't I get published, may have many answers. [No question mark needed.]
LESS CONFUSING: The question of why a writer can't get published may have . . .

2. *Multiple questions within one sentence.* Each needs its own question mark but not capitalization—unless the phrase could stand alone.

CORRECT: **What do you do when your strength is gone? when you can't hear God's voice anymore?**

CORRECT: **Carol pondered her choices: Should she stay? Should she go?**

3. *Indirect questions.* Sentences like the following don't need question marks.

He asked who was next.

Mom asked why Kim did that. (Don't moms always ask why?)

4. *Statements versus questions.* Which of the following is correct?

It's beautiful, isn't it.

It's beautiful, isn't it?

Punctuation depends on inflection and intent. The first sentence is a rhetorical question (statement not seeking a response), so use a period. The period implies that the speaker's voice does not rise at the end as it would with a question. If the speaker's voice does rise at the end, as if waiting for an answer, use a question mark.

When statements are turned into questions, sometimes you don't need an interrogatory word or phrase:

This is a novel?

5. *Titles of works.* If the question mark (or exclamation point) is part of the title, tuck it inside quotation marks or parentheses. If not, shoo it outside. If a question ends with a title containing a question mark, one question mark is enough.

INCORRECT: **May I submit my article "How Long Is Your Fuse?"?**

CORRECT: **Have you seen *O Brother, Where Art Thou?***

CORRECT: **Wasn't Jason Robards in *Tora! Tora! Tora!*?**

In the last example, the exclamation point is part of the title, so this question is a rare correct example of two punctuation marks at the end of a sentence.

6. *Requests.* Despite the word *won't*, the following sentence isn't a question. It's assuming compliance in a polite way, so we use a period.

CORRECT: **Won't you please use a tissue instead of your sleeve.**

7. *Dialogue.* Most writers correctly punctuate the following:

"Who put the fried grasshoppers in my cereal?"

The following unconventional use of question marks can characterize an adolescent, for example, whose voice rises as though every statement is a question:

Kristen ran all the way home. Panting, she flopped beside her mom on the couch. "Penny invited me to her party? And she's the most popular girl at school? And I can't believe she asked me? And I know you'd want me to go? So . . ."

Skill Sharpening

Occasional misplacement or misuse of punctuation probably won't incite editors to stamp "Diagnosis Terminal" on an otherwise good story. But editors *do* expect writers to know these basic skills. The fewer errors in your manuscripts, the more editors see you as a professional, an excellent writer, a writer they can trust.

So, during revision and proofreading, make sure you haven't committed a "Duh!"

Chapter 27 Quiz

Correct any sentences below that have faulty terminal punctuation. Put a C beside any that are correct. See answers in appendix A.

_____   1. Chip asked why we gave up?

_____   2. Twenty-five clowns squeezed into a VW bug.

_____   3. You sent out a manuscript to a magazine you've never even looked at?!

_____   4. "Chris doesn't want to come, does he?"

_____   5. The Bible says, "Jesus wept." (John 11:35)

_____   6. Which animal asked, "What crass intruder dared to slumber upon my Sealy Posturepedic?"

_____   7. Who directed the musical *Mama Mia*?

_____   8. Jeb raised his shotgun. "Don't take one step closer," he hollered.

_____   9. "Have you ever!"

_____   10. Did you answer your grandson's question, "Why do cows take so long to eat their dinner?"?

References

Periods
    The Chicago Manual of Style, Sixteenth Edition: 6.12–15
    The Christian Writer's Manual of Style, Fourth Edition: p. 263
    The Associated Press Stylebook: See Period
    MLA Handbook for Writers of Research Papers, Seventh Edition: 3.2.11
    Publication Manual of the American Psychological Association, Sixth Edition: 4.02

Exclamation Points
    The Chicago Manual of Style, Sixteenth Edition: 6.71
    The Christian Writer's Manual of Style, Fourth Edition: p. 173
    The Associated Press Stylebook: See Exclamation Point
    MLA Handbook for Writers of Research Papers, Seventh Edition: 3.2.11

Question Marks
    The Chicago Manual of Style, Sixteenth Edition: 6.66–70
    The Christian Writer's Manual of Style, Fourth Edition: pp. 321–22
    The Associated Press Stylebook: See Question Marks
    MLA Handbook for Writers of Research Papers, Seventh Edition: 3.2.11

Watch Out for "Slash"-ers

28

If I gave you a word-association test, what would the word *slash* bring to mind? I'm sure many a shrink would delight in psychoanalyzing my response. My thoughts first ran to the Hollywood slasher films of the '70s and '80s that seemed to procreate like rabbits.

Their grotesque progeny still dominate TV programming so much every October that I hardly dare turn on the tube. A mere glimpse of the movie trailers during commercial breaks in perfectly normal shows can spawn a plethora of nightmares. For the life of me, I cannot see any entertainment value in the bloody gore of the darkest sides of psychopathic serial killers.

So I think we need a more positive association for the word *slash*. And to preserve my ability to sleep tonight, I shall alternate the use of various synonyms for the slash (/), such as *forward slash, diagonal, slant, solidus, oblique,* and *virgule.* Keep in mind while reading this chapter that all those words mean the same thing. Ah, I'm feeling better already!

The Lead Role

The solidus frequently plays the role of the word *or.* It indicates a choice, notably in the expression *and/or.*

> CORRECT: **Martha told her teenage grandson he could have a submarine sandwich and/or pizza for lunch.**

Obviously, we wouldn't write *and or or.* To avoid confusing readers, the slant replaces the first *or* in that expression.

157

However, in writing for many publications, we might rewrite the sentence this way:

ALSO CORRECT: **Martha told her teenage grandson he could have a submarine sandwich, pizza, or both.** (As a growing teenager, he probably chose both.)

All the following examples are correct, but we could substitute *or* for the oblique (slash):

Let me know if/when you get published.

When your blood pressure reads significantly over/under recommended readings, call 911.

Studying the life of Saul/Paul [two names for the same person] **teaches us much about God's grace.**

A good student in any field knows he/she needs to learn the tools of the trade.

We might better rewrite the latter sentence using plurals:

Good students in any field know they need to learn the tools of the trade.

That's less awkward to read.

Please avoid, at all costs, the dreaded nonword *s/he*, the illegitimate offspring of political correctness.

An oblique also occasionally stands for the word *and*. Usually those examples still convey "a sense of alternatives," according to *The Chicago Manual of Style, Sixteenth Edition*, the standard used by most book and many magazine editors. Here are two excellent examples from that book:

an MD/PhD program
a Jekyll/Hyde personality

For the most part, however, keep the *or* clue in mind. For instance, you may be writing an article about someone who is a singer *and* a songwriter. No matter how strong the temptation, be strong. Stand your ground. Refuse to join the two words with a virgule. Opt for a hyphen instead.

INCORRECT: **singer/songwriter**
CORRECT: **singer-songwriter**

Chris Tomlin isn't a "singer *or* a songwriter." He's a singer *and* a songwriter, so use the hyphenated term *singer-songwriter*.

Remembering the *or* factor also prevents this error:

INCORRECT: **Clyde Finkelstein received a promotion to vice president/publishing.**

CORRECT: **Clyde Finkelstein received a promotion to vice president of publishing.**

Supporting Roles

In addition to its leading role as a substitute for *or* (and occasionally *and*), we also use an oblique in other roles:

- designations of time spans:

  the 2013/14 school year [slash only used for two-year time spans; otherwise use en dash (see chapter 26).
  Israel's late first-temple period / early second-temple period

In the latter example, when dealing with compound terms such as these, we need a space before and after the diagonal (/). Otherwise, don't use a space.

- in place of the word *per*:

  $1,000/month
  limit one coupon/person
  100 km/sec

Many publications follow a more formal style and don't use the slant in these expressions, opting for the word *per* instead. Follow your target publication's style.

- expressions such as *c/o*, meaning *in care of*. Notice that both the *c* and *o* are lowercase, not capitalized.

- Internet URLs. For example, my author bio at the end of an article might say this:

  You may find out more about the books Joyce has published by checking out the author section of her website: http://www.joycekellis.com/authorjke.

Notice that the formal URL is preceded by *http*, a colon, then two forward slashes. However, generally, you can drop everything before the *www*. If a URL must spill onto another line(s), break it after the double forward slash or a single slash. Don't worry about how long a URL is or how it looks in your document. Never add a hyphen to a URL to signify a line break. Also beware of inadvertently using the computer programmer's backward slash (\) in place of the forward slash.

Dating Roles

In informal writing, we may use the oblique to indicate dates. So July 4, 1776, becomes 7/4/1776. However, our writing may reach around the world, where many cultures put the day before the month—i.e., 4/7/1776. To avoid possible confusion, in most writing for publication, spell out the month.

Mathematical Roles

In informal writing, we use a solidus for fractions, such as 1/2 or 1/4. Microsoft Word software automatically turns some fractions into what are called single glyphs (symbols), such as ½ or ¼—entire fractions in one space. (To turn that feature on or off, check the Help feature for Auto Correct options as you type.) Be consistent.

However, in writing for publication, we spell out such fractions in text.

CORRECT: **MollySue ate one-half of the pie.**
CORRECT: **One-fifth of those surveyed supported the measure.**

Doing so is especially important when writing dialogue.

INCORRECT: "I have 1/3 of a mind to toss you out on your keister!" he shouted.

CORRECT: "I have one-third of a mind to toss you out on your keister!" he shouted.

Poetic Roles

As I've noted elsewhere, securing permission to quote from a song or poetry can be expensive, so most writers avoid it. However, if you've secured permission or you're quoting from public-domain material, a series of obliques can save space, particularly in an article.

For example, one of the first poems I memorized in childhood, "My Shadow," comes from Robert Louis Stevenson's *A Child's Garden of Verses* (in public domain). We could save space quoting it this way:

"I have a little shadow that goes in and out with me, / And what can be the use of him is more than I can see. / He is very, very like me from the heels up to the head; / And I can see him jump before me, when I jump into my bed."

In such quotations, notice that we use a space before and after each virgule. But remember this is an unusual case.

So now, with all these practical guidelines to boost your confidence in using this punctuation mark correctly—whether you call it a forward slash, diagonal, slant, solidus, oblique, or virgule—may a slash never prevent you from getting a good night's sleep.

Chapter 28 Quiz

Correct any errors below as needed in writing for publication. Put a C beside any sentences that are correct. See answers in appendix A.

_____ 1. The journalist/politician ran a surprisingly clean campaign.

_____ 2. Sir Walter Scott wrote, "Oh, what a tangled web we weave,/When first we practise to deceive!" (Note: *practise* is the correct British spelling.)

_____ 3. When an editor asks you to submit something, don't fail to send it to him\her.

_____ 4. Sherri says that when she grows up she wants to be a rocket scientist and or a pig farmer.

_____ 5. Brandilyn was elected the organization's secretary/membership.

_____ 6. "The baby ate ¾ of my candy bar!" Bobby cried.

_____ 7. Francis Scott Key wrote "The Star-Spangled Banner" after watching American forces triumph in the bombardment of Fort McHenry during the Battle of Baltimore on 9/13 to 9/14/1814.

_____   8. When a garbage collector comes home, s/he makes a big stink.

_____   9. You can find some great grammar resources at www.grammarly.com/handbook.

_____   10. The forward slash/virgule/diagonal/slant/oblique/solidus can be a useful tool.

References

Use of Slashes
   The Chicago Manual of Style, Sixteenth Edition: 6.103–10, 13.27, 13.32
   The Christian Writer's Manual of Style, Fourth Edition: pp. 356–57
   The Associated Press Stylebook: See Slash
   MLA Handbook for Writers of Research Papers, Seventh Edition: 3.7.3, 3.2.10
   Publication Manual of the American Psychological Association, Sixth Edition: 4.11

Teach us to number our days, that we may gain a heart of wisdom.

—PSALM 90:12

Paint-by-Number Writing

Proper Expression of Numbers

Some say there are two categories of people in the world: those who divide folks into two categories and those who don't.

I used to classify everyone as either a numbers person or a words person. Then I found out my husband straddles both categories. For this, my checkbook (which he monitors) and my manuscripts (which he proofreads) are eternally grateful.

I confess, when it comes to using numbers in my writing, I often have to look up how to represent them because my brain's electrical system goes haywire with all things technical and numerical. To complicate matters, various publications differ in how they handle numbers.

But let's look at some basic rules. We are basing our guidelines on *The Chicago Manual of Style (CMoS 16)*, the industry standard for style for book publishers and many magazine publishers. And as I have said before, *The Christian Writer's Manual of Style* (*CWMS 4*) belongs within arm's reach of every writer's workspace, and it deserves to be consulted *often*.

By contrast, newspapers and some magazines—including the *Christian Communicator*, in which much of the material in this book first appeared as columns—use *The Associated Press Stylebook* (*AP*).[1]

If you can't tell which stylebook a publication uses, at least be consistent within your manuscript. But you can delight editors if you study your target publications sufficiently to figure out their style.

Cardinal and Ordinal Numbers

Cardinal numbers include those used in counting, expressing quantities, and citing statistics (rendered below per *CMoS 16* guidelines):

- numbers as numerals: **1, 2, 3, 7.5, 100, 1,000**
- numbers written out: **The three little pigs had half a mind to initiate legislation banishing the hundreds of big, bad wolves in their forest.**

Ordinal numbers include those used to express order or ranking:

- **second on Amazon's bestseller list**
- **the classic film *The Third Man***
- **the twenty-first century**
- **the 104th agent who rejected his novel**

Note: The last example uses numerals instead of words because the number is greater than one hundred. Per *CMoS 16*, be careful that the letters in ordinal numbers don't appear as superscripts. We use *104th* rather than *104th* (which Microsoft Word will do automatically unless you change the settings).

Dates

Generally, for dates we use cardinal, not ordinal, numbers.

> INCORRECT: **At the nonagenarian's birthday party on July 3rd, guests shot off bottle rockets.**
> CORRECT: . . . **on July 3, guests shot off bottle rockets.**

News Stories

In new stories covering current events, don't include the year designation. For example, a newspaper story about an upcoming fund-raiser to train numerically challenged writers might phrase it this way:

> **On March 7** [not March 7, 2017 (or current year)], **the Society for the Prevention of Cruelty to Numerically Challenged Word People (SPCNCWP) hosted a fund-raising bowling tournament to help writers score better in their spare time.**

Numerals or Words?

When do we use numerals (*1, 2, 3*) and when do we spell out numbers (*one, two, three*)? This situation can be confusing, but here are some general guidelines.

- According to *CMoS 16*, spell out all numbers between one and ninety-nine, as well as round numbers like one hundred, two thousand, three hundred thousand, four million. Publications that follow *AP* style, however, only spell out one through nine. It's our job to sleuth out who does what. (One website that may clarify differences between the two styles is www.apvschicago.com.)
- Hyphenate spelled-out numbers such as thirty-eight.
- In normal text, use numerals before percentages. Then use the word *percent* instead of the percent symbol.

CORRECT: **A poll of the kingdom's pigs showed that 100 percent of them favored the wolf-ban legislation.**

Do use the percent symbol (%) for statistics in charts, graphs, and sidebars. Then snuggle the percent symbol next to the numeral (no space between) like this: 13%.

- Never use a numeral to begin a sentence. Either spell out the number or rewrite the sentence to eliminate a numeral at the beginning. (I'm using the numeral 3, which would normally be spelled out anyway, for demonstration—and humor-attempt—purposes only.)

INCORRECT: **3 unarmed pigs offed their rapacious intruder and enjoyed wolf stew for dinner.**
CORRECT: **Three pigs enjoyed wolf stew. Or: The three unarmed pigs enjoyed wolf stew.**

Plurals for Numbers

When writing the plurals of numbers, think of the numbers spelled out. For instance, imagine we are writing a scene in which the three little pigs are counting their winnings after gambling on a game of Go Fish.

INCORRECT: **One pig asked another if he had five $100's for a $500.**
CORRECT: **One pig asked another if he had five $100s for a $500.**

We don't need an apostrophe because there's no possessive involved, only a plural. So, when pluralizing numbers, beware of those sneaky apostrophes that keep butting in where they don't belong.

Common Expressions

Some numerical phrases also present quandaries. The following are written correctly:

9/11 observances
my six-year-old granddaughter
the six-year-old
in chapter 12
one-fourth of the student population

However, note the way we express more complicated fractions, such as in dimensions:

CORRECT: **Sheila knitted a baby blanket that ended up a little large: 36½" x 48".**

Type the first number (36), space, the fraction (1/2), double quotation marks ("). Your word processing program will likely change 1/2 to ½, what's called a single glyph. (If it doesn't, you can teach it to do that in Word's settings (File, Options,

Proofing, Auto Correct Options, Auto Format). Then let the first number and the fraction snuggle up next to each other—no space between.

Dialogue

Generally, we spell out numbers in dialogue unless they become large and unwieldy, such as in years and dates. The numbers in the following dialogue are written correctly.

> "According to my calculations," said the first little pig, "we have more than three hundred and fifty wolves in the kingdom—"
>
> "And they're all big and bad," the second pig said.
>
> The third pig thought for a moment. "Tomorrow, April twenty-third," he declared, "I, as the duly elected chairpig of the kingdom's Homeland Security Administration, shall seek legislation declaring next year open season on big, bad wolves."

Scripture References

In decades past, we used roman numerals to differentiate between Bible books this way:

> I and II Kings
> I and II Thessalonians

Now we use arabic numerals:

> 1 and 2 Samuel
> 1, 2, and 3 John

But because we don't begin sentences with numerals, here are some options:

- First Peter 5:7 says, "Cast all your anxiety on [God] because he cares for you."
- In 1 Peter 5:7, Peter wrote, "Cast all your anxiety on [God] because he cares for you."
- Peter wrote, "Cast all your anxiety on [God] because he cares for you" (1 Peter 5:7).

When referring to specific chapters and verses in Scripture, use numerals. Spelling them out makes them more difficult to find.

> INCORRECT: In verse eight of chapter four, James encourages us to take the initiative and come near to God.
>
> CORRECT: In verse 8 of chapter 4, James encourages us to take the initiative and come near to God.

For more help in this area, see chapter 33.

Statistics

In today's culture, people can manipulate stats to prove almost anything. But Christians committed to truth are especially responsible to use statistics carefully and not "spin" them to say what we want them to say.

Often statistics can bog down an article or book chapter, however. So consider featuring them separately in a sidebar—a related miniature article or list of facts featured alongside the main article in a separate column or box.

But remember, whether using stats in the text of an article or chapter or in a sidebar, writers who are pros double-check all facts and figures and handle them with integrity.

Summary

Whether you're a numbers person or a words person or one of those particularly blessed people who straddles both camps, the importance of handling numbers correctly in your writing is one more reason to study your target markets.

We often describe excellent writing as painting word pictures, but we can also learn the beauty of skillfully "painting by numbers."

Chapter 29 Quiz

Put a C beside any sentences that are correct, and rewrite any that require correction. See answers in appendix A.

_____ 1. The man, in his 90's, loved pig stories.

_____ 2. The 3 little pigs' wild victory party trashed the inside of the 3rd little pig's brick house.

_____ 3. It took 12 firefighters to extinguish the chimney fire caused by cooking wolf stew.

_____ 4. The distraught pigs asked fifteen contractors to submit bids for reconstruction.

_____ 5. More than 90% of the bids were outrageous.

_____ 6. [In sidebar or box] Almost 80 % of church members contributed to missions last year.

_____ 7. "I found encouragement in memorizing 1 John," Bodie said.

_____ 8. Lois printed out her query letter on good-quality 8½" x 11" paper.

_____ 9. Sharon worked feverishly to meet her deadline for the 9-11 anniversary article.

_____ 10. The pastor asked, "Did everyone memorize Joshua chapter 1, verse 9 this week?"

References

Cardinal and Ordinal Numbers
The Chicago Manual of Style, Sixteenth Edition: 9.6
The Christian Writer's Manual of Style, Fourth Edition: p. 370

Writing Out Dates

 The Chicago Manual of Style, Sixteenth Edition: 6.45, 6.106, 9.36–37

 The Christian Writer's Manual of Style, Fourth Edition: pp. 368–71

 The Associated Press Stylebook: See Dates

 MLA Handbook for Writers of Research Papers, Seventh Edition: 3.5.5

 Publication Manual of the American Psychological Association, Sixth Edition: 4.31

Numerals versus Words

 The Chicago Manual of Style, Sixteenth Edition: 9.2–7, 13.42

 The Christian Writer's Manual of Style: pp. 253–56, 368–69

 The Associated Press Stylebook: See Numerals

 MLA Handbook for Writers of Research Papers, Seventh Edition: 3.5.2

 Publication Manual of the American Psychological Association, Sixth Edition: 4.32–33

Plural Numbers

 The Chicago Manual of Style, Sixteenth Edition: 9.54

 Publication Manual of the American Psychological Association, Sixth Edition: 4.38

Scripture References

 The Christian Writer's Manual of Style, Fourth Edition: p. 331

 MLA Handbook for Writers of Research Papers, Seventh Edition: 7.7.1

Large Numbers, Percentages, Fractions, Money, and Inclusive Numbers
(Especially for Page Numbers)

 The Chicago Manual of Style, Sixteenth Edition: 9.8, 9.13–15, 9.18, 9.21, 9.25, 9.58–60

 The Christian Writer's Manual of Style, Fourth Edition: pp. 254, 256–67

Ascribe to the LORD the glory due his name; worship
the LORD in the splendor of his holiness.

—PSALM 29:2

Getting Possessive

Showing Possession

One of my favorite movies is a Disney film of stunning intellectual depth, *Finding Nemo*.

Okay, maybe it's just fun to watch. But I love the scene where Marlin, the distraught clown fish father of the "missing" young title character, teams up with Dory, the vibrant blue tang with short-term memory issues. They set off to track down Nemo and eventually find themselves flopping around on a dock in a marina full of sailboats.

Literally two fish out of water, they seem like a fast-food delivery to a flock of waiting, hungry seagulls. A nearby gull calls out, "Mine!" Immediately, a compassionate pelican tries to convince Marlin and Dory that he'll save them from the gulls if they'll hop inside his beak.

The two fish understandably balk. But then the whole flock of gulls swoops down to attack, crying out, "Mine, mine, mine!"

The pelican quickly scoops the fish into his beak and flies off, the gulls in hot pursuit. Through his deft aeronautic maneuvers, the pelican slips through the space between the mast and the sail of one of the boats. The pursuing gulls quickly impale themselves on the sail by their beaks.

The moral? Possessiveness gets us into trouble.

Likewise, the not-so-deft use of possessives often gets writers into trouble. I've covered similar material in chapter 22, "Stamp Out Apostrophe Abuse," but the incorrect use of possessives, especially pronouns, shows up often enough in manuscripts that a review and some specifics regarding possessives are in order. The topic is bigger than simply when to use apostrophes to show possession. And I suspect some people will skip around in the book, so you may not have read the other chapter yet.

Let's look at some easier questions of proper usage of possessives (with and without apostrophes) and build toward some of the trickier ones.

Most challenges or indecision in the Land of Possessives come in the area of pronouns. Some grammarians lump all those possessives together. Others divide them into two categories: possessive adjectives and possessive pronouns.

Fittingly, possessive adjectives modify nouns. Possessive pronouns can stand alone.

POSSESSIVE ADJECTIVE: **Downsizing, I sold my antique typewriter.**

My modifies *typewriter* (a noun), so it serves as an adjective.

POSSESSIVE PRONOUN: **That typewriter was mine for decades.**

The pronoun *mine* stands alone. Possessive pronouns can serve as subjects or direct objects of verbs.

USED AS SUBJECT: **Mine was well used.**

USED AS DIRECT OBJECT: **I sold mine at a garage sale.**

Seldom Misused

I mention some of the following in other places, but the guidelines—and even some examples—bear repeating. Most writers have no trouble writing correctly that Seth's computer is *his*, not *hi's*. But for some reason, we'll sometimes see examples like these:

INCORRECT: **That VeggieTales notebook is her's.**
INCORRECT: **Those pens are their's.**
INCORRECT: **The moo goo gai pan is your's.**
INCORRECT: **My husband's books and mine are our's.**

No need for apostrophes in these examples. The "words" *her's, their's, your's,* and *our's* do not exist except in the mind of the careless writer. Use *hers, theirs, yours,* and *ours.*

However, possessives of indefinite pronouns (such as *one*) and of reciprocal pronouns (such as *each other*), do need apostrophes.

CORRECT: **In Galatians 6, Paul tells us to bear each other's burdens.**
CORRECT: **Later, he says one is to bear one's own load, a distinction worth studying.**

Sometimes Misused

Here are some trickier decisions:

1. ***The words*** **it's** ***and*** **its.** When I've surveyed editors about the most common errors in manuscripts, this one comes at or near the top of their lists. *It's* is a legitimate word, but *it's* is not a possessive word. It's a contraction for *it is* or *it has*. Note these examples.

CORRECT: **It's [contraction for *It is*] not easy to get published.**

CORRECT: **Its [possessive] likelihood can increase, however, if you diligently study the craft and markets.**

Similarly, note the difference between *you're* (contraction for *you are*) and *your* (a possessive adjective).

CORRECT: **The Nielsen ratings can measure what you're [not *your*] watching.**

CORRECT: **They monitor your watching habits.**

2. ***Plurals often cause confusion.*** I can't tell you how many times our family has received mail addressed to *The Ellis's*. If people want to send something to all of us, they need a plural, not a possessive—unless, perhaps, they intended to address the envelope to the Ellises' maid, for instance, should someone wish to volunteer for that position. The plural of *Ellis* is *Ellises*. So the possessive of that plural would be *Ellises'*.

Possessives of most plurals use only an apostrophe after the pluralizing *s*—e.g., the *boys'* pranks, the *pickles'* acidity, and the *Christians'* efforts.

3. ***Possessives of two or more nouns or pronouns can also introduce errors.*** Is the following example grammatically correct?

I could not have done this without you and your sister's help.

Sometimes it helps to break the sentence into the two parts discussed:

I could not have done it without your sister's help, and I could not have done it without your help [not *you help*].

So that example is not correct. Instead, write it like this:

I could not have done this without your and your sister's help.

4. ***What about nouns ending in the letter* s?** When creating a possessive of a noun ending in *s*, such as *business* or *octopus*, treat it as any other noun with an apostrophe and an *s*—such as the *business's* quarterly earnings, the *octopus's* flailing tentacles.

For proper nouns ending in *s*, such as *Mavis* and *Travis*, use *Mavis's* and *Travis's*.

EXCEPTIONS: For many years writers and editors have made exceptions to this rule for Jesus and Moses. Perhaps because we generally don't vocalize a second *s* (making a third syllable), we wouldn't write them that way either. Instead, we may write about *praying in Jesus' name* or about *Moses' cranky followers in the wilderness.*

The sixteenth edition of *CMoS* and the fourth edition of *CWMS* say that we should treat everyone alike, so to speak. So they recommend *Jesus's* and *Moses's*, just as we would write *Judas's* and *Thomas's*.

This is another area where I believe writers can at least ask editors if they may use previous common practice here.

Some publishers have taken exception to *CMoS 16* on this one and use *Jesus'* and *Moses'*. And if consistency is the goal, using *Jesus's* and *Moses's* is inconsistent with commonly used Bible translations and paraphrases, such as those quoted in this book. *CWMS 4* does make this allowance: "If an author has a strong preference for *Jesus'* or other similar forms, then that should be honored."[1]

So it's worth asking. If you're self-publishing, you may establish your own style on this issue, but be consistent.

Frequently Misused

Often, if I ask my husband what I should write my column about, he says, "Write about gerunds." For some reason, that's a funny word to him. And it's true that some writers don't have a clue what a gerund is, much less how to use one properly. So this section's for you, Babe.

1. *Beware the gerund.* A gerund is an –*ing* verb (action or state of being) transformed into a noun. In today's vernacular, we've become adept at "verbing" nouns—such as *he officed out of his pickup*.

But a gerund does the reverse. It "nouns" a verb, turning a verb into a noun form. In the following example, *being* and *whining* are gerunds used in two different ways.

Being [subject] negative is prohibited, so quit whining [object].

What do gerunds have to do with possessives? If you're going to use a pronoun before a gerund, proper English usage calls for a possessive.

INCORRECT: You being tall [meaning, the fact that you are tall, or your tallness] doesn't necessarily make you a star basketball player.
CORRECT: Your being tall doesn't necessarily make you a star basketball player.

Note: The pronoun precedes *being*, a noun that looks like a verb—a gerund.

But we also need to differentiate between a gerund and a participle –*ing* verb that remains a verb, not a noun). Use the possessive for pronouns preceding gerunds, but not for pronouns preceding participles.

GERUND: His singing grates on my nerves.
PARTICIPLE: We heard him singing again yesterday.

2. *Beware the typo.* Once again, as I say often, don't rely solely on your computer's spell-checker. In many emails and manuscripts we find writers have inadvertently typed *you* when they meant *your*.

SLOPPY PROOFREADING: "Please check you manuscript for typos," the editor said.
THE PRO'S PROSE: "Please check your manuscript for typos," the editor said.

Proofread, proofread, proofread! And get someone else to look over your work to catch errors easily missed.

No honest writers will sugarcoat it: good writing is hard work.

So, in the end, the moral of this chapter, much like that of the seagull scene, is this: don't get possessive in your work unless you learn how to steer clear of the dangers.

Chapter 30 Quiz

Choose the correct word in brackets in each of these sentences. See answers in appendix A.

1. [Their's/Theirs] was the victory.

2. God shrank [Gideons/Gideon's] army to three hundred.

3. The Gideons/Gideon's/Gideons'] have distributed Bibles in hotels and elsewhere for many years.

4. The [Gideons/Gideon's/Gideons'] ministry has brought many to faith in Christ.

5. The editor got fed up with [him/his] missing so many deadlines.

6. We live next door to the [Browns/Brown's/Browns'].

7. "I can't stand [you/your] using neon-colored paper for your manuscripts," the editor ranted.

8. Tara fears submitting her manuscript because she doesn't know whether [its/it's] publishable or not.

9. Eddie extended [him/his] and his company's congratulations on the book contract.

10. Jennifer found her book with [it's/its] spine out on the bookstore shelf, so she arranged a copy with the cover facing outward to catch [browsers'/browser's] attention.

References

Possessives

The Chicago Manual of Style, Sixteenth Edition: 7.15–28
The Christian Writer's Manual of Style, Fourth Edition: pp. 297–99
The Associated Press Stylebook: See Possessives
Publication Manual of the American Psychological Association, Sixth Edition: 4.12

Jesus said to him, "... It is written: 'Worship the Lord your God, and serve him only.'"
—MATTHEW 4:10

"Quotable Quotes for 2000, Alex"

Handling Quotations Correctly

31

You're a big *Jeopardy!* fan. One night you're dreaming you finally made it onto the thinking-person's quiz show. You stand before Alex Trebek, signaling button in hand, ready to beat the other two brainiac contestants to the punch.

The game proceeds to the Double Jeopardy! round with the lead constantly changing. You're currently in third place, but only a few hundred dollars separate the three of you. Time is running out. You need a miracle. You're running the category of Quotable Quotes, and you announce your next selection to the host and millions of viewers around the world: "Quotable Quotes for 2000, Alex."

An electronic whiz-bang sound fills the studio as the clue—the usual yellow numbers on blue—is replaced by a dazzling, multicolored Daily Double square. With a correct answer, you could double your money and conquer first place. But if you blow it, you're dead.

Sweaty hands. Dry throat. You check your score again: $10,000 but still trailing the other two cerebral heavyweights. You clear your throat. "I've always wanted to say this, Alex. Let's make it a true Daily Double."

The audience laughs and applauds. You're already mentally spending the $20,000. The blue square appears, and Alex reads the clue: "In the King James Bible . . ."

You relax. It's a Scripture quotation. You say to yourself, "I've racked up so many hours in personal and small-group Bible study that this should be a lock."

Alex continues, "King Solomon warns his son that 'pride goeth before' this."

You squeeze your signaling device. *Too easy*, you tell yourself. *Who wouldn't know this one? Make sure you frame it in the form of a question*, you remind yourself.

"What is a fall?" you blurt out quickly.

"Oh, sorry. Incorrect," Alex replies. "It's often misquoted. The correct answer is *destruction*. 'Pride goeth before destruction, and an haughty spirit before a fall.' That drops you down to zero."

A buzzer sounds, announcing the end of the round. No, the buzzer is your alarm clock. Your nightmare ends, but the irony of the quotation haunts you.

Though we may never compete on *Jeopardy!*, as conscientious writers, we want to handle quotations from people, print sources, and electronic sources with accuracy, clarity, integrity, and correct formatting. It's all part of professionalism—what we're aiming for as we write with excellence for our Master. (Dollar amounts in the subheads below do not connote relative importance.)

"Accuracy for 200, Alex"

Answer: "It's the best way to ensure accuracy in your quotations."

Question: "What is 'Never type what you can copy and paste'?"

One great way to avoid quotation errors is to use the technology of downloadable Bible software and online resources. At BibleGateway.com, for instance, you can search—and copy and paste from—about fifty English translations (and many other languages). So we have no excuse for misquoting what "pride goeth before."

Again, avoid errors: Never, ever, ever type a quotation if you can copy and paste. Highlight the desired material with your cursor, copy (Ctrl+C), and paste (Ctrl+V) where you want it. Delete individual verse numbers in the text, and be sure to give the correct reference and version in parentheses. Note: on the Bible-Gateway site, at the gear symbol, you can turn verse numbers, as well as footnotes and cross references, off and on. You don't want to copy and paste any of these in your Scripture citation.)

When quoting from a book or a magazine article, take advantage of electronic sources. Many books and magazines are online, so it's easy to copy and paste that material.

In addition, you can download an ebook to a smartphone, tablet, or computer. On both my Kindle and my computer I can highlight what I want to quote, select the copy option, then paste it into a file. I have even used this method with ebooks borrowed from my local library. The Kindle program also adds (to the document you're pasting into) source information, such as author, publisher, copyright date, title of book, and sometimes page number.

When quoting a person, using a digital recorder for the interview—and then transcribing and proofreading carefully—can help ensure accuracy.

"Clarity for 400, Alex"

Answer: "It's the best way to avoid confusing the reader with a poorly constructed quotation."

Question: "What is 'Quote judiciously without changing the meaning of the original'?"

- Use only what you need, and paraphrase briefly where necessary. Use quotations sparingly to support the points you're trying to make, and keep them as short as possible while still conveying the author's thought.
- Delete lead-in phrases, such as *therefore, for that matter,* and *in other words.* Get to the heart of what the author (or Scripture passage you're quoting) is saying. Those connective phrases serve as transitions to what came before. But if what came before isn't there, we don't need the transition.

> SHORTENABLE: "So then, just as you received Christ Jesus as Lord, continue to live your lives in him" (Col. 2:6).
>
> SHORTENED: "Just as you received Christ Jesus as Lord, continue to live your lives in him" (Col. 2:6).

Repeating the counsel of *The Elements of Style,* "Omit needless words." In many cases, "needless words" can confuse the reader.

- We use ellipses to indicate omitted words in the middle of a quotation, but we don't generally need them at the beginning or end. Just make sure you're not changing the writer's meaning with what you're omitting.

Compare these two renderings:

> MISLEADING: "You could go ahead with the project . . . ," the governor said. "We have enough money in the coffers."
>
> ORIGINAL: "You could go ahead with the project, though I would advise against it," the governor said. "We have enough money in the coffers."

This example is extreme, but excellent writers always make sure they preserve the spirit and intent of the quotation.

- We create ellipses by typing three periods with spaces between them, as demonstrated above. If the omitted text is within a sentence, only the standard three periods are necessary. Use four periods if the thought—before the omitted text—is complete.

"Integrity for 600, Alex"

Answer: "It's the best way to maintain godly integrity in your writing and treat other writers' work fairly."

Question: "What is 'Learn the ins and outs of public-domain material, fair use, and permissions'?"

Public-domain works are materials you may quote from without seeking permission. Anything published before January 1, 1923, is in the public domain. Most of the old hymns qualify, for instance, but check copyright dates. The criteria get more complicated after that, but Cornell University has created a helpful, up-to-date chart available at http://copyright.cornell.edu/resources/publicdomain.cfm.

If at all in doubt, ask a reference librarian at your public or university library (they love to help!) or do a copyright search with the Copyright Office (www.copy-right.gov). A few hours of investigation are far better than a lawsuit.

Fair use describes how much a writer may quote fairly without seeking permission from the original writer or publisher. Here's the guideline from *CWMS 4*: you need to seek permission for 300 words or more from a single book-length source,[1] although publishers' permission varies from 50 to 500 words.

However, fair use also considers the proportion of the original from which you're quoting. Here's an extreme example: quoting 300 words from a 200-page biography should cause no problem. But quoting 300 words from an 800-word magazine article—without permission—could result in a lawsuit. Securing permission is the writer's responsibility.

The Chicago Manual of Style, Sixteenth Edition, (*CMoS 16*, the authority for most book publishers) gives this general guideline: "One should never quote more than a few contiguous paragraphs of prose or lines of poetry at a time or let the quotations, even if scattered, begin to overshadow the quoter's own material." *CMoS 16* characterizes such practices as "taking a free ride on the first author's labor."[2]

Alert! Stories from the legal trenches admonish writers to avoid quoting even one line of a poem or song without permission. And that permission may cost you dearly.

One final note on this topic: To avoid unintended plagiarism, always note source information at the time you're capturing the quotation. I've collected little notes with wonderful quotable quotes on them, but I've had to throw many away because I don't know if they were my brilliant thoughts or someone else's. I have been able to locate some via the Internet, but we all know how reliable the Internet is!

"Formatting for 800, Alex"

Answer: "It's the best way to show professionalism in formatting quotable quotes."

Question: "What is 'Learn when to use block quotations, when to work quotations into normal paragraphing, and how to format both'?"

Because we want to keep quotations brief, keeping readers engaged, most quotations work best as run-ins. We work them into a regular paragraph, formatted like this: *Strunk and White advise, "Omit needless words."*

But if we wish to include a longer complete thought, we format it as a block quotation. Most style manuals advise a block style for extracts of a hundred words or more.

To format correctly, begin a new line of type and indent the entire quotation. Do not further indent the first line of the block quotation; but if the quotation runs longer than one paragraph, indent subsequent paragraphs. Using the block style replaces the need for quotation marks at the beginning and end of the extract, so don't insert them. You'll look like an amateur.

Final Jeopardy!

Today's Final Jeopardy! category is Professionalism in Twenty-First-Century Writing.

Answer: "These four aspects of quoting from the work of others make a writer stand out from the crowd."

Fully awake, you reply (in the form of a question, of course), "What are accuracy, clarity, integrity, and correct formatting?"

Alex Trebek would be pleased.

More importantly, so would our Master.

Chapter 31 Quiz

Reword sentences 1–5 to put them in the best form, following the principles of this chapter. Put a C beside any that are correct. Then answer questions 6–10. See answers in appendix A.

_____ 1. In 1 Timothy 6:6, Paul wrote, "But godliness with contentment is great gain"

_____ 2. I lift up my eyes to the mountains—where does my help come from?[2] My help comes from the LORD, the Maker of heaven and earth" (Psalm 121:1–2).

_____ 3. "The author or speaker from whom you learn the most is not the one who teaches you something you didn't know before, but the one who helps you take a truth with which you have quietly struggled, give it expression, and speak it clearly and boldly,"[3] wrote Oswald Chambers.

_____ 4. I wonder, was Solomon writing from personal experience when he wrote, "Pride goes before a fall" (Prov. 16:18 NIV)?

_____ 5. AW. Tozer wrote this: "We can afford to follow Him to failure. Faith dares to fail. The resurrection and the judgment will demonstrate before all worlds who won and who lost. We can wait."[4]

6. What's wrong with the following quotation as given here? "My Father will give you whatever you ask. . . . Ask and you will receive" (John 16:23–24).

7. Most style manuals say to create a block quotation when quoting about _____ words or more.

8. When does a block quotation need quotation marks around the whole thing?

9. According to *CWMS 4* what is the general rule of thumb for how much you can quote—cumulatively—from another source without securing permission?

10. What four aspects of quoting from the work of others make a writer stand out from the crowd?

References

Block Quotations
    The Christian Writer's Manual of Style, Fourth Edition: pp. 327–28

Fair Use
    The Christian Writer's Manual of Style, Fourth Edition: pp. 174–75

Public Domain
    The Christian Writer's Manual of Style, Fourth Edition: p. 265

Quoting Accurately
    The Chicago Manual of Style, Sixteenth Edition: 2.30, 13.6–10, 13.20–22
    The Christian Writer's Manual of Style, Fourth Edition: p. 265
    The Associated Press Stylebook: See Quotations
    MLA Handbook for Writers of Research Papers, Seventh Edition: 1.6.2, 3.7.1
    Publication Manual of the American Psychological Association, Sixth Edition: 6.06

Quoting with Permission
    The Chicago Manual of Style, Sixteenth Edition: 4.77–87, 13.3–5
    The Christian Writer's Manual of Style, Fourth Edition: pp. 264–65
    The Associated Press Stylebook: See Use of Others' Material
    Publication Manual of the American Psychological Association, Sixth Edition: 6.10

Using Ellipses
    The Chicago Manual of Style, Sixteenth Edition: 13.48–54
    The Christian Writer's Manual of Style, Fourth Edition: pp. 161–62

Citation Citings

Footnotes, Endnotes, and Other Source Citations

A coworker of my husband's walked into his house after work, where, unbe-
knownst to him, his wife had already started dinner in the kitchen. He greeted her
with a kiss, sniffed, then made a face. "Do you have something on your shoes?"
he asked.

Not a wise question. I suspect he either slept on the couch that night or she
made him take her out for dinner—or both.

This has become a standing joke in our family. Whenever some malodorous
smell assaults our nostrils, we make some comment about what stinky substance
one of us may be inadvertently carrying on our shoes.

Again, I can hear, "How is she going to get to a Write-with-Excellence topic
from that illustration?"

Here we go: Our manuscripts sometimes need to "carry" source information
or notes not part of the main text—sometimes at the "foot" of the page. And some
writers find that process odious, maybe even odorous. (I can hear the groans now.)

But over the years in my work as a magazine editor and freelance book editor,
one of the biggest stinkin' errors I've come across is inconsistent or improper formatting of footnotes, endnotes, and source citations within the text.

So how do we present this information in a way that doesn't make editors hold
their noses? By following two guidelines:

1. Pay attention to source citations as you read publications in which you want
   your writing to appear.
2. Learn proper formatting.

Citing Sources

When do we have to cite sources?

We mostly cite sources in the fact-fertile land of nonfiction, primarily articles and books. Bottom line: whenever quoting from someone else's material or from an interview, and whenever drawing research from another source (e.g., statistics, poll results, case studies), tell where you found it.

Where do we cite sources?

We document our sources in one of three places:

1. "On the foot" . . . er . . . "at the foot" of the page. We call those footnotes—amazing! Some magazines use them. Many nonfiction books use them. (Okay, it's a stretch to get from "something on your shoes" to something on the foot of the page, so I obviously need to watch where I step.)

2. At the end of the article, the book chapter, or the entire book. Ironically, we call these endnotes. Or simply notes. Those at the end of the book, we list by chapter.

3. Inserted directly into the text of the book chapter or article. Although not technically an in-text citation, as used in more formal writing, we can insert attributions of a quotation into books or articles for a popular readership like this:

   Writers often battle fears about writing, but Luci Shaw, in her book *The Crime of Living Cautiously*, wrote, "Feel the fear, but do it anyway."

If I were using a footnote, I would include the following information: (Downers Grove, IL: InterVarsity Press, 2005), 48.

Again, notice, in this example, that when writing for a general audience (as opposed to a scholarly crowd), we need only author and title in the text. (Page numbers, publisher, etc., in the body of the text would impede the flow.)

Writers who are pros also provide publication data to the editor in a separate document for fact-checking. Better yet, if the editor would prefer, we can email photocopies or digital scans of the original source to simplify the editorial staff's fact-checking process even further.

Scholarly writing has its own rules, so consult the style manual of your target publication.

When do we do what?

Study your target market to determine when and where to cite sources. Pick up a copy of the publication you are targeting for your writing and determine whether they use footnotes, endnotes, or citations within the text. Then, in King James Scripture-speak, go and do thou likewise.

Many Christian magazines and books weave the information into the text, at least for Scripture quotations. Enclose references in parentheses after the closing quotation marks, like this:

"In the beginning was the Word" (John 1:1).

Some periodicals use parentheses for Scripture references but use footnotes or end-notes for other source citations. Other publications use footnotes or endnotes to cite both Scripture and other sources.

When writing a book, you may be able to choose your preferred citation type, depending on the publisher. Check with the editor, but always be consistent.

So which way is best?

Some readers find footnotes distracting. Others hate having to hunt several pages or even to the end of the book to find out why the writer felt the need to insert an endnote. But it often comes down to the writer's preference, publisher's style, and target audience.

How do we cite sources?

Creating proper documentation format shows editors you're a pro. Whenever you're unsure, don't guess—look it up. Here's a quick, easy way to remind yourself of proper format: Grab a nonfiction book from a *major publisher* off your shelves, and follow the documentation format it uses. (Caution: Avoid using self-published books as models. They may not use proper formatting.)

Here are the basics:

- *Footnotes.* Many magazines and most book publishers use *Chicago Manual of Style* (*CMoS 16*) as the standard for note formats. Writers for the Christian market will also want to refer to *The Christian Writer's Manual of Style* (based on *CMoS 16*), which includes topics unique to Christian writing. Citation basics include author, title, facts of publication, and page number(s) or on-line URL—in that order.

  Let's say I wanted to quote the following pun from a vintage humor book: "Max Beerbohm declined to be lured into a hike to the summit of a Swiss Alp. 'Put me down,' he said firmly, 'as an anti-climb Max.'" Ba-dum pum.

  After the closing quotation mark, I click on Microsoft Word's References menu then click on Insert Footnote. This will insert a superscript number and bring me to the bottom of the page. There I footnote the quotation in this format:

[1] **Bennett Cerf, *Bennett Cerf's Treasury of Atrocious Puns* (New York: Harper & Row, 1968), 77.**

The number *77* indicates page number, so we don't insert the letter *p* or the word *page* in front of it.

Footnotes or endnotes may use the superscript (as used above) or a number in regular (roman) font followed by a period:

1. Bennett Cerf . . .

Microsoft Word automatically inserts the next footnote number in a super-script form.

If I wanted to use a quotation from an article in *Today's Christian Living*, for example, I could footnote it with the superscript as shown above, or I could insert the quotation this way: "Lee Strobel's [nonfiction] books read like riveting detective novels. From the very first page, readers are captivated by fascinating details expertly woven together with vivid imagery."

I would then format the footnote this way:

2. **Ken Walker, "Lee Strobel Touches Countless Lives,"** *Today's Christian Living*, **November 2015, 22.**

And excellent writers always make sure to include all necessary data.

- *Endnotes/Notes.* Use the same formatting as footnotes. We simply move them to the end of the chapter or the end of the book. For the latter, we break them down by chapter.

Nonprint Media

Obviously, I can't cover all media. So I advise buying, studying, and frequently consulting *The Christian Writer's Manual of Style, Fourth Edition*,[1] which covers many more situations peculiar to our profession. It is a Christian writer's bookshelf essential. It's worth the investment to become a professional writer that editors can trust.

Bibliographies

Bibliographies—sometimes called *sources*—appear at the end of a book. They compile, alphabetically, into one place, all the sources you cited (along with any particularly relevant sources you consulted while writing the book).

A bibliography listing contains essentially the same information as footnotes/notes, but the format looks like this for a book entry:

Cerf, Bennett. *Bennett Cerf's Treasury of Atrocious Puns.* **New York: Harper & Row, 1968.**

Notice the hanging indent for lines after the first line. (See Microsoft Word's help feature to create hanging indents.)

Getting It Right

We can save ourselves time later if we record all the source information and page numbers at the time we're doing our research—or whenever we come across an interesting piece of information we might use some day in our writing.

If we're conscientious writers and copious information-capturers, with a little diligence in formatting we can present a lovely offering—a fragrant, not noxious offering—to editors: a well-written, well-documented piece that fits their editorial needs.

Chapter 32 Exercise

1. Find a nonfiction book that has footnotes or endnotes. Copy one book and one magazine citation from those notes that show all the information needed and the way to format it properly.

2. Using either an article of at least eight hundred words that you have already written (or one you write for this exercise), insert at least two pertinent quotations or statistics from outside sources to support some of your points: one from a book and one from a magazine article. Footnote them properly.

3. Compare your findings with the members of your critique group.

References

Citing Sources

The Chicago Manual of Style, Sixteenth Edition: 2.61, 14.1–3, 14.68–69
The Christian Writer's Manual of Style, Fourth Edition: pp. 245–52
The Associated Press Stylebook: See Quotations
Publication Manual of the American Psychological Association, Sixth Edition: 6.01–32

Bibliographies

The Chicago Manual of Style, Sixteenth Edition: 14.56–67
The Christian Writer's Manual of Style, Fourth Edition: pp. 73–76
MLA Handbook for Writers of Research Papers, Seventh Edition: 1.5.2, 1.5.6, 6.5.2

> Concentrate on doing your best for God, work you won't
> be ashamed of, laying out the truth plain and simple.
> —2 TIMOTHY 2:15 (*THE MESSAGE*)

Handling Scripture Carefully and Correctly

33

On a trip to Israel, I visited the Shrine of the Book, an extraordinary museum displaying some of the Dead Sea Scrolls. God miraculously preserved these manuscripts for centuries until their "accidental" discovery in several Qumran caves in 1947. Ancient scribes painstakingly copied those Scriptures so we could have God's Word with astounding accuracy.

Awed by those scrolls, I realized the great responsibility today's Christian writers have. In practical terms, how can we be careful scribes, handling God's precious Word?

Handle with Care

Careful scribes need keen discernment. God calls us each of us to be a diligent student of the Bible, "rightly dividing the word of truth" (2 Tim. 2:15 KJV), or put another way, one "who correctly handles the word of truth" (NIV).

First and foremost, consider the context of a verse or passage. We can rightfully claim numerous promises and principles in Scripture, but it's easy to become disillusioned—even wander into heresy—if we don't carefully examine the context when applying God's Word.

For instance, it would be foolish to believe all the counsel of Job's supposed friends, applying everything they said as truth.

Understand That Less Is More

Don't overwhelm the reader with Scripture. Often writers essentially string together Scripture quotations with only a few sentences or original thoughts in between. If I want to read long portions of Scripture, I'll turn to my Bible. Readers come to your article or book to discover what insights the Lord may have given you into a topic or passage.

Here's a diagnostic tool: Go through your manuscript, highlighting all your Bible quotations with your computer's highlighter. You'll quickly see what percentage of your work is yours and how much you're quoting.

Important fact: Much as we may not want to admit it, readers often skip over long quotations. So streamline your quotations for maximum impact. By focusing precisely on the specific point you want to make, you'll more likely touch the reader's heart.

Your readers may get lost in the "hedge maze" of everything I've quoted here from Joshua 1:7–9:

> Be strong and very courageous. Be careful to obey all the law my servant Moses gave you; do not turn from it to the right or to the left, that you may be successful wherever you go. Keep this Book of the Law always on your lips; meditate on it day and night, so that you may be careful to do everything written in it. Then you will be prosperous and successful. Have I not commanded you? Be strong and courageous. Do not be afraid; do not be discouraged, for the LORD your God will be with you wherever you go.

The whole passage is wonderful, but what do you want readers to focus on? Being strong and courageous? Obedience? Meditating on Scripture? Success? Not fearing? God's presence with us everywhere we go?

Clarify through selectiveness. If your article or book chapter aims to encourage Christians to be strong in difficult times, use only the first sentence: "Be strong and very courageous." Or if you want to emphasize God's presence with us in scary, discouraging times, skip down to the last sentence: "Do not be afraid; do not be discouraged, for the LORD your God will be with you wherever you go."

If you want to unpack the whole section, so to speak, do it a phrase at a time.

Selectiveness! Your readers will thank you for it, and those words will more likely make a greater impact.

Quote Accurately

Be careful—extremely vigilant—in replicating a quotation. As I've said before, you can eliminate errors by never *typing* a Scripture passage. Instead, use the copy-and-paste feature of your word-processing program to copy the text directly from a reliable online Bible site, such as BibleGateway.com, or a Bible software program, such as Logos. Then highlight the passage in your manuscript and change the font to Times New Roman/Times Roman (the font you're using in all your manuscripts, right?). Then be sure to delete verse numbers given in the text of the online source. This process not only eliminates typos but saves time.

I prefer BibleGateway.com when I have Internet access. That site features most major Bible translations and paraphrases; and you can quickly search by topic, word, or reference.

Accuracy is paramount, as illustrated by these two examples:

- A copyist in the 1600s left out one three-letter word. But his slipup rendered God's commandment in Exodus 20:14 this way: "Thou shalt commit adultery." It got published that way!
- Around 1700, another copyist—perhaps a bitter, aspiring writer with wandering thoughts—messed up when copying the psalmist's lament about mistreatment in Psalm 119:161. In the King James version, it reads, "Princes have persecuted me without a cause: but my heart standeth in awe of thy word." The inattentive scribe's manuscript got published this way: "Printers have persecuted me without a cause."

Although, as writers, we may feel that way about publishers sometimes, this copyist also "adulterated" God's Word.

The egregious errors of a few and the vigilance of the vast majority of scribes over the centuries inspires us to be faithful—obsessive—checking everything: word for word, punctuation for punctuation.

Again, be careful with ellipses too. If you leave out words and replace them with ellipses, make sure you don't change the original meaning.

7 Essential Principles for Handling Scripture Carefully and Correctly

1. Approach God's Word with reverence. You are holding in your hands the words breathed from the mouth of God (2 Tim. 3:16–17). I once held—with gloved hands—a small diary written in pencil by a Civil War soldier on the battlefield. I turned the pages with great awe that his thoughts and feelings had survived almost 150 years. How much more awesome that we get to work with the very words of Almighty God!

2. Develop the lifestyle of the Bereans in the book of Acts (17:11), searching the Scriptures daily to develop discernment, making sure you're thinking and writing biblically.

3. Avoid prooftexting. Don't come up with an idea and then run to a concordance or Bible-search program, looking for a verse to prop it up. Let your ideas grow out of a consistent devotional life and careful Bible study (2 Tim. 2:15).

4. Rely on the Holy Spirit to open your eyes to God's truth (Ps. 119:18).

5. Take time to listen, so God can make his meaning and applications clear. Pray like Samuel: "Speak, for your servant is listening" (1 Sam. 3:10).

6. Let Scripture interpret Scripture. Make sure that any idea you're putting forth doesn't contradict something else in the Bible (2 Peter 1:20–21).

7. Remember, you are personally accountable for everything you're learning and passing along through your writing and/or speaking (James 3:1–2). As I once heard Charles Swindoll say on a radio broadcast, avoid "trafficking in unlived truth."

See appendix C for more resources related to using Scripture accurately.

Use Proper Mechanics

First, when writing a book manuscript, indicate at the beginning of the book (usually on the copyright page) the predominant Bible translation you'll be using. Consult *The Christian Writer's Manual of Style, Fourth Edition* for its listing of the proper wording necessary to credit various Bible translations and paraphrases (see Permission Guidelines: The Bible).

Including this information simplifies your references throughout. Quotations from this predominant version need no translation credit at the point of reference. We indicate quotations from *other* versions this way: "God so loved . . ." (John 3:16 KJV).

Use proper mechanics in every aspect of your Scripture quotations. Buy and thoroughly study *The Christian Writer's Manual of Style* so that proper mechanics become second nature.

Here are a few mechanics for starters:

- Omit unnecessary lead-in words (e.g., *for, whereas, as, so, even as, just as, therefore, but*). They often confuse readers or create an incomplete sentence.

    CONFUSING: **In Matthew 20:28, Jesus says, "Just as the Son of Man did not come to be served, but to serve, and to give his life as a ransom for many."** This is an incomplete thought—a sentence fragment.

    CLARIFIED: **In Matthew 20:28, Jesus says, "The Son of Man did not come to be served."**

- Use ellipses for material deleted in the midst of a quotation and brackets to fill in gaps for clarification:

    CORRECT: **"The Son of Man [came] . . . to give his life as a ransom for many."**

- Don't use ellipses to indicate words left out at the beginning or end of a quotation.

    UNNECESSARY PUNCTUATION: **Paul tells us, ". . . the gift of God is eternal life . . ." (Rom. 6:23).**

    MORE POWERFUL: **Paul tells us, "The gift of God is eternal life" (Rom. 6:23).** (Note that we capitalize *The* in this instance though it isn't capitalized in its context. It's the beginning of a sentence here.)

- Don't use letter designations to indicate a part of a verse—such as John 3:16a or Romans 6:23b—unless required in a scholarly work. Generally, the number reference is sufficient.

- When referring to a specific verse or range of verses (in parentheses after a quotation), use *v.* (not *vs.*) for *verse* and *vv.* (not *vs.* or *vss.*) for *verses*.

    At the beginning of John 1 we see the Word—who is Jesus—as Creator (v. 3) and as the Light of the World (vv. 4–5).

- To indicate a range of consecutive verses within a chapter of the Bible, as above, or between chapters with no verse references—use an en dash (not a hyphen):

Encouraged to memorize whole chapters of the Bible, Claire made John 1–10 her goal.

- If your Scripture reference includes verse numbers and spans more than one chapter of a book, use an em dash:

  Claire only managed to memorize John 1:1—6:59.

  For more information about creating en dashes and em dashes, see chapter 26.

- For books of the Bible containing only one chapter, such as Jude, publishers vary in how they indicate the passage. *CWMS 4* gives these guidelines: "The clearest way to reference them in text is either the first verse of Jude or verse 1 of Jude. If the reference is parenthetical after a quotation, then use this form: (Jude v. 1)."[1]

- Today we use arabic numerals, not roman numerals, to designate books like 1 Kings, 2 Timothy, and 3 John (as opposed to I Kings, II Timothy, and III John).

- Use italics, not boldface, for emphasis within a quotation. (Never use all caps for emphasis either.) Then add the words *emphasis added,* or *italics mine,* after the reference:

  "Be strong and courageous and *get to work.* . . . The Lord my God is with you. . . . He will see to it that everything is finished correctly" (1 Chron. 28:20 TLB, emphasis added).

- Book publishers typically prefer Bible book names to be abbreviated in parentheses after a quotation—as I've done in the previous example. For magazine articles, study your target publisher or publication to determine whether to spell out or abbreviate Bible book names when referencing them in parentheses. Use the correct abbreviations as given in *The Christian Writer's Manual of Style.* Academic works and some study Bibles use a more concise scholarly style of abbreviations, which are also listed in *CWMS 4.*

- Always spell out book names in the regular text of your manuscript (when not in parentheses that follow a quotation).

- Use proper punctuation and style when setting up Scripture quotations. The following examples are correct. (Some words are omitted to save space.)

  1. **First Corinthians 13:1 reads, "If I speak in the tongues of men or of angels, but do not have love, I am only a resounding gong or a clanging cymbal" (NIV).** Because we can't begin a sentence with a numeral, we need to spell out *First* here.
  2. **In 1 Corinthians 13, Paul wrote, "If I speak . . . cymbal" (v. 1 NIV).** Note: We don't put a period at the end of the *quotation* but save it for the end of the *sentence.* Because we've already given the book and chapter number in the sentence, we only need the verse designation in the parentheses.
  3. **In 1 Corinthians Paul wrote, "If I speak . . . cymbal" (13:1 NIV).** Here we need to

designate both chapter and verse in the parentheses, but not the name of the book.

4. **Paul wrote, "If I speak . . . cymbal" (1 Cor. 13:1 NIV).** Note that unless we're using the predominant version, we always add the translation or paraphrase abbreviation in caps per CWMS 4 within the parentheses—after the reference. A few publications insert a comma between the reference and abbreviation **(1 Cor. 13:1, NIV),** but most don't.

- Remember: No punctuation before the closing quotation marks (unless the quotation requires a question mark or exclamation point). Save the period for the end of the sentence.

Delight an Editor

Few things delight editors of Christian publications more than finding a well-written manuscript with strong biblical content—material that needs little work on mechanics. Our careful handling of Scripture helps editors feel they can trust us in other areas as well.

So be a dependable scribe. Be professional. Though I've already used 2 Timothy 2:15 in this chapter, it bears repeating here as we make Paul's admonition our goal: "Do your best to present yourself to God as one approved, a worker who does not need to be ashamed and who correctly handles the word of truth."

Chapter 33 Quiz

In the following sentences, correct any errors you find. Mark a C beside any sentences that are correct. Use BibleGateway.com to verify that all biblical quotations are correct—word for word, punctuation for punctuation—per the translation cited. (For demonstration purposes in this exercise I have intentionally retained the translation designations of Scripture references in the NIV even though that's the predominant translation of this book.) See answers in appendix A.

_____ 1. For years, I Samuel 12:24 has been one of my life-motivation verses: "But be sure to fear the LORD and serve him faithfully with all your heart; consider what great things he has done for you" (NIV).

_____ 2. John wrote that "The blood of Jesus, [God's] Son, purifies us from all sin" (1 John 1:7 NIV).

_____ 3. Peter urged us toward spiritual maturity when he wrote, "Like newborn babies, you must crave pure spiritual milk so that you will grow into a full experience of salvation. Cry out for this nourishment." (1 Peter 2:2 NLT).

_____ 4. Later in that chapter, Peter related our suffering to our Savior's: "Christ also suffered for us, leaving us an example, that you should follow in his steps" (1 Peter 2:21 NKJV).

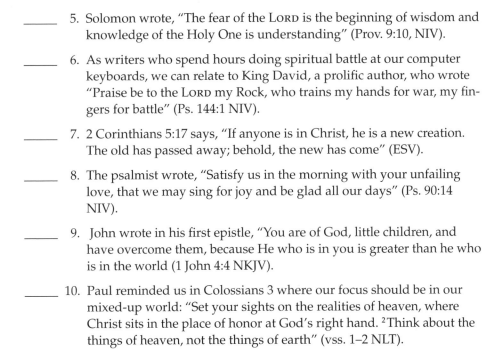

_____ 5. Solomon wrote, "The fear of the Lord is the beginning of wisdom and knowledge of the Holy One is understanding" (Prov. 9:10, NIV).

_____ 6. As writers who spend hours doing spiritual battle at our computer keyboards, we can relate to King David, a prolific author, who wrote "Praise be to the Lord my Rock, who trains my hands for war, my fingers for battle" (Ps. 144:1 NIV).

_____ 7. 2 Corinthians 5:17 says, "If anyone is in Christ, he is a new creation. The old has passed away; behold, the new has come" (ESV).

_____ 8. The psalmist wrote, "Satisfy us in the morning with your unfailing love, that we may sing for joy and be glad all our days" (Ps. 90:14 NIV).

_____ 9. John wrote in his first epistle, "You are of God, little children, and have overcome them, because He who is in you is greater than he who is in the world (1 John 4:4 NKJV).

_____ 10. Paul reminded us in Colossians 3 where our focus should be in our mixed-up world: "Set your sights on the realities of heaven, where Christ sits in the place of honor at God's right hand. ²Think about the things of heaven, not the things of earth" (vss. 1–2 NLT).

References

Abbreviations: Bible Books and Related Material
    The Christian Writer's Manual of Style, Fourth Edition: pp. 21–24

Bible Versions and Translations, Types of
    The Christian Writer's Manual of Style, Fourth Edition: pp. 53–55

Bible Versions in English
    The Christian Writer's Manual of Style, Fourth Edition: pp. 55–64

Quoting the Bible
    The Christian Writer's Manual of Style, Fourth Edition: pp. 330–36

Style, Usage, and Other Considerations

style \stī(-ə)l\ *n* **1:** Your own unique, personal distinctive, superterrific way of writing that makes someone say, "Hey, that sounds just like you." It distinguishes your way of writing from the way others write. (In other words, don't even think about trying to copy someone else's style.) **2:** the way word choice, grammar, and punctuation come together in an acceptable way so that readers understand what in the world you're trying to say.

Stylin'
What Is Style?

The Devil Wears Prada, a fish-out-of-water story, portrays a naive college graduate, Andrea Sachs, seeking to jump-start her journalism career by working as an editor's assistant at *Runway*, a top-notch fashion magazine. Unfortunately, she's never read the magazine. And her idea of style, judging from what she wears to the interview, seems to consist of dark-wash jeans, buckskin blazer, white shirt, and blue sweater. In fact, one coworker mistakes her for the "before" of a before-and-after story.

It makes sense for a fashion magazine to expect a certain level of sartorial savvy on the part of its employees. But in an effort to fit in, Andrea lets relationships slide and undergoes a makeover of both wardrobe and values.

In Happily-Ever-After Land, protagonists come to their senses sooner or later. And, predictably, Andrea soon finds happiness in her own relationships and style—being who she is, not what someone else expects her to be.

Ah, style! So far in this book I've focused primarily on matters of grammar and punctuation, so it's high time I tackled the style issue. What is it? How do you develop it? And why is it important to understand it?

Two Types of Style

Eighteenth-century essayist Philip Dormer Stanhope, Earl of Chesterfield, distilled *style* this way: "Style is the dress of thoughts."

In general, I believe that *what we say* is content. *How we say it* is style.

Specifically, in the writing world, we use the word *style* in two different ways— writing to *fit in* (accepted style) and writing *to be you* (personal style).

1. *Accepted Style*

Accepted style is that which is acceptable and expected in the use of the English language, so as not to be thought of as a hick from Rubesville who don't know nuthin' 'bout puttin' sentences t'gither. Used this way, style includes such things as grammar, punctuation, capitalization, and proper word usage. It's a matter of learning the rules of the English language.

This is the "fitting in" kind of style. Learning these rules increases your likelihood of getting published (if the content is also there) because editors love to see manuscripts that don't need much work. Some star-quality writers break the rules at times. But as teachers often say, you have to know the rules in order to know when you can break them.

Each periodical and publishing house chooses a recognized style manual to be its standard. (See sidebar on page 200.) When editors make changes to our manuscripts, they aren't sadistically hacking up our slaved-over prose to get their daily dose of jollies. Editors follow the rules in their designated style manuals.

In addition, they also develop what's called "house style," which codifies decisions they have made that either aren't addressed elsewhere or differ from the standard. Editors follow style-manual guidelines to smooth out our prose and help us communicate more effectively. Insert my personal shout of thankfulness here.

2. *Personal Style*

Personal style is your natural way of expressing yourself. Sometimes we talk about someone having a breezy style or contemplative style, a humorous style or ponderous style—or many others. Some writers' styles inspire a genre, like the hardboiled style of a Raymond Chandler novel. I pulled a few books off my shelf to find examples of various styles I would label in these ways:

- Breezy:
  "He was a professional thief. His name stirred fear as the desert wind stirs tumbleweeds. . . . His weapon was his reputation. His ammunition was intimidation. . . . His presence was enough to paralyze" (Max Lucado).[1]

- Much different but still breezy, maybe even quirky:
  "I walk along defending myself to people, or exchanging repartee with them, or rationalizing my behavior . . . or pretending I'm on their TV talk show or whatever. I speed or run an aging yellow light or don't come to a full stop, and one nanosecond later am explaining to imaginary cops exactly why I had to do what I did, or insisting that I did not in fact do it" (Anne Lamott).[2]

- Contemplative (writing about risk):
  "If we let ourselves be paralyzed by fear, we will not experience the mountain view, nor the thrill of finding our way into a wide meadow full of sunlight . . . nor even the newly increased sensitivity of our ears and nose that comes when our eyes have been temporarily deprived of clear vision. Our risking in faith and obedience brings joy to our Master's heart" (Luci Shaw).[3]

- Humorous (hearing about a "real prayer warrior"):

   "I cringed with guilt, imagining this saint who has worn out countless pairs of pantyhose at the knee, praying for lost causes and hopeless cases. . . . I feel puny and pathetic, for you see, I'm not a prayer warrior at all. I'm a prayer wimp.

   "Problems like the water heater exploding don't send a prayer warrior running from the house, in her ratty pink bathrobe and fuzzy purple slippers, screaming, 'Help, Lord! Save us!' No, a warrior never loses her cool like that.

   "'Thank you, Lord, for this opportunity to wash the basement floor,' she intones" (Mary Pierce).[4]

- Ponderous:

   "In after days, when because of the triumph of Morgoth Elves and Men became estranged, as he most wished, those of the Elven-race that lived still in Middle-earth waned and faded, and Men usurped the sunlight" (J. R. R. Tolkien and Christopher Tolkien).[5]

- Hard-boiled:

   "It was about eleven o'clock in the morning, mid October, with the sun not shining and a look of hard wet rain in the clearness of the foothills. . . . I was neat, clean, shaved and sober, and I didn't care who knew it. I was everything the well-dressed private detective ought to be. I was calling on four million dollars" (Raymond Chandler).[6]

These examples demonstrate that personal style includes word choice, sentence and paragraph length, sentence complexity, density of expression, and more. It's the "feel" of the piece, how it flows, how much effort it takes the reader to understand it, how clearly it communicates, and how much it entertains.

Varied Styles and Hybrids

We don't need to confine ourselves to a finite list of style categories. If you start pulling books off your shelf, trying to describe the author's style in a single word, you may get frustrated. We find many hybrids. Some authors write primarily in a simple and direct style with a dash of satire. We might classify others as mixing a conversational style with dry wit.

Styles, in general, have changed over the years too. Charles Dickens, for example, may not have found a publisher if he had lived in today's publishing climate—or he may have faced heavy editing.

And because various magazines have differing styles, you may also need to vary yours to fit in as Andrea Sachs did in the movie. But you shouldn't need to sell your soul over doing so. In other words, you might have to spiff up your outfit but not change your personality.

Accepted style and personal style are not mutually exclusive. The more we write and learn what's acceptable, the more we'll start seeing a blossoming of our own personal style that communicates well with the reader.

Think of style as the right amount of salt in our writing, drawing out the natural flavor of the content without overpowering it.

Style Manuals

Here's a list of the most commonly used style manuals, noting who uses them:

- *The Elements of Style*, by William Strunk Jr. and E. B. White (a little book affectionately known in writing circles as *Strunk & White*). Short, succinct, basic guidelines for acceptable English grammar and usage. Used by many writers in various areas of publication. Frequent reading and study recommended.
- *The Associated Press Stylebook* (*AP*), by Associated Press. Used primarily by newspaper and some magazine editors.
- *The Chicago Manual of Style, Sixteenth Edition* (*CMoS 16*), by The University of Chicago Press. It's the standard used by most book editors and many magazine editors.
- *The Christian Writer's Manual of Style, Fourth Edition* (*CWMS 4*), edited by Robert Hudson, published by Zondervan. Used by many book and magazine editors. Based on the principles in *CMoS 16*, it delves deeper into specifics of style that Christian writers and editors deal with. This manual belongs on the desk of every Christian writer and editor—within arm's reach. Frequent study recommended.
- Writing style manuals are dictated by discipline, such as Modern Language Association (MLA) for English and the humanities, and the American Psychological Association (APA) for psychology, among others.

Which should you use? The answer is like those in *Jeopardy!*—in the form of a question—two questions, actually:

What do you write?

What does your target publication or publishing house use?

Figuring that out is part of studying the publication or house. Pick a few items, such as style of subheads and use of numerals versus spelling out numbers, where CMoS 16 and AP differ; and determine which your publication follows.

Consistency is paramount! If you consistently use one style throughout, you look more professional than if you cap every word in a subhead in one chapter but then only cap the first word of subheads in other chapters.

Developing Your Style

Our own personal style develops as we read and write. It's like osmosis in plants. Everything we read soaks into our being and subtly shapes our style. We never try to mimic another person's style, but our own personal style may reflect some of what we read. And the more we write, the more our natural personal style will emerge. Though we adapt slightly to fit in here or there, our writing personality will still shine through.

Katherine Anne Porter, the Pulitzer Prize–winning author of *Ship of Fools*, encapsulated style this way: "Aristotle said it first, as far as I know. . . . It is one of those unarguable truths. You do not create a style. You work, and develop yourself; your style is an emanation from your own being."[7]

It's more fun to write and then see how others describe our style. Like Andrea Sachs, quit worrying about your style. And be you.

Chapter 34 Exercise

Along with others in your critique group or class, write 100 to 150 words in a style that comes naturally to you (or select a passage from something you've written), and read it to your group. Ask them to characterize your writing style. Discuss strengths, weaknesses, inconsistencies, and/or ways you think each of you could adapt to the publications you're targeting for your writing.

Don't Use That Tone with Me
Avoiding Preachiness and Other Reader-Offensive Tones

35

A retired preacher named Phil became frustrated with Dudley, a younger pastor he mentored. Dudley put little effort into his sermon preparations, and his delivery often fell flat. Phil pointed out elements that needed strengthening, Scripture references Dudley could have used, and even body language that could emphasize a particular truth.

One day Phil peeked at Dudley's notes for the coming Sunday's sermon. The outline looked decent—until Phil came across this handwritten notation in the margin: "Weak point: Pound pulpit."

Speakers may have the luxury of pounding the pulpit, whether their points are weak or strong. But excellent writers employ subtle techniques to get their points across.

In fact, readers don't want sermons. They look to writers for a "good read" that isn't preachy. Yet editors reject many manuscripts because of the tone—often too preachy or too angry. So how do we recognize and remedy these maladies that turn off readers?

Remedies for a Preachy Tone

1. *Use the word* **we,** *not* **you.**

I'll never forget the look on one insecure writer's face when it dawned on him that readers identify with us writers better in our pain and mistakes than when we pretend we've got it all together. Transparency in his story could actually help others.

In Christian material, especially, readers relate to us better when we come alongside them and our writing says, as my grandmother often said, "I've been there and spent the day."

We approach the topic we're writing about as fellow travelers, instead of as judges ordering readers around. Fellow travelers use *we* language instead of *you* language. Here are some examples.

> PREACHY *YOU* LANGUAGE: **When you are going through difficult days, you must trust the Lord. You should give all your cares to him because he cares for you (1 Peter 5:7).**

You language often leads to preachy words, such as *must* and *should*, which popped up in the above example.

> SLIGHTLY SOFTER *WE* LANGUAGE: **When we are going through difficult days, we must trust the Lord. We should give all our cares to him because he cares for us (1 Peter 5:7).**

That's the first step toward "unpreachifying" the sentence, but the preachy words continue to stalk us. (For more preachy-word examples, see sidebar on page 206.)

We can convey the same truth in *we* language—and eliminate preachy words—by telling a personal story about God helping us through a difficult time. Then we can make the broader application something like this:

> UNPREACHY, YEA, EVEN ENCOURAGING: **As I trudged through those difficult days, I discovered we can trust the Lord and give all our cares to God because he cares for us (1 Peter 5:7).**

Softer, right? Readers don't feel bludgeoned to death by what they have to do. They feel encouraged to follow a path someone else has learned to take.

2. *Use possibilities, not edicts.*

You know you're getting old when your speed-dial list (or favorites list on your smartphone) includes more doctors than friends. And, unfortunately, the older I get, the closer I'm getting to that reality. But I weary of doctors who have only one cure for all of one's maladies: lose weight.

One day I visited a new specialist, and he surprised me with his approach. Instead of chewing me out for not losing more weight, he showed me medical complications I could avoid by changing a few lifestyle habits. Instead of preaching at me, he showed me possibilities. Much more effective.

We can do the same thing for our readers. Instead of taking a Godlike "Thou shalt . . ." approach, commanding readers to do something, we can show the positive results of obedience, trusting, serving, and more. Here's an example:

> EDICT-SPEWING: **If you want to bear fruit for the Lord, you have to abide in Jesus, the Vine.**
>
> ENVISIONING THE POSSIBILITIES: **As we learn to abide in Jesus, the Vine, he produces the fruit he wants to see in us.** (Of course, explain what it means to abide in Jesus.)

Now we're understanding that God's commands come to us for our good. We see the positive results of abiding, rather than being told what we have to do. Readers see the possibilities.

3. *When to use the word you.*
Sometimes there is a place for *you* language. Here are a few examples:

- *Instructional material.* You will notice that, for variety, I switch between *you* language and *we* language in this book. Other how-to writers do the same. But it's a more conversational *you* than a laying-down-the-law *you*. Read through this chapter again (and pay attention when reading other columnists' and how-to writers' work) to see the difference.
- *How-to articles.* Whether writing about how to make a beaded bracelet or how to spark new romance in a dying-embers marriage, writers assume an authoritative tone—that of a teacher (not preacher). We may use imperatives (command forms) such as these:

    BEADY IMPERATIVE: After you have strung your beads on the wire, take your crimping tool and . . .

    ROMANCE IMPERATIVE: First, you need to identify what attracted you to each other in the first place and then . . .

- *Dialogue in fiction.* To create unlikeable characters who are always telling people what to do, go for the gold in preachiness when crafting their dialogue. Let them spew edicts as much as their personalities allow.

But, for the most part, avoid a preachy tone and walk alongside the reader with *we* language, avoiding preachy words.

Remedies for an Angry Tone

I have seen manuscripts that ooze anger. Yes, the writers had suffered (or observed) a deep wound. But they railed endlessly against evildoers and a society that allowed such injustice. Anger can overpower "message" and block empathy. That's when readers quit reading.

Often we need a first draft to vent the anger, purging ourselves of the vitriol that has built up during the hurtful experience. But then a raging bonfire provides a good place to "file" that draft. Afterward, we can take a step back, pray for perspective, and begin again.

Remember the fundamental writing advice: Show, don't tell.

Adjusting the tone dial in a manuscript often means showing an injustice or offense through "story," rather than simply telling us how awful the situation was and what should be done to rectify it. Movies like *Erin Brockovich* demonstrate that story can draw far greater attention to an issue than a raging letter to the editor or an opinion piece—though that type of writing has its place.

We call this "putting a face on an issue." Instead of writing an angry treatise on abortion or human trafficking, tell us the story of the lingering emotional pain of one teenager pressured into an abortion or one precious eleven-year-old sold into prostitution.

Now we'll discover the injustice along with you. We'll feel the pain and empathize, envisioning our daughter or granddaughter being treated that way. Now readers will more likely get involved than if you write an angry piece, saying, "This must be stopped!"

Preachy Words and Phrases to Avoid

must	ought to	should	It is essential that . . .
have to	You are required to . . .	got to	It is necessary to . . .
need to	It is imperative that . . .		

Remedies That Sell Manuscripts

God certainly nudges some of us to pass along serious, even shocking, exhortations. But we can spur readers to life changes without pointing fingers or pounding the pulpit. And we can motivate readers to action without erupting in anger.

Envision the possibilities!

Chapter 35 Quiz

Try your hand at "unpreachifying" the following sentences. See possible rewrites in appendix A. Put a C beside any sentences that are okay in context. Then analyze a passage of something you're writing. Highlight preachy language and rewrite to unpreachify.

_____ 1. You must receive the Lord Jesus Christ as your Savior to receive forgiveness of sins.

_____ 2. It is essential that we give God first place in our lives.

_____ 3. In order to grow in your faith, you should read your Bible and pray every day.

_____ 4. We all ought to tell others about Jesus.

_____ 5. We need to eat a healthy, balanced diet.

_____ 6. If you want to be a true disciple of Jesus Christ, you have to take up your cross every day and follow him.

_____ 7. Jesus declared, "Go now and leave your life of sin" (John 8:11).

_____ 8. You've been putting off forgiving that person. Do it now!

_____ 9. "There's no excuse for laziness," Mom told Jared. "Get up off the couch and help around the house."

_____ 10. You've got to let go of your sin and follow God.

Many words mark the speech of a fool.

—ECCLESIASTES 5:3

Tight Writing

36

Sitting face-to-face with a highly revered writer, I trembled as she silently read my devotional article. The first time I attended a conference for writers, I had the privilege of a one-on-one appointment with Margaret Anderson, author of *The Christian Writer's Handbook* (the premier guide for Christian writers for decades). I clutched my notebook like a shield over my heart, awaiting her reaction.

Finally, she handed the manuscript back. "This is good," she said. "I think it's publishable. Tighten and polish and send it off."

Ecstatic, I found refuge in a nearby restroom for a quick thank-you-Lord session. Then I realized I didn't have a clue what she meant by "tighten and polish."

I've spent the rest of my career figuring that out. It's a problem for many writers. So I'll focus on tightening here and discuss polishing in the next chapter.

In these challenging times, we're familiar with economizing. And with shrinking publishers' budgets and readers' attention spans, we can increase our PQ (publishing quotient) if we learn to economize with words. Here are nine ways to start cutting back.

1. Stay Focused

Begin with the big picture. What is the purpose of your book, article, or fiction scene? Write, in one sentence, what the book or article will say (not what it's about). Some call this a thesis statement. I use a more descriptive term: article-in-a-nutshell sentence.

Similarly, know the purpose of every scene of your fiction piece. How will a given element move the plot forward, contribute to character development, set a mood?

This focus becomes the standard for measuring everything else in the manuscript: Does each sentence, paragraph, anecdote, quotation, and statistic support the article's focus? In fiction, is every action, dialogue exchange, and setting description essential to that scene's purpose?

If not, cut it. (But save it in another file. You may be dumpster-diving for ideas someday and find a way to recycle what you discarded before.)

2. Eliminate Redundancy

Once we shape the big picture, we can start hacking away at smaller pieces of "deadwood," such as these redundancies:

- *dwindled down.* Have you ever heard of anything dwindling *up*? Eliminate *down*.
- *ecstatic with joy.* Could we be ecstatic with sadness? *Ecstatic* is sufficient.
- *in close proximity. Proximity* means to be *close*. Delete *close*.
- *down through the long centuries.* All centuries consist of exactly one hundred years, none longer than another. We need neither *down* nor *long. Through the centuries* will do.
- *mischievous grin on her face.* Where else would she be wearing it?
- *He stood up.* Unless specifically referencing standing down from office or in warfare, we can simply write *He stood*.
- *She nodded yes,* or *he shook his head no.* When going over these redundancies in writing workshops, I say, "Look at me." I nod. "This means yes, right?" Then I shake my head. "This means no, right? So we don't need the *yes* and *no*."

I repeat for emphasis: Nodding means yes. Shaking one's head means no. So we can chop the *yes* and *no*.

Take note: axing a word here and there can leave room in your word count for something more important.

3. Pick One

Writing flows better with wise word choices. Often we use too many words, trying to ensure readers understand, and we wind up sounding like the *Amplified Bible*. That reference work provides unique insights, but it's awkward to read.

So, painstakingly pick the best word.

EXAMPLE: **Through Christ we experience the joy and delight of our salvation.**

How much difference is there between *joy* and *delight*? I often tell writers that when they find what I call multiple-choice synonyms in their writing, I want them to hear my bell-like voice in their head, chiming, "Pick one."

OTHER EXAMPLES: **joy and rejoicing of our hearts**
sins and transgressions
sorrow, sadness, and grief

Unless you're differentiating between multiple terms, pick one.

4. Streamline

Wordiness tires readers. Keep them engaged by streamlining expressions such as these:

WORDY: **If we keep from doing that . . .** [6 words]
STREAMLINED: **If we avoid that . . .** [4 words]

WORDY: **Diane inquired as to his reason for coming.** [8 words]
STREAMLINED: **Diane asked why he came.** [5 words]

WORDY: **The doctor warned Ana that she had better quit smoking.** [10 words]
STREAMLINED: **The doctor warned Ana to quit smoking.** [7 words]

WORDY: **Jesus often used stories as an effective means of making abstract truths understandable.** [13 words]
STREAMLINED: **Jesus often used stories to make abstract truths understandable.** [9 words]

WORDY: **The Jews in Berea who believed in Jesus searched the teachings of the Scriptures every day to see if the teachings of Paul were in sync with them.** [28 words]
STREAMLINED: **The Berean Jewish believers daily searched the Scriptures to determine the trustworthiness of Paul's teachings.** [15 words]

WORDY: **We need to take time to reflect on what we read. As we do this, we will receive new insights into what God has to say to us.** [28 words]
STREAMLINED: **As we reflect on what we read, God will provide new insights.** [12 words]

Note: If you want to emphasize taking time, you might retain that part. However, *reflecting* implies taking time.

Though I'm mathematically challenged, I believe we have saved forty-one words in these few examples. That could give you another brief paragraph to develop an important point elsewhere.

We don't want to change a nuance of meaning when cutting, but streamlining can help us choose precise words.

5. Restructure Prepositional Phrases

Prepositional phrases can also indicate a place to simplify. For example, we wouldn't write *the favorite planet of Janet*. We'd turn it into a possessive: *Janet's favorite planet*.

But when a proper noun isn't involved, we often miss an opportunity to write tight. Note these examples:

ORIGINAL: **the actions of the extraterrestrials**
RESTRUCTURED: **the extraterrestrials' actions**

ORIGINAL: **opportunity for self-advancement**

RESTRUCTURED: **self-advancement opportunity**

ORIGINAL: **her address in London**
RESTRUCTURED: **her London address**

ORIGINAL: **tablets of stone**
RESTRUCTURED: **stone tablets**

Little by little, we whittle and whittle—tightening our writing.

6. Write Lean

Often we ease into a statement instead of hitting it dead on, even in fiction.

WORDY: **Michael decided to get even with the bully.**

The decision isn't the important thing here, so we can delete that whole sentence. In context, we will know what Michael decided when we read what he did.

BETTER: **Michael punched the bully in the stomach.**

Note this point-of-view issue:

WORDY: **Sandra saw a roach crawling across the tablecloth and jumped.**

In this scene, the writer has already established that we're in Sandra's viewpoint. So we don't have to say she saw the roach. We can simply narrate.

BETTER: **Sandra jumped. A roach was crawling across the tablecloth.**

Redundancies to Avoid

Redundant	Replace with
sum total	sum
all throughout	throughout
end result	result
empty void	void
vanished out of sight	vanished
in close proximity	in proximity
exact same word	same word
deposed from office	deposed
sinlessly perfect	sinless
gingham-checked apron	gingham apron
postponed to a future time	postponed
"Thanks," he said gratefully.	"Thanks," he said.

Depending on context, you might be able to drop the tag *he said* and simply write *"Thanks."*

7. Watch for Trigger Words

Other expressions that slow the flow include these:

one of the
it is/was
there is/are/were
in considering
it's interesting to note that

I call them trigger words because they trigger a need for "surgery."

SURGERY CANDIDATE: **One of the fears many of us experience as a reality in our lives is the fear of being alone.**

We can cut that twenty-word sentence to five:

HEALTHIER: **Many of us fear solitude.**

SURGERY CANDIDATE: **There are many people who have never read the Bible through.**
HEALTHIER: **Many people have never read the Bible through.**

SURGERY CANDIDATE: **It is who he is that gives fragrance to what he does.**
HEALTHIER: **Who he is gives fragrance to what he does.**

SURGERY CANDIDATE: **It is interesting to note that God didn't rebuke Peter when he began to sink.**
HEALTHIER: **God didn't rebuke Peter when he began to sink.** (Let the reader decide whether it's interesting or not.)

SURGERY CANDIDATE: **In considering holiness we often equate it with performance.**
HEALTHIER: **We often equate holiness with performance.**

8. Clean Up Qualifiers

I address this issue more fully in chapter 13, but here are some brief guidelines. You can slash most qualifying words, such as these: *very, slightly, almost, nearly, just, really,* and *seem to.*

RIDICULOUS EXAMPLE: **I *just* want you to know that I *really* don't like to see so many qualifiers in your writing. They *seem* to be *very* distracting and *almost* always make me *slightly* nauseated.**
CLEANED UP: **Eliminate nonessential qualifiers. They're distracting, even sickening.**

Qualifiers have a place in our language, but cut any that aren't essential.

9. Go on a *Which* Hunt

Use your word-processing program's search feature to find the word *which* (also *who, whom, that*) in your manuscript. Often they can go bye-bye:

- **conversations which are replete with stories**

- people whom we have known
- Teenagers don't enjoy the same activities that they did when they were younger.

The more we read good writing, participate in critique groups, and carefully edit our own work, the more ways we'll learn to tighten our writing—to communicate clearly and hold reader attention.

Bottom line? Eliminate nonessentials.

Chapter 36 Quiz

Streamline the following sentences, following the principles in this chapter. Mark a C beside any that are acceptable. See answers in appendix A.

_____ 1. Shelli was apprehensive and nervous about her interview for college.

_____ 2. There are eleven donuts remaining.

_____ 3. Blend together the ingredients, pour into a greased pan, and put into an oven that has been preheated to 350 degrees.

_____ 4. The painting disappeared from sight.

_____ 5. The goal of the unscrupulous financial planner was to abscond with the life savings of his clients and head for the Cayman Islands.

_____ 6. Jordan plans to head out for her backpacking venture at 3:15 a.m. in the morning.

_____ 7. Erin crouched beside the fire escape across the street from the jewelry store. She saw the burglars run out the door on the side of the store, and she scrammed.

_____ 8. Sharie's children's book was a bit too cutesy for the publishing house she targeted.

_____ 9. If Pierre hadn't been so eager and anxious to impress the girls, he might not have belly flopped like a potbelly pig at the diving meet.

_____ 10. The SWAT officer picked up a bullhorn and told the dirty scumbag he was completely surrounded.

References:

Tight Writing/Eliminating Redundancies
    The Chicago Manual of Style, Sixteenth Edition: 5.220
    The Christian Writer's Manual of Style, Fourth Edition: pp. 365, 392–94
    Publication Manual of the American Psychological Association, Sixth Edition: 3.08

May the favor of the LORD our God rest on us; establish the work
of our hands for us—yes, establish the work of our hands.

—PSALM 90:17

Spit-Polished Writing

One of my most cherished possessions is the pith helmet my father wore in World War II. He returned from the war with two incurable diseases: hyperdisciplinarianism and superinflated perfectionism. I need not go into the painful details of the corporal punishment issue. But Dad could spit shine black dress shoes till he could see his reflection in them. And the master polisher shined our Sunday-go-to-meeting shoes each Saturday night to his "pro" standards.

Writers, too, need to be master polishers. Spit polishing manuscripts is a sign of a true professional. And editors like to work with true professionals. In the previous chapter I mentioned a respected author telling me my article was good, but I needed to "tighten and polish" it. In that chapter I looked at what it means to "tighten" writing. Here I'll talk about ways to "polish" it, so it will stand out from dull writing that boomerangs back with a does-not-meet-our-needs note attached.

Put the Pro in Proofreading

Good proofreading is invisible. Bad proofreading sticks out like a botched haircut. Spell-checkers can point out some errors, but they don't catch legitimate words incorrectly used: *their* instead of *there* or *they're*, *for* instead of *four*, *discreet* instead of *discrete*. One writer asked readers to search their *soles*. We might wonder if we're supposed to look for secondhand gum or what? Whenever you're in doubt on spelling or exact meaning, look it up.

Always proofread a hard copy of your manuscript before sending it to an editor. Typos and other errors diabolically hide on computer screens. You need periodic breaks from that life-sucking machine anyway, so sit back with your favorite beverage, mark up the hard copy, then make the corrections on screen.

- Watch for omitted words and punctuation. I know this is like saying, "Start seeing motorcycles." It's tough to see what you don't see. And often, when reading our work, our minds automatically fill in things we've left out. But slow down. Read carefully. Word for word. Letter for letter. The following error even slipped by professional proofreaders and made it into a published book: "It had been raining off an on all day."
- Read it aloud. Because you're a writer, your family probably already thinks you're nuts anyway; so go off by yourself and read your work aloud. Sometimes you'll hear errors when you can't see them.
- Get help. Never submit anything you haven't had someone else proofread too. A fresh set of eyes can pick up errors when your familiarity with the material blinds you to them.

Employ Parallelism

Using parallelism puts words, phrases, and other elements in parallel form. Doing so delights readers. It brings structure, cohesiveness, and rhythm to our writing.

> NONPARALLEL: *Praying* in the name of Jesus means to *pray* with all the authority in that name.
>
> PARALLEL: *Praying* in the name of Jesus means *praying* with . . .

Parallelism, using an *-ing* word in both phrases, creates a better rhythm in that sentence and gives it a cohesive feel.

> NONPARALLEL: Music can lift our spirits, and the feeling of despair is gone.
>
> PARALLEL: Music can lift our spirits and banish despair.

Putting this sentence in parallel form, using two strong verbs, eliminates a pesky *to-be* verb (*is*), which we want to avoid whenever possible. We also tighten the sentence, cutting four unnecessary words.

Parallelism can bring sentences into alignment as well. Look at this paragraph:

> When bills mount, we worry. When kids make wrong choices, we wonder where we went wrong. And we're tempted to give up when we can't see God working.

We'll create a better flow if we revise the third sentence this way, continuing the parallelism:

> And when we can't see God working, we're tempted to give up.

Put numbered or bulleted lists in parallel form as well. In an article about how to prepare for a writer's conference, for example, a nonparallel list might look like the following.

> NONPARALLEL:

- Be praying that God will give you a teachable spirit.
- Which editors do you want to talk to? Decide beforehand.

- Check the Internet to learn the types of things the attending editors publish.
- Creating and rehearsing a brief overview of your article or book idea gives you confidence.
- Polished manuscripts to show to editors are a good thing to bring.

Extreme example, but those lines begin in different formats: a *to-be* verb, a question, a command, an *-ing* word, a noun. We can choose any of those to follow through with, but a command form may work best.

PARALLEL:

- Pray for a teachable spirit.
- Decide beforehand which editors you want to talk to.
- Check the Internet to learn the types of things the attending editors publish.
- Create and rehearse a brief overview of your article or book idea.
- Polish and print manuscripts to show to editors.

Scrutinize Word Choice

Mark Twain wrote, "The difference between the almost right word and the right word is really a large matter—it's the difference between the lightning bug and the lightning."[1]

That's exaggeration for humor's sake. But make sure you're using precise words. One writer said he would like to *coerce* readers to grow in their faith. Sounds like strong-arm tactics to me. How about using *encourage* instead? Another writer described a *jagged-edged* knife when the correct term is *serrated* knife.

Other subtle nuances of language often keep our writing from shining.

POOR EXAMPLE: Are we focusing on God's sovereignty, or are we trying to handle things ourselves?

This sentence may look and sound fine. But in context, the writer was contrasting whether we're trusting in God or our own ability. The word *focusing* doesn't get to the heart of that. We can focus on God's sovereignty in worship or Bible study or other ways. But the issue was where we're putting our trust.

BETTER: Are we trusting in God's sovereignty or trusting our own ability to handle things?

There, repeating the word *trusting* also emphasizes that word.

So make sure you're using the precise word you want, but don't fall in love with your thesaurus.

Alluding to being paid by the word, Twain also wrote, "I never write metropolis . . . because I can get the same price for city."[2]

So use *often* instead of *frequently*; *used* instead of *utilized*; and, of course, *wink* instead of *nictitate*. Use a common word to communicate, rather than a fancy one to impress.

Use Fresh Imagery

Sometimes writers struggle to tell the difference between fresh and fitting word pictures and those that stick out like a throbbing appendage of the hand. It's important not to interrupt the flow of an article, a book chapter, or a fiction piece with long, elegant comparisons of the way the sun sets or a possum sleeps.

But the perfect simile or metaphor adds richness and texture.

1. *Similes* compare things, using the word *like* or *as*.

    EXAMPLE: **After the editor panel, conferees pounced on the panelists like hungry lions seeking whom they may devour.**

2. *Metaphors* compare things without using the word *like* or *as*. In essence, the thing we're describing "becomes" the descriptor, and vice versa.

    EXAMPLE: **An anvil of a man, Henry stood guard at the bank entrance.**

In your quest for fresh imagery, beware of clichés.

Today's clichés are yesterday's clever sayings. The simile *fresh as a daisy* isn't fresh anymore because we've heard it so often. Root out clichés, such as *ran like the wind, as fat as a pig,* and *like water off a duck's back*.

Readers love to come across a perfect word picture that doesn't *unnecessarily* call attention to itself but fits the scene perfectly—something new or a twist on something familiar.

Bill Myers writes in a novel that a junior high classroom "grew so quiet you could hear a press-on fingernail drop."[3] That's polish! (Pardon my pun.)

Find the Right Placement

Today many readers skim more than read. So to make sure readers grasp something, place it at the beginning or end of a sentence and/or paragraph. Doing so creates emphasis. Don't bury it in the middle.

It takes time to polish our writing, and many writers quit much too soon. But when we spit shine our manuscripts, readers may see the reflection of the Master Polisher there. And isn't that what we want?

Chapter 37 Quiz

Nail the Right Word

Choose the right word within the brackets. If either is correct, write *E* before the sentence. See answers in appendix A.

_____   1. Van wanted to travel [further/farther] that day, but the kids were getting antsy.

_____   2. Editor Meenstreek [inferred/implied] to us that Cassandra's manuscript stank.

_____   3. We finished a task that was [literally/virtually] impossible.

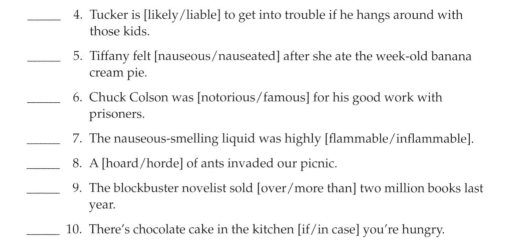

_____ 4. Tucker is [likely/liable] to get into trouble if he hangs around with those kids.

_____ 5. Tiffany felt [nauseous/nauseated] after she ate the week-old banana cream pie.

_____ 6. Chuck Colson was [notorious/famous] for his good work with prisoners.

_____ 7. The nauseous-smelling liquid was highly [flammable/inflammable].

_____ 8. A [hoard/horde] of ants invaded our picnic.

_____ 9. The blockbuster novelist sold [over/more than] two million books last year.

_____ 10. There's chocolate cake in the kitchen [if/in case] you're hungry.

References:

Proofreading

    The Chicago Manual of Style, Sixteenth Edition: 2.86–87, 2.107–15

    The Christian Writer's Manual of Style, Fourth Edition: pp. 314–17

    MLA Handbook for Writers of Research Papers, Seventh Edition: 3.1.1–2

    Publication Manual of the American Psychological Association, Sixth Edition: 8.02

Word Choice

    The Chicago Manual of Style, Sixteenth Edition: 5.220

    The Christian Writer's Manual of Style, Fourth Edition: pp. 388–89, also all of Part 2: "The Word List," pp. 400–597

Parallelism

    The Chicago Manual of Style, Sixteenth Edition: 5.212–15

    Publication Manual of the American Psychological Association, Sixth Edition: 3.09, 3.23

Similes and Metaphors

    Publication Manual of the American Psychological Association, Sixth Edition: 3.10

Walk with me and work with me—watch how I do
it. Learn the unforced rhythms of grace.
—MATTHEW 11:29 (*THE MESSAGE*)

Got Rhythm?

Several cellmates had been together so long on the same cellblock that they knew everything about each other. They had exhausted all topics of conversation. They even knew each other's jokes. In fact, they got to the point that they numbered them.

A prisoner would call out, "Number forty-two." Everyone laughed uproariously. Another would shout, "Sixty-seven." Everyone appropriately groaned. Still another would holler, "Twenty-three." And a polite chuckle echoed through the halls.

One day a new, young convict landed unceremoniously on the cellblock. Informed about what was going on, he sat back, intrigued at this bizarre means of sharing funny stories. In time he persuaded his cellmates to teach him the jokes and their corresponding numbers. Finally, he felt ready to join the jokefest. "Number forty-two," he called out.

No response.

Thinking the others hadn't heard him, he shouted a little louder, "Number forty-two!"

Still no response.

"I said, number forty-two," he tried again at the top of his lungs.

Dead silence.

Bewildered, he turned to one of his cellmates. "What's wrong?" he asked. "Why didn't anyone laugh? That's usually a knee-slapper."

The cellmate draped his arm over the new inmate's shoulders and said, "Some people know how to tell a joke, and some don't!"

In jokes, as in many areas of life—including writing—timing is everything.

- Good writers take the time to craft a pleasant rhythm and create a good flow in what they write.

- Mediocre writers write what they want to say, do a little rewriting and proofreading, then submit.
- Poor writers tend to think everything they write is fine. It's usually this category of writers that claims a direct pipeline to the Creator's inspiration, warning editors not to touch a word. Don't be like that. God gives us editors to keep us from embarrassing ourselves.

Editors tend to accept more writing that's well-crafted, writing that creates a pleasant rhythm, writing that flows. Mediocre and poor writers often end up singing the jailhouse blues over enough rejection slips to paper a cellblock.

So how can we create a pleasant rhythm and flow in our writing? And what are some trouble spots to look for? I'll address rhythm in this chapter and tackle flow in the next chapter.

Varying Sentence Structure

Analyze how you begin consecutive sentences throughout your manuscript.

Don't use all subject-then-verb sentences. In personal-experience articles and books, beginning sentence after sentence with *I*, then a verb, makes a piece sound self-centered.

> NOT FUN TO READ: I prayed to the Lord about the problem day after day, but he didn't answer. I couldn't believe God didn't care about this. I asked my friends for advice, but no one seemed to have any insights. I was a spiritual wreck.
>
> VARIED SENTENCE STRUCTURE: Day after day, I prayed about the problem. No answer came. Didn't God care about this? When I asked my friends for advice, no one had any insights. I was a spiritual wreck.

This more interesting arrangement of words creates a better rhythm. Using introductory phrases, such as *Day after day*, and dependent clauses, such as *When I asked . . .*, creates variety. Even throwing in a question helps. And, fortunately, the *I* gets buried in the middle of sentences.

In fiction and third-person narrative, we may have the same issue without the *I* problems. When writers and editors get behind in their deadlines, they often miss rhythm breakers like the following disguised excerpt from a published novel:

> He'd been too tired to keep his eyes open. He had been lulled to sleep by the clickety-clack of the commuter train.
>
> He exited the train at the stop near a favorite bakery from his childhood. The line to the bakery extended way out the door. And the prices were much higher than he remembered. He didn't want to buy stock in the place, just grab some breakfast.
>
> Finally, he reached the counter and opened his wallet to buy a latte and a cruller. He couldn't afford more with his last ten-dollar bill. A cab picked him up and dropped him off at his favorite park. He sat alone on a bench for a long while.

Notice that every sentence begins with a subject then verb. Although we have one transition word (*Finally*) and a sentence that begins with *And* (which is allowed

Sentence Types Refresher Course

- **A *simple sentence*** doesn't have to be short, but it's comprised of only one independent clause (subject and verb). Though a relatively long sentence, full of prepositional phrases, the following is a simple sentence (subject is underscored, verb is double underscored):

    At the age of seventy <u>Kristoff</u> <u>flew</u> on a plane for the first time without any anxiety [independent clause]. (Note the ambiguity. Was this the first time Kristoff flew or the first time he flew without anxiety?)

- **A *compound sentence*** has two or more independent clauses and no dependent clauses:

    <u>Kristoff</u> <u>flew</u> for the first time [independent clause], and <u>he</u> <u>wasn't</u> anxious at all [independent clause].

- **A *complex sentence*** has one main independent clause (subject and verb that can stand by themselves) and at least one dependent clause (subject and verb that can't stand by themselves but are dependent on the main clause—subject of dependent clause underscored, verb double underscored):

    When his first <u>grandson</u> <u>was</u> <u>born</u> [dependent clause], Kristoff flew on a plane [independent clause].

    Or

    Kristoff's son encouraged him to fly to Chicago [independent clause] although <u>Kristoff</u> <u>hadn't flown</u> before [dependent clause].

    The tip-off is a subordinate conjunction—*when* in the first sentence, *although* in the second. Note: Generally, when the dependent clause comes *before* the independent clause, we use a comma to separate the two clauses (comma after *born* in first example). When Mr. Dependent comes *after* Ms. Independent, we don't use a comma (no comma before *although*).

- **A *compound-complex sentence*** has two or more independent clauses and at least one dependent clause:

    When his <u>son</u> <u>invited</u> Kristoff to visit [dependent clause], <u>Kristoff</u> <u>hesitated</u> briefly [independent clause], but [coordinating conjunction] his <u>desire</u> to see the baby <u>erased</u> any misgivings about flying [independent clause].

Using a variety of sentence structures makes your writing more interesting.

these days), most sentences begin with *He.* The author could have at least used the guy's name once.

So we might vary the sentence structures, something like this:

Kip surrendered to the clickety-clack of the commuter train as it lulled him to sleep.
Arriving at his destination, he found his favorite bakery from childhood, but the line extended way out the door. The prices were much higher than he remembered. He didn't want to buy stock in the place. Just grab some breakfast. When he reached the

counter, he opened his wallet to buy a latte and a cruller—the only treat doable with his last ten-dollar bill.

A short cab ride later, Kip sat alone on a bench in his favorite park for a long while.

Note the various sentence types I used. I even threw in a sentence fragment (*Just grab some breakfast.*), which is also allowed occasionally in today's writing. Refresh your memory regarding sentence types, and use variety to create a pleasant rhythm. (See sidebar: "Sentence Types Refresher Course.")

Varying Sentence Length

Using sentences all about the same length creates an effect similar to the soporific clickety-clack of Steve's commuter train. And we don't want our readers succumbing to sleep. So try to balance short, medium, and long sentences—yes, even occasional fragments—to create a smooth, engaging rhythm for the reader. The length of sentences also helps with the flow of a piece. (See excerpt from Kirk Livingston's article in sidebar.)

Count the number of words in each sentence in the following excerpt. What does the writer accomplish with this great contrast? (Note: In the longest sentence, the author intentionally pushes the envelope on punctuation rules by omitting some commas.)

"Stop the World, I Want to Get Off"
by Kirk Livingston

"Urgency is the calling card of our culture. Life's pace is not only demanding, it is strident, it is in our face. It is phone calls that give way to faxes, followed by emails and more phone calls and couriers knocking at your door wondering why you don't come to answer even though you are in the middle of supper with your family, which is the first time you've sat down together all week because of various things like soccer practice and dance team that seem to run on night after night, leaving you exhausted so that by the end of the week you no longer function as a human but rather as a kind of automaton that knows nothing of kindness and barks out orders to equally exhausted children who are even more prone to show their tiredness as prickly anger.

"Whew. Stop it. Stop the world. Stop the revolving, the demanding, the circle of needs from everyone I come in contact with. Stop the urgency. Not everything can be that terribly urgent. Not everything is a No. 1 priority."[1]

Using Parallelism

I touched on this topic in the previous chapter, but it's important to mention it again here. Keep "like elements" of a sentence in the same form.

RHYTHM BREAKER: **The clowns kept piling out of the VW Bug, tooting their horns, and they repeatedly sprayed the crowd with seltzer water.**

RHYTHM MAKER, EMPLOYING PARALLELISM: **The clowns kept piling out of the VW Bug, tooting their horns, and spraying the crowd with seltzer water.**

We don't need to micromanage rhythm to the point of obsession in an article or a book. But look for places where readers may stumble over words, be put to sleep, or become distracted instead of enjoying the rhythm of a well-crafted piece.

Then you'll never hear the criticism, "Some people know how to tell a story, and some don't."

Chapter 38 Quiz

Rewrite these examples to add rhythm to the writing. If you belong to a critique group or class, compare your results.

1. When polishing a manuscript, you may come across something like this poorly written example:

   She walked into the kitchen and looked around. She stood still for several minutes. She couldn't remember what she had walked into the kitchen to do. She knew it was important, whatever it was.

   Try using other sentence structures to make this example more interesting. Hint: In addition to varying sentence types, you may use direct thoughts or add another character and create dialogue.

2. Sentences that don't begin with the same word may still need varied sentence structure. Note this example:

   Writers at conferences get a little kooky sometimes. A few of them played a practical joke on Ginger, their favorite magazine editor. They wrote a manuscript filled with grammatical errors, inserted Ginger's by-line, and filled out a cover sheet for a manuscript critique. One conferee wrote Ginger's name on the critique form. Another signed Ginger up for a consultation with a book editor to see how that faculty member would respond to such a terrible submission from a respected editor. The book editor had a good laugh and tossed the manuscript. Ginger never found out, fortunately. The writers were disappointed.

   In this made-up scenario, each sentence has a different subject. But throughout the paragraph, each sentence still begins with subject-verb construction. Try rewriting this paragraph, varying the sentence types. Then compare it with the possible rewrite in appendix A.

References:

Sentence Structure
   Publication Manual of the American Psychological Association, Sixth Edition: 3.08

Compound Sentences
   The Christian Writer's Manual of Style, Fourth Edition: See Comma, pp. 131–32; Semicolon, p. 352)

Sentence Fragments
   The Christian Writer's Manual of Style, Fourth Edition: p. 354

Flow Gently, Sweet Manuscript   39

I love clever character names. Some of my favorites come from the Disney film *Finding Nemo*. In the dental-office aquarium scene, what better name for a blowfish than Bloat? And the fish named Deb, seeing her reflection in the glass, thinks she has a sister and calls her Flo.

Deb and Flo. (Identical twins?) I love it!

From there, my twisted mind leaps to this pronouncement: The "ebb and flow" of a piece of good writing "reflects" well on the writer, communicates well, and creates an enjoyable reading experience.

Could we find any better example in classic literature than the beginning of Charles Dickens's *A Tale of Two Cities*: "It was the best of times, it was the worst of times, it was the age of wisdom, it was the age of foolishness, it was the epoch of belief, it was the epoch of incredulity"?

Can you feel the ebb and flow? Yes, Dickens repeatedly used the dreaded word *was* that editors advise writers to strengthen. And these words are only the first 36 of a long first sentence (at least for twenty-first-century readers) of 119 words. I have heard editors say that today's readers generally tire after an average sentence length of about 17 words.[1]

But the rhythm Dickens used reinforces the contrasts he made. Like a tide, the flow pulls us into the story. Let's look at ways we can do the same.

Flow Makers

1. *Sentence Length*

In the previous chapter, I discussed ways we can vary sentence length to create a pleasant rhythm. But when we realize what the *relative* length of each sentence can do, we may also see new ways to facilitate the flow of manuscripts, keeping readers engaged.

Long sentences, judiciously used, sweep readers along as if they were lazily floating down a quiet river on an inner tube. Overly long, run-on sentences can create a breathless feel—especially if readers can't read the sentence in a single breath. (Remember, some people still read to one another aloud.)

If you haven't read it yet, go back to the previous chapter and read "Stop the World, I Want to Get Off" by Kirk Livingston. His usually not-recommended run-on sentence of more than 100 words captures today's one-thing-after-another breathless pace. Perfect! We certainly wouldn't plagiarize this, and we would use this device sparingly, but what an impact it makes.

Short sentences and sentence fragments can, ironically, do the same thing. A series of short sentences and/or fragments in quick succession can convey urgency and danger. The staccato rhythm quickens the reader's heartbeat. Great for action scenes.

Some years ago I wrote an article about a small-town fire chief who was sucked up into a tornado and lived to tell about it. Setting the scene with Cal arriving home, I showed him seeing an outbuilding behind his house breaking up. He jumped out of his truck to unlock the main garage door, but flying debris assaulted him. He didn't know if he dared hop back in the pickup and drive it in:

> He took one peek. Nothing coming. Two giant, running steps. He jumped in the pickup. Debris pelted the truck again, but he got it into the garage. Shut it off. Locked the door. Grabbed his radio. Headed to the basement.

Through these short sentences and fragments, readers read faster. The pulse quickens. They want to know how Cal escapes this peril. I could have written it this way:

> He took one peek, but there wasn't anything coming. He took two giant, running steps and then jumped into the pickup while debris continued pelting the truck. But he got it into the garage, then shut it off and locked the door. He grabbed his radio and headed to the basement.

But I worked hard, trying to capture what Cal felt—that jerky, chaotic feeling.

On the other hand, a series of short sentences haphazardly thrown together can create a choppy, distracting, even childish reading-primer sound.

> CHOPPY: **Scotty wanted a new car. His wife objected. They had college tuition to think about. After all, they had seventeen kids.**
>
> FLOWING GENTLY: **Scotty wanted a new car, but his wife reminded him they needed to save for college tuition. After all, they had seventeen kids.**

In the revision, smoothly combining the ideas in the first three sentences sets us up for the zinger—the final short sentence.

Medium sentences provide a buffer between long and short sentences, also contributing to a smooth flow.

2. *Transitions*
In his book *The Magazine Article: How to Think It, Plan It, Write It*, journalism author-

ity Peter Jacobi wrote this: "Words do not create transition. Ideas do. Words serve only as tools."[2]

A well-written manuscript provides a smooth, logical progression of thought and ideas, first of all. Then specific words or phrases can guide readers through nonfiction points or fiction scenes. We will examine these further in chapter 41, but I'll mention some briefly here.

- Numbered points: To "chunk" information, you may use the words *first, second, third*. Or use phrases such as *in addition* or *besides that*. Or simply use arabic numerals (1, 2, 3) to keep your reader oriented.
- Time markers: Transitional phrases, such as *weeks later, when he finished his homework,* and *the next day,* not only provide transition but compress time—especially useful in narrative passages of both fiction and nonfiction.
- Repetition of a phrase or concept: Be careful not to overdo this device, but here's an example:

  End of one paragraph: **She prayed they would see the error of their** *religion.*
  Beginning of next paragraph: *That religion* **had held her in its grip too long.**

- Cause/effect: *because, therefore, so, consequently, as a result.*
- Contrast: *however, on the other hand, by contrast, despite.*
- Subheads: Readers often skim over these potentially powerful tools. That's why we need Jacobi's advice. But subheads can provide a strong path for the reader to follow through the article or book chapter. Editors or designers may change them, but creating our own subheads can give us a logical framework. And putting them in parallel form also helps the flow of the piece.

The "Glory of Threes"

How many little pigs fought bravely against Señor Big Bad Wolf? How many bears unwittingly hosted Goldilocks? How many billy goats suffered from a gruff disposition? And what's the minimum number of legs required for a stool to stand by itself?

For some reason, three elements feels complete. Perhaps it's rooted in the Trinity. Maybe it's a clue to the famous three-point sermon pastors love.

You can use three words or phrases that go well together.

EXAMPLE: **He prayed for wisdom, decisiveness, and patience.**

But to avoid redundancy, make sure they're not just synonyms of each other. Craft three sentences within a paragraph that present your idea well without undue repetition.

EXAMPLE: **The wisdom he prayed for came from his father's counsel. The decisiveness came from the assurance he was doing the right thing. The patience came from knowing God would do the right thing.**

Devise three subheads that cover your topic well, using parallel construction when possible. These can create a steady, three-legged framework for your piece.

During the Y2K computer-culture hysteria, I wrote an evangelistic article titled

"Facing the Impossible." Using the following three subheads, I could emphasize the role of hope in uncertain times:

A Needed Hope
A Solid Hope
A Lasting Hope

To capitalize on the glory of threes further, I transitioned from an anecdotal lead to the body of the article with this sentence: "We sure could use a bit, a byte, a gigabyte of hope." This imagery fit the context, and the three elements offered a settled feeling amid the threatened chaos.

Flow Breakers

We could, as discussed in chapter 38, call the opposite of flow makers, obviously, *flow breakers*:

- too many short, choppy sentences
- too many overly long sentences
- a lack of parallelism

But one of the worst flow breakers is unclear meaning. Anytime readers have to back up and read a sentence two or more times, we've cut off the flow and invited readers to quit reading.

When you take time to revise, remember the visual image of Deb and Flo in the aquarium. A good ebb and flow in our writing *reflects* well on us—and our Creator. It also keeps readers turning pages.

Chapter 39 Quiz

Revise the sentences below to maximize flow and pacing. Put a C beside any that are okay. See answers in appendix A.

_____ 1. "Slowly I turned. Step by step. Inch by inch."

_____ 2. Signing the megabucks-earning author filled the agent's heart with thankfulness and gratitude.

_____ 3. First, we give our hearts wholly to God. . . . Secondly, we seek his guidance, moment by moment.

_____ 4. Gunther tried to get Brunhilda out of his mind. He loved her. She was his soul mate. They were perfect for each other. Three months passed. He barely slept. He was devastated.

_____ 5. The Supreme Court made a questionable ruling. And huge crowds of protestors marched outside the courthouse.

_____ 6. While house hunting, the couple considered three primary criteria: price, floor plan, and where it was located.

_____ 7. Blythe stared down the intruder. Her hand trembled. She squeezed the trigger. Click. Nothing happened.

_____ 8. Those trying to live healthy lives have a difficult time knowing what to eat and what not to because one day butter is bad for you and the next day margarine is suspect followed by recommendations that olive oil is best and now it's coconut oil, so how can a person know what to believe?

_____ 9. Lack of alertness to the activities of possible homegrown terrorists, insensitivity to the strategies of Satan, underfunding of our military, a carelessness about following God's ways, failing to train our youth for spiritual warfare, and fear of speaking up when our lawmakers, in effect, overturn God's laws—all make us vulnerable as a nation.

_____ 10. Diana sprawled on the lawn of the castle. She stared up at the thin, wind-swept clouds. She finally felt free. And she praised God. Never again would she be plagued by the horrors of her past.

References:

Readability
    The Christian Writer's Manual of Style, Fourth Edition: pp. 339–40

Sentence Length/Flow
    Publication Manual of the American Psychological Association, Sixth Edition: 3.08

Transitions
    Publication Manual of the American Psychological Association, Sixth Edition: 3.05–6

> When [Jesus] had spit on the [blind] man's eyes
> and put his hands on him, Jesus asked, "Do you see anything?"
> He looked up and said, "I see people; they look like trees walking around."
> Once more Jesus put his hands on the man's eyes. Then his eyes were
> opened, his sight was restored, and he saw everything clearly.
>
> —MARK 8:23–25

Come to Your Senses
Captivating Readers with Sensory Detail

40

On a particularly stressful day, I saw a woman giving chair massages in a mall. So I treated myself to a never-before-experienced, professionally induced, five-minute relaxation session. The therapist said to tell her if anything she did hurt me, and she would work a different area. All went well for about thirty seconds. Then I said, "Ow."

She kept massaging the same place, so I protested a little louder. "Ow." Since the torture continued, I hollered, "Ow!"

"Oh, did that hurt?" she asked. Moving to the other side of my back, she soon hit another trouble spot. Again we went through the three levels of "Ow."

Meanwhile, she chattered about her employer—a chiropractor. "You should get him to work on your back. He does miracles with all kinds of trouble areas," she said. "I *used* to have a *hearing* problem."

I couldn't wait to run outside and laugh out loud.

Seriously, if one of your sensory organs has ever gone out of whack, you know how much you come to appreciate the proper functioning of all five precious senses our Creator has given us: sight, hearing, smell, touch, and taste.

Touch the Heart

Too often, writers write as though readers have only two senses: sight and hearing. But years ago at a writer's conference, an author by the name of Bob Slosser honed in on three words that have stuck in my head like a burr on a wool sweater—and they changed my writing.

I read *Child of Satan, Child of God*, the memoir he wrote for Susan Atkins, a member of Charles Manson's creepy, murderous gang. In this riveting story of her journey to faith in Christ, Slosser certainly followed his own three-word advice: "Take me there!"

A reader once wrote to an author and said she was so engrossed in his novel that when she put the book down to go outside to get the mail, she grabbed her umbrella. The sun shone brightly in her neighborhood that day, but it was raining in the scene she had just read. So she still lived in that fictional world.

Whether we're writing fiction or nonfiction (narrative, anecdotes, and illustrations), vivid sensory detail can transport our readers into the story and touch the emotions. Often even a fragrance can trigger a tearful memory.

I'll never forget the day my coworker Debbie Doubek and I learned that a precious friend had been killed in an automobile accident. Debbie held my hand as we prayed together for the family, and ourselves, in our grief. Throughout the day, as I tried to work, the sweet vanilla aroma of Debbie's hand cream lingered on my hands.

Today a whiff of vanilla can transport me to that day—twenty years ago.[1]

In our writing, "reader transport" takes intentionality. When we write, we want to create 3-D moving pictures with sounds and textures, aromas and flavors.

Here are some "Take me there!" ideas.

Pay Attention

Remember leaf collections and rock collections for school? I often asked others to help me find spectacular specimens to boost my grade from a C (average) to what my parents expected (an A+).

I think working on such collections made me more attentive. To this day I'm delighted to identify a ginkgo tree by its fan-shaped leaves. And I get excited if I find an igneous rock—because I love the word *igneous*.

Writers become collectors too. We become attentive through all five senses: what we see, hear, smell, taste, and touch (including textures). And we draw inspiration from our "observation collections" while painting our own word pictures for readers.

Years ago, while working on a middle-grade novel about a horse-crazy tween, I took horseback riding lessons to immerse myself in the culture—so I could take my readers there. One day, driving home, I noticed a baseball game involving kids the age of a main character in my book who played baseball.

I pulled into the gravel parking lot. [Hear the crunching sound you would have missed if I only had said *parking lot*?] Then I climbed into the bleachers to soak up some Babe Ruth League baseball culture: the feel of the hot, aluminum bleachers [touch]; nearby, a big man in a barely buttonable gray suit and cowboy boots [sight]; his foul cigar smoke [smell]; his hollering at the umps [sound]. Unfortunately, there wasn't a concession stand to provide "tastes."

I took notes furiously. Much of that scene—including some of that big ol' guy's exact words—appeared in one of *Snowmobile Trap*'s baseball scenes. It's worth the work to give readers a vicarious sensory experience.

On the Food Network's *Food Network Star* competition, producers look for a contestant's ability to describe how their food smells and tastes. The cooks can't say it's delicious, fantastic, or awesome. Such words tell the viewer nothing. Instead, contestants must tap into flavors and textures: sweet, pungent, rich, gooey, crunchy, even the char of peppers roasted on a gas-stove burner.

Writers can work to find just-right words too. So always be ready with notepad, smartphone, or tablet so you can find lovely new samplings for your sensory-detail collection.

Listen to Everyone

When my husband and I go out for dinner, he knows he can't count on much conversation. I'm often discreetly listening to the people around me for speech patterns, topics people are talking about (that I could be writing about), memorable bits of dialogue, and more.

And I urge you, fellow writers, to raise your right hand—right where you're sitting—and recite with me my "Eavesdropper's Pledge for Writers." (See sidebar on page 237.)

Okay, pardon my "tongue-in-cheekness," but remember that describing well what you want your readers to *hear*—as well as see, smell, touch, and taste—can transport them to the scene and touch their emotions.

Learn from the Masters

We can learn a lot by reading masters of the writing craft. By *masters*, I don't necessarily mean authors whose bodies are already a-molderin' in the grave. I mean writers—classic and contemporary—who transport you into their story. What kinds of sensory description do they employ—and how?

1. *Specificity.* Some of us might have written a story in which a rat goes to the fair and forages for food. But in *Charlotte's Web*, E. B. White *takes* us to the fair. We watch Templeton, a rat, discover specific sights, smells, and textures inside a discarded, folded newspaper: "Inside it were leftovers from somebody's lunch: a deviled ham sandwich, a piece of Swiss cheese, part of a hard-boiled egg, and the core of a wormy apple. The rat crawled in and ate everything."[2]

I'm there!

2. *Metaphorical language.* Using metaphors and similes can help your reader *experience* the scene.

> NO READER TRANSPORTATION HAPPENING: **I drank in the beautiful stillness of the beach.**
>
> TAKING ME THERE (author Anne George describing a fog at the beach): **"The horizon disappears, and you can't tell which is water and which is sky. Vapor swirls around you as you walk, and gulls huddle together on the sand as if the weight of the air were too much for their wings."[3]**

Here are a few more vivid descriptions I've collected over the years:

- *Sight* and *sound.* Philip Yancey, describing the 2011 tsunami in Japan, helps us *see* the debris and bodies washing in and back out seventeen times, "like water sloshing in a bathtub." Then he captures the *sound*: "Sixteen of the times they heard frantic cries for help, then at last a loud sucking sound as if from a huge drain, then silence."[4]

We don't need long descriptions. Novelist Martin Cruz Smith referred to the "oboe calls of crows."[5]

- *Touch.* Note C. S. Lewis's characteristic mastery: "Jill was lying so close to the creature [Aslan] that she could feel the breath vibrating steadily through its body."[6]
- *Smell, sound,* and *taste* combined. C. S. Lewis again: "the hissing, and delicious smell of sausages . . . and not wretched sausages half full of bread and soya bean either, but real meaty, spicey ones, fat and piping hot and burst and just the tiniest bit burnt."[7] Isn't your mouth watering now?

Weave Skillfully

Many readers skip over long descriptive passages, so don't do a "description dump." Be selective, and skillfully weave in descriptions like bright highlights in a tapestry—avoiding purple. Purple prose, that is. Avoid overwriting.

Often less is more.

Remember my oft-repeated axiom: Write to communicate (and, I would add, to transport the reader), not to impress.

Above all, we don't want our readers to have a "hearing problem"—or a problem seeing, tasting, smelling, or touching. We want them to experience fully the story we're telling.

Answer their cry, "Take me there!"

Chapter 40 Quiz

Zero in on one or two aspects of the following items and describe them briefly to "take me there." You get extra credit if you create a context for the description. But don't wander into purple-prose danger zones. Compare your answers with those of your critique group.

1. your favorite dessert (taste and/or texture)

2. a lake on a windy day (sight and/or touch)

3. sunlight penetrating a forest (sight)

4. a bird's song (sound)

5. the Fourth of July (smell)

6. rain (sound)

7. a beach (smell)

8. snowfall (sight and/or touch)

9. an old, cherished, worn-out baby blanket (sight and/or texture)

10. hot chocolate on a wintry night (smell and/or taste)

References:

Sensory Detail
  Publication Manual of the American Psychological Association, Sixth Edition: 2.06

Metaphors and Similes
  Publication Manual of the American Psychological Association, Sixth Edition: 3.10

Eavesdropper's Pledge for Writers[8]

I, _____ [insert name],
do hereby acknowledge
that I not only have a license
but a responsibility
to eavesdrop
on every conversation
within my hearing.
And I hereby pledge to do so
from this day forward
until death
or deafness
or the rapture
ends my listening days here on earth.

This is what the LORD says to you: "Do not be afraid or discouraged because of [the opposition]. For the battle is not yours, but God's."

—2 CHRONICLES 20:15

Putting the Transit into Transitions
The Importance of Smooth Transitions

41

An old duffer headed out one Saturday morning for his weekly game with his golf buddies. As usual, he kissed his wife and told her he'd be home before noon. By one o'clock she started to worry. By two o'clock she was frantic. At 2:47 p.m. her husband—hot and sweaty—schlepped into the house and set down his golf bag. When his wife asked why he was so late, the old guy replied, "Well, on the fourth fairway Ted died of a heart attack. So for the rest of the game it was 'Hit the ball, drag Ted.'"

This groaner describes well the way many a project or relationship progresses—or doesn't progress. We feel we have to pull the deadweights along in order to get anywhere. But this concept especially applies to the way we often shape—or fail to shape—our writing. We may "tee off" well with a great introduction to an article or fiction piece, and the ball soars well down the fairway. Then we get sidetracked, dragging Ted (deadweight) into the game. And we lose our readers, maybe leaving them "teed off."

Or the opposite. We may jerk the reader around with too many ideas or images or plot lines without a logical progression.

Early in my writing career I received a *personal* rejection letter (rarely sent to writers) from a prominent Christian magazine. After expressing regrets that my article didn't "fit their editorial needs at this time," the editor cited a few reasons. His metaphors have stuck with me: "You have sails and anchors."

As I looked over my article, I understood. Some parts flowed well. Others dropped anchor, stalling reader interest or jerking readers around. Similar to the golfing illustration, parts of the article were dragging the reader behind, like poor Ted.

Creating Transitions

A great way to avoid "anchors" and facilitate flow in our writing is to create transitions purposely. Although I touched briefly on this topic in chapter 39, let's examine how to be more purposeful in their use.

Transitions are signposts that guide our readers from thought to thought or scene to scene. How we do that contributes to our style and readability.

Remember the observation of Peter Jacobi in chapter 39? Here's a little more of what he said: "If linkage [of thoughts] is weak, you'll lack transition despite the use of transitional words. *There must be connective informational tissue.* Words do not create transition. Ideas do. Words serve only as tools" (emphasis added).[1]

Arranging our ideas logically often begins with sketching an informal outline. Then we can go back and intentionally work on structure and transitions. I sometimes need to start writing before the logical progression emerges. But the beauty of shaping our writing with transitions is that we can do it at any stage of the writing process.

Just as public transit moves travelers along geographically, transitional words and phrases move readers along in their thought processes. Here are some ways we can do that.

1. *Subheads.* Because I will address subheads in chapter 45, I'll touch on them only briefly here. In articles and nonfiction books, well-thought-out subheads can serve as effective tools, guiding readers from one point to another. Unfortunately, subheads are virtually invisible to some readers. So don't rely on them exclusively. Consider partnering subheads with other options below. Note that transitions often work best at a paragraph break.

2. *Numbered points.* In nonfiction, numbered points work especially well for logical arguments or steps in a process.

> EXAMPLE: **First, open your heart to God's will. . . . Second, seek his will through prayer. . . . Third, listen to ways the Lord may be indicating his will through the counsel of godly mentors. . . .**

Use numbers in the text spelled out (*first*, not *1st*) to emphasize sequence or importance. Be sure to keep these transitions parallel in form.

> EXAMPLE FAILING TO IMPRESS: **First . . . secondly . . . thirdly**

Most of us wouldn't use the word *firstly* to maintain parallelism, so keep it simple.

> EXAMPLE WORTH A GOLD STAR: **First . . . second . . . third**

We can also use arabic numerals (1, 2, 3), such as I've used in this part of the chapter. They make information easily accessible and keep readers oriented as we move through various points or options. Lead-ins to the numbered points also play a part in transitions. They set up readers for what's coming, such as I did before this numbered list.

3. *Time markers.* We want to avoid clichés the equivalent of "meanwhile back at the ranch" in both fiction and nonfiction narrative (storytelling, personal experience). But time markers are vital tools.

> EXAMPLES: **before, later, after the war, once aboard, when they got home, by two o'clock**

As I mentioned before—but it bears repeating—time markers can also compress the story, deleting large segments of time and unnecessary details to keep readers reading.

Cut anything that doesn't move the story forward. Transitions can be our best friends in that cutting process.

I've often become frustrated when evaluating a manuscript because the beginning doesn't create a good sense of time and place and/or the sequence of events isn't clear as the story unfolds. Especially when starting a story at a high point of conflict and then going back to fill in the details, plant brief time cues throughout the narrative to keep readers oriented. Any time readers have to back up to figure out the timing of what's happening, you've given them an excuse to quit reading.

4. *Repetition of a phrase or concept.* If I were writing an article focused on Solomon's temple, I might end one paragraph with this sentence:

> **David passionately desired to build a temple for God.**

Then I might begin the next paragraph this way:

> **A place of worship couldn't be built by a man of war, God told him.**

By using the synonym *place of worship* I'm maintaining focus on the temple theme.

Beware of overusing this type of transition, especially repeating a word close to its previous use.

5. *Cause and effect.* If ideas create transitions (and they do), we can only help readers follow a logical progression of thought when we are *thinking* clearly. Incident B occurring after incident A doesn't necessarily mean A caused B.

But, when appropriate, we can use words and phrases such as *because, therefore, so, consequently, as a result,* and *in response to.* These transitions help readers see relationships between events and ideas, motivating further reading.

On the other hand, in fiction a misunderstanding about whether or not A caused B can create a great plot twist.

6. *Summary or return to theme.* Using this type of transition presupposes that we *have* a theme—something lacking in many articles and books.

In my view, what the project is *about* relates to topic—such as an article about the topic of joy. But what the project is *saying* relates to the theme. For example, an article about the topic of joy might *say* that joy is possible when we . . . (fill in the blanks for the structure of your article: keeping our focus on Jesus, not our circumstances; acknowledging God's sovereignty; and going out of our way to bring joy to others).

In both fiction and nonfiction—even personal experience articles and memoirs—readers need to see a thread holding the narrative together and moving it forward. The following phrase examples may spark ideas for ways to tie your story back to the theme periodically: *everywhere they went, no matter what they tried, another way.*

7. **Contrasts.** In fiction we can often convey contrasts among such elements as mood, setting, characters, and point of view by a change of paragraph or leaving extra space between paragraphs. Add time markers when appropriate.

In nonfiction, words and phrases such as *however, on the other hand, by contrast,* and *despite* can direct readers to make a U-turn in their thinking.

Creating Microtransitions

On a sentence level, using subordinating conjunctions (such as *because, since, if, when*) and coordinating conjunctions (such as *and, or, but*) can clarify our writing as we "direct the traffic flow" of ideas.

Minding the Gap

Some years ago, when my husband and I visited London, we took the tube (subway) to transit from one "sightseeing must" to another. Freed of maneuvering a rental car in traffic going the opposite direction from what we were used to, we could relax and enjoy the ride. But we were also amused by signs warning passengers to be careful of the space between the train and the platform: Mind the Gap.

We can improve the pieces we're writing and enhance our readers' "transit" experiences by identifying (minding) the gaps in the presentation of our thoughts as well as the anchors—a.k.a. "dead Teds"—that drag the piece down. Then we can keep readers reading by creating transitions that will bridge the gaps, put wind in the sails, and revive Ted.

Chapter 41 Exercise

Using an article of 800 to 1,500 words that you have already written or that you write for this assignment, pay special attention to transitions.

1. On a printed copy of your manuscript, mark any gaps or anchors (a.k.a. "dead Teds") you find.

2. Insert at least two or three appropriate subheads, using parallel form if at all possible.

3. Look for material that needs to be rearranged now that your subheads create a framework for the article.

4. Look for places you can better use transitions, such as numbered points or bullets, time markers, contrasts, cause and effect, or any of the others listed above (including what I call microtransitions).

5. If you belong to a critique group, devote one whole session to the area of transitions. Help each other find ways to create better transitions in each manuscript.

Here I am, preaching and writing about things that are way over my head, the inexhaustible riches and generosity of Christ. My task is to bring out in the open and make plain what God, who created all this in the first place, has been doing in secret and behind the scenes all along.

—EPHESIANS 3:9 (*THE MESSAGE*)

Beware the Jargonaut

Purging Jargon from Your Writing

42

I love looking up word derivations and coining words of my own.

If an astronaut (think: *nautical*) is one who sails into outer space and a cybernaut is one who sails through the expanse of cyberspace, I've decided a jargonaut is one who sails through life, perpetuating jargon—seldom uttering or writing a fresh thought.

Jargon is the shorthand an in-crowd uses. It's quite useful—to those who understand it.

Professional Jargon

My bridge-engineer hubby, who worked for the Department of Transportation (DOT) for forty-three years, whispers sweet nothings in my ear about torsion, shears and moments, and elastomeric bearings. And he almost never uses the word *asphalt*. In DOT-speak, a blacktop road is made of *bituminous*.

After we were married, I briefly worked for the DOT also. In my clerical role I saw the letters *TH* everywhere. Not wanting to seem totally ignorant, I asked Hubby, not Mr. Bossman, what they stood for and learned that is the abbreviation for trunk highway. To this day I don't understand the difference between a trunk highway and a plain old road. So, in case I'm not the only one ignorant of that jargon, whenever my hubby writes out directions to our house for someone, I ask him to use the word *highway*, not *TH*.

Despite jargon's helpful shorthand quality within a profession or group, it excludes those who don't understand it. And good writers write to communicate, not to impress, exclude, or make readers feel dumb.

So if I were writing a profile about a surgeon or a waste-management expert,

I would need to research that person's specialty to learn the jargon. I might start in the children's section of a library because nonfiction writers for children have to learn the jargon well enough to explain it to youngsters.

Then, during the interview, if I hear unfamiliar terminology, I need to request an explanation. Better to ask than to realize during the writing process that I don't know what the person was talking about.

Finally, I have to find the right wording to convey these profession-specific elements without writing down to my readers.

Scrabble-Tile Jargon

Sometimes a more technical article by someone weaned on jargon starts resembling all ninety-eight letter tiles of a Scrabble game, dumped out.

> EXAMPLE: **The EPA's DSB within the OEI sent out new EIS forms to the DOI and the DNR, saying they would report to the DOJ any infractions of the EO regarding the proper disposal of KL.**

> TRANSLATION: **The Environmental Protection Agency's Data Standard Branch within the Office of Environmental Information sent out new Environmental Impact Statement forms to the Department of the Interior and the Department of Natural Resources, saying they would report to the Department of Justice any infractions of the Executive Order regarding the proper disposal of Kitty Litter.**

Okay, I made that up. You probably knew some of those abbreviations (except the last one, which I threw in for fun). But pity the reader who doesn't have a clue.

Some people might call these abbreviations acronyms. But technically, according to *CMoS 16*, acronyms create a new word, such as scuba (*s*elf-*c*ontained *u*nderwater *b*reathing *a*pparatus), laser (*l*ight *a*mplification by *s*timulated *e*mission of *r*adiation), and AIDS (*a*cquired *i*mmune *d*eficiency *s*yndrome).

Identifying initials such as EPA and DNR are called initialisms. We don't want to throw too many of these Scrabble-tile dumps within a small space, and it's unwieldy to keep repeating the entire name of an organization or department throughout an article. So, what if we're writing about the cooperation of several Christian organizations on an evangelistic project? How do we handle those initialisms deftly?

The first time you refer to an organization or entity, spell it out. Then insert the identifying initials in parentheses:

> **Leaders from the Billy Graham Evangelistic Association (BGEA), Salvation Army (SA), and Every Home for Christ (EHC) met to strategize.**

Every time after that, you can simply use the initialism:

> **Dick Eastman, president of EHC, said . . .**

However, if you have several unfamiliar initialisms in an article, occasionally spell out what they stand for to keep readers oriented.

Christian Jargon

In the movie *The Hiding Place*, Jeannette Clift George played the role of Corrie ten Boom, whose family members hid many Jews in their home during the Holocaust. At the time of filming that movie, Jeannette was a new Christian trying to understand her new "believer" friends. Also dealing with some personal issues, she turned to these friends for help. Unfortunately, they said things like, "You just have to have more faith."

"I didn't know what that meant," Jeannette said as she gave her testimony later. "But I suspected it had something to do with the eyebrows because whenever people said it, they spoke louder and raised their eyebrows."

Those believers were talking about something as simple as *faith*! What words and phrases do we Christian writers take for granted? To newbie Christians, we may as well be speaking Swahili or Urdu.

Unfortunately, Christians number among the worst jargon offenders. Yet how many readers understand the insider language? According to a 2014 Barna Group study, the extent of biblical illiteracy in America is appalling. Although 69 percent of adults consider themselves moderately or somewhat knowledgeable about the Bible, only 43 percent correctly named the first five books of the Bible. The rest either answered incorrectly or said they weren't sure.[1]

College professor Kenneth Berding offers this anecdotal example of biblical illiteracy. While teaching at a New York college, he asked his students to write a biographical sketch of an Old Testament character. One student wrote this about Joshua, the great leader of Israel: "Joshua was the son of a nun."

"This student," Berding writes, "clearly didn't know that Nun was the name of Joshua's father, nor apparently did he realize that Catholic nuns weren't around during the time of the Old Testament. But I'm sure it created quite a stir at the convent!"[2]

That story reminds me of my daughter's college roommate who said she wanted to learn the stories in the Bible so she could tell them to her kids someday. "Like . . . wasn't there a guy who built a big boat . . . for lots of animals?" she asked.

"Uh, that would be Noah," my daughter replied.

Another Barna Group survey, in 2009, "found that many people who say they have heard of spiritual gifts were not necessarily describing the same gifts outlined in the Bible." Some claimed to possess the "spiritual gifts" of a sense of humor, life, a job, a house, creativity, and clairvoyance, among others.[3]

So we cannot assume our readers know what we're talking about when we use Christian terminology familiar to us.

In addition, I often see manuscripts that conclude something like this: "When I truly learned to trust the Lord, he began to bless me beyond belief." That's jargonaut talk.

What does it look like when someone "truly learns to trust the Lord"? Usually articles like these spend 98 percent of the space telling us about the pain the writers were going through before God brought them to a turning point, followed by a sentence or two of Christian jargon.

We can help our readers more if we show specific ways our newfound trust helped us respond to a crisis or fear differently. What did that trust look like in daily-living terms?

And what does it mean that God *blessed* you? Eliminate that nebulous word (and its cousin, *blessing*) from your manuscripts as much as possible—or at least give examples. In what way did that blessing manifest itself?

Jargon severely minimizes takeaway value.

Fresh illustrations and fresh Christian terminology are like footprints you leave behind for readers to follow, taking their own steps toward Christian maturity.

Audience-Tailoring

Study your target markets too, noting the level of Christian terminology the editors assume their readership understands.

When writing for non-Christian audiences, purging Christian jargon becomes even more important. In a profile of musician Phil Keaggy for an evangelistic magazine, for example, I looked for a fresh way to express the transaction that occurred when Keaggy, in his teens, "accepted Christ." I finally came up with this: "Phil took to heart the good news that Jesus Christ died to give him hope."

A quotation from Keaggy followed: "When Christ came into my life, fear was dealt a major blow. There was a sense of burden and release and cleansing."

Whenever you identify Christian jargon, consider what readers will think if they take it literally. Keaggy's quotation uses some Christian terminology, yet even if readers take it somewhat literally, they understand what's he's talking about.

What literal images may come to the uninitiated reader's mind, however, if we write about "applying the shed blood of Christ to our sinful hearts"?

Communicating Clearly

Writers have a responsibility to communicate clearly. And excellent Christian writers strive for clarity especially in the spiritual realm. We enrich the reader's takeaway value—if we vigilantly guard against being jargonauts.

So what kind of sweet nothings do I communicate into engineer-hubby's ear? Initialisms, abbreviations, and acronyms—or sometimes diphthongs, diacritical marks, and dangling participles. It's only fair.

Chapter 42 Exercise

Christian Jargon Revision

Are you sensitive to jargon in your writing? Read through the Christian jargon examples below. Either on your own or with your critique group, see how many more examples you can identify.

Choose at least five, and write a passage in which you make each concept clear to readers unfamiliar with it.

ask Jesus into your heart	propitiation
bear your cross	sanctified
give it all to God	saved
God blessed me	shed blood of Christ
I felt burdened to pray	spiritual gift
I felt led to . . .	spiritual warfare
justified	substitutionary atonement
Lamb of God	thorn in the flesh
Lion of Judah	trust and obey

References

Acronyms and Initialisms
> The Chicago Manual of Style, Sixteenth Edition: 10.2
> The Christian Writer's Manual of Style, Fourth Edition: pp. 35–37

Jargon
> The Christian Writer's Manual of Style, Fourth Edition: pp. 219–20
> The Associated Press Stylebook: See Jargon
> Publication Manual of the American Psychological Association, Sixth Edition: 3.08–9

Every item of your new way of life is custom-made by the Creator, with his label on it. All the old fashions are now obsolete. Words like Jewish and non-Jewish, religious and irreligious, insider and outsider, uncivilized and uncouth, slave and free, mean nothing. From now on everyone is defined by Christ, everyone is included in Christ.

—COLOSSIANS 3:10–11 (*THE MESSAGE*)

Exclusive All-Inclusives
Avoiding Gender and Other Types of Exclusivity

43

When the Bible-college professor walked into the classroom, he caught his students telling ethnic jokes. So he decided to set them straight.

"We don't want to offend anyone by telling ethnic jokes," he said. "If you want to tell a lighthearted story about a people group, choose one that no longer exists. For instance, as far as we know, there are no Hittites left on earth. You can tell Hittite jokes."

The students laughed.

"So," the prof continued, "there were these two Hittites named Sven and Ole . . ."

Ba-dum pum!

Here's another consideration. You've probably seen alluring all-inclusive vacation ads on TV. They attack our computers with pop-ups too.

"Annoying little attention grabbers!" your humble grammar geek mutters.

But what enticements! Beautiful people—with tanned, toned bodies sporting neon-yellow bikinis or flowing, exotic beachwear—sprawl on sugary beaches and drink deep-red wine from crystal stemware.

Another ad shows a wife distraught when her husband discovers on the way to an all-inclusive resort that he left his wallet behind. But, ta da! No worries! Everything is included. He doesn't *need* a wallet!

Ah, all-inclusives.

Then you peek at the price per person, per night; and you discover these resorts are quite *ex*clusive!

In our writing world, some word choices can make our readers feel excluded—or worse, offended. I still can't figure out who the political-correctness (PC) police are, where their headquarters exist, or who dictates the laws they enforce. On the other hand, I don't want anything I write to exclude any readers or turn them off.

The apostle Paul took this approach with his life, his ministry, and obviously his writing: "I try to find common ground with everyone, doing everything I can to save some" (1 Cor. 9:22 NLT).

So what is exclusive or biased language? What are various ways it can sneak up on us? And how can we avoid it?

Christian Jargon

I looked at jargon more fully in the previous chapter, but a review in this context may be helpful. If someone unfamiliar with the Bible picks up something I've written that's filled with Christian insider phrases, I may push that reader further from God, rather than closer to him. What a tragedy!

Some people call such jargon Christianese, and you'll find examples in the previous chapter's exercise. But here's another short list of Christianese words and phrases we can avoid—or at least make plain in the context—instead of assuming everyone knows what we mean:

sin	discipleship
accept Christ as your Savior	the Godhead
salvation	the rapture
glorified	filled with the Holy Spirit
to God be the glory	only begotten Son
spiritual formation	the triune God
getting into the Word	walking by faith

Find fresh, new ways of expressing spiritual truth. Imagine you're chatting with a non-Christian coworker. How would you change your vocabulary to express these potentially foreign concepts? With some alterations, you'll clarify concepts for those unfamiliar with Christian jargon. And you'll probably also perk up the ears of those so familiar with the words that they're no longer firing any synapses in the brain.

Rusty Wright is a gifted communicator to the less-biblically literate among us. In his article "Paris Hilton and What We Want," he demonstrated ways we can apply scriptural principles to contemporary cultural issues without hitting readers over the head with the Bible. Here's an excerpt:

> Attractive and even worthwhile pursuits can become enslaving. Amassing the most "toys"; rat-race schedules; obsession with career, job, education, sports or even friends can insulate people from facing their own mortality.
>
> The biblical book of Hebrews presents a similar analysis of the human dilemma, reasoning that people "have lived their lives as slaves to the fear of dying."[1] It claims that Jesus died to "deliver" people from this slavery so they might connect with God in time and eternity.
>
> It seems morbid to always be thinking about your own death. But could avoiding it altogether constitute unhealthy denial?[2]

Notice Rusty's style: no long Scripture quotations, easy on the Christianese.

But Christian jargon often manifests itself in another way. It shows up in the writings of people who love Greek and Hebrew—oh, and don't forget Aramaic. Both seminary graduates and the self-taught have been known to throw in an overabundance of words from the Bible's original languages. Beware of bogging down the flow of the writing and creating that "exclusivity embarrassment" we want to avoid.

One of my favorite parts of the movie *My Big Fat Greek Wedding* is the father's insistence that all vocabulary comes from the Greek: "Give me a word, any word," Gus Portokalos says, "and I show you that the root of that word is Greek."

Someone throws out the word *kimono*. He hesitates for a moment. Then, in his broken English, he says, "Ha! Of course! Kimono is come from the Greek word *himona*, is mean winter. So, what do you wear in the wintertime to stay warm? A robe. You see: robe, kimono. There you go!"

Don't make your manuscripts laughable—or overwhelm readers with the ancient languages. Yes, we can gain deep insights when we dig into these rich vocabularies. But be selective. Don't flaunt your knowledge. Instead, consider your readers. An occasional reference to nuances in the original language can create a greater impact than using a plethora of them. We don't want to look like we're showing off.

The target audience for a manuscript will determine how much or how little we can appropriately use. I cannot say this too often: Write to communicate, not to impress.

Racial Bias

Bias of any kind can distract readers, so we want to avoid it whenever possible. The editors of *The Chicago Manual of Style* (*CMoS 16*) wrote, "Biased language that is not central to the meaning of a work distracts readers, and in their eyes the work is less credible."[3]

To be as inclusive as possible, avoid racial stereotypes. Know your audience in any magazine you're targeting. Would they prefer the term *African-American*? *Black*? Which terminology is correct for another readership—Latinos? Hispanics?

Always stay away from pejorative, inflammatory, or potentially offensive terms.

Some readers have even asked why white authors only mention the race of characters if those characters *aren't* Caucasian. Something to think about.

Gender Bias

CMoS 16 also says, however, that "to call attention to the supposed absence of linguistic biases . . . will also distract readers and weaken credibility."[4]

In one of the ubiquitous TV ads for medication, Ms. Average speaks to the camera, saying, "I talked to my doctor and *she* said . . ." You'd think there weren't any male doctors anymore, judging from the majority of today's pill-pushing commercials.

In the twenty-first century, some women are doctors, lawyers, firefighters, military officers, and construction workers. But let's not pretend men don't exist. Horrors! Let's provide balance.

My author friend Gayle Roper uses the word *guys*, as in "Listen up, guys," to refer to both men and women. "It's a good, generic term," she says.

I love it! As I was growing up, I also thought nothing of someone using the masculine *he* as a generic term. However, our language is changing (for better or worse), and we need to avoid the distractions words such as *guys* can be for our readers. So, in fiction, let *one* character talk like Gayle Roper, if you want. But otherwise, beware.

Other Issues

Despite the common use of expressions such as *You go, girl, girls' night out,* and *girlfriend,* today's vernacular prefers *women* over *girls* and *ladies.* In fiction dialogue, however, you can use these distinctions for characterization.

We also avoid suffixes such as *–ess*. So we no longer refer to an *actress, waitress,* and *stewardess*. They are *actors, servers,* and *flight attendants*. And we no longer differentiate between a *comedian* (male) and *comedienne* (female). They're all a bunch of comedians. Of course, if you have an old biddy of a fictional character who's stuck in the past, feel free to let her talk the way an old biddy would talk.

Even though we may not like the PC police, if we want to be caring writers, we'll try to make our writing as inclusive as possible.

I recently ate a meal on a college campus and found that the chef had revamped the menu to accommodate food sensitivities, allergies, and medical conditions—from diabetes to peanut allergies to gluten intolerance. Similarly, with heightened awareness, if we want to reach the broadest audience and avoid offending even extinct people groups such as the Hittites, we'll explore creative ways to avoid turning readers off before they can hear the truth.

When our greatest desire is to see the truth of Jesus Christ presented plainly, we want our writing to be as all-inclusive as possible.

Chapter 43 Exercise

Revise the following sentences to avoid any exclusive or biased language. Suggest options if the issue is not cut and dried. Put a C beside any sentences that are acceptable. See answers in appendix A.

If you are in a critique group or class, compare your answers with one another's. You may want to devote a session to compiling a list of exclusive language to watch for (Christianese and other types). Then focus on rooting out these words and phrases in your manuscripts.

_____ 1. Jesus died for all men.

_____ 2. Dwight motioned for the waiter and complained about the fly in his vichyssoise.

_____ 3. On the hottest day in the summer, the black minister preached on and on till half his congregation fell asleep.

_____ 4. Whenever my critique group comes over, I refer to them as "the girls," even though we all qualify for Medicare.

_____ 5. Justin said that when he gave God priority in his life, the Lord blessed him for that commitment.

_____ 6. Sandra Bullock is one of my favorite actresses.

_____ 7. The nurse pulled a pen out of her pocket and signed the discharge form.

_____ 8. We don't fear eternity because we're under the blood of the Lamb.

_____ 9. Jesus asked Peter three times, "Do you love me?" The first and second times, Jesus used the word ἀγαπᾷς (*agape*). Peter responded with a different word: φιλῶ (*phileo*). The third time, Jesus used a form of the word Peter himself used: φιλεῖς (*phileo*). And Peter used the same word he had all along: φιλῶ (*phileo*).

_____ 10. The flight attendant announced that she would come through the cabin to collect service items.

References:

Gender, Racial, Religious Bias
   The Chicago Manual of Style, Sixteenth Edition: 5.221–30
   The Christian Writer's Manual of Style, Fourth Edition: pp. 187–91
   The Associated Press Stylebook: See Man; Peoples, Persons; Race; Religious References; Religious Titles; Woman/Women
   MLA Handbook for Writers of Research Papers, Seventh Edition: 1.10
   Publication Manual of the American Psychological Association, Sixth Edition: 3.12–16

Touché, Clichés!   44

Anyone who knows me well knows I love the movie *The Princess Bride*. As a rule, I don't enjoy prolonged sword-fighting scenes, such as the old black-and-white Errol Flynn swashbuckling flicks. But the swordplay between Westley, a.k.a. the Man in Black (MIB), and Spaniard Inigo Montoya makes me laugh every time.

In the middle of an acrobatics-filled sword fight between the two lefties, the Spaniard starts smiling. When the MIB asks him why, Montoya says he knows something his opponent doesn't: "I am not left handed." He throws his sword into his right hand and fights even more skillfully. At that, Westley confesses he is not left handed either, tosses his weapon into his right hand, and takes the advantage in the duel. Great screenwriting!

Drop the *s* from *swordplay*, and you find another of my favorite bits of entertainment: wordplay. Aspiring excellent writers love holding up ideas as if they were prisms, then watching sunlight refract those ideas into colorful images to share with readers.

We employ a simile here, a metaphor there, and a clever turn of phrase in another passage. All the while, we make sure our vivid word choices don't blast our readers but, rather, clarify and delight.

But sometimes, in an attempt to be clever, we reach into the repository of our imaginations as if we were drawing a winning raffle ticket. We blindly grab any entry our thoughts land on. The mind pulls out a dog-eared phrase, an insipid idiom, or a vapid comparison. And we declare it a winner.

Prolific writer King Solomon, however, took time to discover a fresh image for finding the right words:

"A word fitly spoken [or written] is like apples of gold in settings of silver" (Prov. 25:11 NKJV).

Nice simile when he wrote it. But even this lovely picture has, to some extent, lost its luster with frequent use.

Unfortunately, sometimes we enjoy a fitting phrase so much—or we hear it so often—that it becomes our go-to expression. But wordsmith William Safire ironically warned, "Avoid clichés like the plague."

What is a cliché?

As I like to say, today's clichés are yesterday's clever sayings. Clichés are overused, tired, lazy expressions that lull readers into semicomatose states. We derive them from a variety of sources—from ancient proverbs to popular song lyrics to TV-character catchphrases.

They may or may not be similes or metaphors. But they're like potato chips from a bag left open too long. They're stale. No longer enticing.

Less-than-conscientious writers fill their writing with phrases like these:

- Idealistic young women, "as fresh as a daisy," flouncing into the parlor for croissants and tea
- Retired gentlemen returning to work—"back in the saddle again"
- Politicians "throwing their hats into the ring"

Or writers may transition to a new scene with nauseatingly overused phrases the equivalent of "as the sun slowly sank in the west," "meanwhile, back at the ranch," or "at the crack of dawn."

Why avoid clichés?

Here are five reasons to avoid these "little foxes that spoil the vine" (this phrase from Song of Solomon 2:15 has itself become a cliché, especially in some Christian circles).

1. *Clichés can be invisible.* If we write in a testimony article that someone was at the end of her rope, hanging on for dear life (a double-whammy cliché), readers may skip over that part (pardon the pun). Well-chosen imagery, on the other hand, helps transport readers to the scene we're trying to describe. How could *you* capture that end-of-our-rope feeling in a fresh way?

2. *Using clichés robs us of opportunities to create perfect, memorable images in readers' minds.* In *Finding Your Promise*, author Jane Rubietta briefly described the beginnings of creation. She could have simply said that God hung the moon and stars in place—a bit of a cliché. But instead she delights readers with this line: "The very God of the universe . . . hung the . . . moon for a nightlight."[1] What a lovely thought! And it sets a mood, doesn't it?

Note: The moon here isn't *like* a nightlight (a simile). It *becomes* a nightlight (a metaphor). Either would have worked, but I find the moon becoming a nightlight a stronger image.

Similarly, note this memorable imagery from Randy Singer's novel *The Advocate*, set in first-century Rome. Theophilus's mentor, Seneca, is helping him write a letter to Emperor Tiberius, aiming to persuade him to outlaw the brutal gladiator games. "In real life," Seneca said, "people are persuaded by stories. Facts get stuck in the head, *shielded* by our biases and *struck down* by the *swords* of our preconceptions. Stories go straight to the heart" (emphasis added).[2]

What great imagery! Notice the words I italicized—so appropriate to the times and situation.

3. *Using clichés may confuse readers—or stop them from reading—if we inadvertently create mixed metaphors.* In an earlier draft of this chapter, the paragraph above that uses a raffle-drawing example contained several images competing with that word picture. I wrote of pulling something out of our writers "tool kit" (a carpenter or mechanic allusion) and "plugging in" (an electrical allusion) the expression that comes most quickly to mind. Mixed metaphors. Yikes! Rewrite required. Stay focused to help your readers stay focused.

4. *Trying to transliterate a cliché may muddle—or even destroy—the imagery.* To transliterate is to translate a word, letter for letter, from one alphabet to another. For example, as we saw in the previous chapter's quiz, the Greek word for unconditional love is transliterated as *agape*.

Borrowing that concept, I call it transliterating a cliché when we try to create a new expression by simply substituting a different word for each one in a cliché—or close to it. For instance, trying a spin-off of Solomon's quotation about finding the right words, an inept writer may proffer "Like apples of scarlet displayed on a Christmas plate of emerald-green . . ."

Such a sad cleverness attempt.

If a writer ventures a loose takeoff on "as soft as a baby's behind," he may nauseate readers with "Her face was as pockmarked as the derriere of an infant with diaper rash." Ewww!

Make your mind work until it finds the right words that are your own. But don't make the image so bizarre that it jars your readers.

5. *Using clichés signals to the editor and the reader that we don't care enough to search beyond the obvious.* Editors often list clichés among the most common symptoms of poor writing. If writers can't come up with something fresh, editors ask, in essence, why should we bother to publish it?

Self-published books (without benefit of good editing) are often *drowning* in tired clichés that make tired readers give up the will even to tread water.

Are clichés ever okay?

We can use clichés sparingly—in situations like these:

1. *We can use clichés in dialogue.* Save clichés for differentiating characters through dialogue. We don't want to overdo it, but occasionally throwing in a certain style of cliché (such as the would-be-erudite-sounding, the country-rube-speak, or the

"My grandma always said . . .") helps readers recognize the speech of a particular character—without the author supplying dialogue tags.

Make such clichés appropriate, however, to the character's age, culture, and geographical location.

And never end on a weak note. Unfortunately, Margaret Mitchell, in *Gone with the Wind*, lets Scarlett O'Hara get away with this cliché as the last words of the novel: "Tomorrow is another day." A feeble conclusion to a page-turner (in my humble opinion).

2. *Twisting or even mangling clichés purposefully can create attention-grabbing titles.* Here are some possibilities:

Crime Doesn't Play
A Stitch in Time Saves Embarrassment
Nothing Ventured, Nothing Maimed

As far as I know, there are no books with these titles. Even if there were, titles can't be copyrighted. So feel free to run with any of these.

But, in general, heed the William Safire dictum to avoid clichés like the _____. That's another diagnostic tool pointing to a cliché. If people can readily fill in the blank and complete the phrase, it's probably a cliché.

So if you sense a cliché coming on, repeat after me: "Touché, clichés! There's something you should know. We writers can wield our verbal weaponry with far more dexterity than with any feeble old clichés."

Let's do it!

Chapter 44 Exercise

1. For a reminder of some common clichés, Google the words *cliché list*. Peruse the examples of onetime clever sayings and famous quotations that have reached cliché status. You'll likely find some you wouldn't have thought of as clichés. Make a list of at least ten you use either in speech or writing.

2. Read through a piece of your writing you want to sharpen. Highlight any clichés you find.

3. Ask your critique group (or someone else you trust) to point out other clichés they see.

4. Don't try to transliterate the clichés (see the dangers above). Instead, dig deep to delight your reader with a word picture or just-right phrase to communicate clearly—without trying to impress.

Worth the Sweat

We're Entitled to a Great Title and Engaging Subheads

45

Jay Leno's "Headlines" segments on TV's classic *Tonight Show* delighted audiences for decades. In case you've been stranded in the Himalayas forever, the segment went like this: Jay would show humorous newspaper headlines or blurbs that have appeared in print and then comment briefly. Here are a few examples:

- Homicide victims rarely talk to police
- Spelling frundraiser a success
- Breathing oxygen linked to staying alive
- Man shoots himself in head, misses vital parts
- Boy saves sister's life. . . . "I wouldn't do it again. She's been a pain this week."

The adage "You only get one chance to make a good first impression" definitely applies to creating attention-grabbing titles and subheads.

Many writers struggle to create engaging titles for their articles and books, but titles have always fascinated me. While working on my high school newspaper, eons ago, I wrote a December humor feature about Santa's little-known fear of small, dark spaces—due to all the time he spends in chimneys. I titled it "Claustrophobia." (I grew up in a family of punsters.)

After more than four decades in this business, I still don't feel I've finished a piece of writing until I've come up with a title that is, in Goldilocks terminology, "just right." I delight in the challenge.

Creating titles is a delicate dance between our style and the style of our target publications or publishing houses. So how do we capture the attention of editors and readers with titles and "fit in" without risking the embarrassment of possible submission to some future "classic headlines" comedy act? To find out, consider a series of questions.

Why sweat titles?

You may say, "I've heard that editors seldom use the title you submit, so why should I sweat over coming up with a good one?"

My immediate response is that I get all goose-pimply when an editor says, "I love your title." I feel more accomplishment if that title survives onto the printed page or a book cover. But, for perspective, I asked a number of editor friends that question. Here are a few of their responses:

- Fiction editor Jan Stob from Tyndale House cited the first-impression element, adding this: "If the title is cheesy, clichéd, or dated, I'm going to wonder if the writing and story delivers more of the same. The title can also help identify the genre. Does the title indicate that this is a romance? Suspense? Women's fiction?"
- Scott Noble, former editor of the *Minnesota Christian Examiner* newspaper, said to sweat over titles "because the title . . . can move your article to the top of the pile."
- Veteran book and magazine editor Jim Watkins quipped, "If you write a great title, *I* don't have to. So *do* sweat!"

Why do editors change titles?

Editors I surveyed cited a number of reasons for changing titles, including these:

- *Knowledge of the market and keying into felt needs of readers.* Andy McGuire at Bethany House noted the difference between straightforward titles for topical books (e.g., *Secrets to . . .* [fill in the blank]) and creative titles for memoir and fiction (e.g., *All She Ever Wanted*). Selecting a strong title tells the editor something about your knowledge of the market—an important trust element for editors. But if that's not there, market-savvy editors and their marketing gurus have to change the title to play to the audience.
- *The style of the publication or publishing house.* Early in my writing career, I submitted an article with what I thought was an intriguing title: "I Felt Like Sarah." The article compared my experience of a dream "apparently denied" to Sarah and Abraham's frustration with infertility. The editor changed my title to a bland one (in my opinion): "Trusting." What I hadn't researched carefully was that particular magazine's style preference for titles. The editor favored short, "label" titles over longer ones that raised reader curiosity.

  We may find that other publications frequently use *alliteration, puns,* or *straightforward titles.* It's part of our job as writers and marketers to notice these things. And we can delight an editor by submitting a well-written article with that type of title.
- *Balance within a publication's content and layout.* In his book *Effective Magazine Writing,* longtime *Decision* editor Roger Palms wrote, "Titles are chosen with care. The editor considers not only your article but also the surrounding articles, making sure your title doesn't clash with an article title on a facing page."[1]

Where do I start?

Some of the best titles come from within the manuscript itself, such as I've done with the "sweat" element in this chapter. But if you're having trouble coming up with an attention-grabbing title, try casting your idea in one of these ways (post these categories near your computer):

- Numbers
  Here are some titles of published books:

  The 5 Love Languages, by Gary Chapman
  30 Ways to Enrich Your Family Fun, by Joyce K. Ellis
  365 Ways to Cook Chicken, by Cheryl Sedaker

- Questions
  "Is There Life after Vietnam?"—an article I wrote about a Vietnam vet who returned from the war a paraplegic—resold several times. Most of the editors retained my original title. A few altered it to fit their style and available space.

  Here's another example: I'll never forget an article on gossip I read years ago, pulled in by this title: "She Did What?"

- Alliteration
  An article titled "Fast Facts on False Beliefs" uses alliteration (clearly setting up reader expectation). Likewise, notice Don Ferguson's classic book, *Grammar Gremlins.*

- Clever turn of phrase or pun
  An article I wrote about a church's car-clinic ministry for single moms bore the title "A Quart of 10W-40 in Jesus' Name."

  Thomas Nelson gave the title *Intentional Walk* to a book about the faith of several St. Louis Cardinals baseball players.

- Startling or arresting statement
  An editor retained my title for a parenting article: "Help! I'm a Parent Run Ragged!"

- Descriptive
  The straightforward description "Raising a Special-Needs Child" keys into a felt need for a specific group within the larger audience of parents.

- Hyperbole/Superlative
  Exaggeration captures attention, such as in these hypothetical book or article titles:

  The Ultimate Camping Experience
  The Most Terrifying Night of My Life

- Oxymoron
  We can create conflict and interest with contradictions in terms, such as Harry Kraus's *Lethal Mercy.*

- Literary allusion
Laura Jensen Walker accomplishes this with the addition of humor in her title, *Dated Jekyll, Married Hyde*.

- Cultural allusion
Some editors particularly like rip-offs of song titles or bestsellers. Someday I'd like to write an article called "Making Up Is Hard to Do." Or maybe a book called *Invasion of the Joy Snatchers*.

- Comparison/Contrast
An article about helping postmodern readers connect with Scripture was titled "Old Book, New Eyes."

    Another type of contrast is what some editors call taking a topic and "standing it on its head." Create an opposite for effect. One of my all-time favorites was an article on strengthening small-group ministries. But it was written (in the reverse) under the title "How to Kill a Small Group."

- Combination
Try combining any of the above. After the movie *Dead Man Walking* came out in the '90s, *Pursuit* magazine (which is no longer being published) used a cultural allusion and question combination to come up with this title for an evangelistic article: "Are You a Dead Man Walking?"

    My book title *The 500 Hats of a Modern-Day Woman* uses a cultural allusion to Dr. Seuss's classic picture book *The 500 Hats of Bartholomew Cubbins* (a number title), combined with a play on words and hyperbole.

    Today many publishers of nonfiction books favor short, attention-grabbing titles, using the subtitle to better describe what the book is about:

American Idols: The Worship of the American Dream, by Bob Hostetler
You'll Get Through This: Hope and Help for Your Turbulent Times,
    by Max Lucado

What's the deal with subheads?

I look at subheads as a title's "little sister." Subheads can be an important part of constructing articles and book chapters. Early in my writing career, no one told me I could write my own subheads. But when I mentioned that to an editor, he said, "It never occurred to me that writers *wouldn't* submit them."

When writing for magazines, it's important to remember that not all of them use subheads. And some periodicals use them only for longer articles.

Subheads accomplish several purposes:

- Organization: succinctly capturing main points and putting them in sensible order.
Veteran editor Sue Kline wrote: "I think you should also sweat over subheads. These small details tell me you really are a magazine writer. They tell me you are clear on your thesis and that you have given thought to how your article is structured."

- Breaking up text: helping with visual appeal.
  We want to keep easily distracted readers engaged.

- Transitions: moving smoothly from one point to the next.
  Beware of relying on subheads exclusively, however. Some readers treat them as invisible spacers. So we still need transitions in the body of our articles and book chapters.

Here are some approaches to writing subheads.

1. Let the subheads grow out of the material and shape it.
   Some years ago, I was writing the testimony of professional race-car driver Lake Speed (his actual birth name) that I referred to in chapter 22. Terminology from the racing world begged me to turn them into subheads:

   Born to Race
   Fast Start
   Spinning Out of Control
   Going into the Turn
   New Partnership
   Checkered Flag in His Sights

   My editor loved them!
   While writing a profile of singer-songwriter Pam Thum, I found that some of her song titles outlined her life perfectly, so the subheads became these:

   A Rising Star
   In the Middle of It All
   Life Is Hard, but God Is Good
   There's a Future for This World

2. Use parallel construction when possible. Try casting your subheads in similar structures, as in the following.

   - All adjective-then-noun combinations:

     Tenuous Faith
     Amazing Strength
     Eternal Perspective

   - All beginning with -ing words, such as the following I used for the Vietnam vet article I wrote about earlier:

     Hitting Bottom
     Rebuilding His Mind
     Reaching Out to Other Vets

   - All questions, as I've done in this chapter:

     Why sweat titles?
     Why do editors change titles?
     Where do I start?
     What's the deal with subheads?

Note: Because *The Chicago Manual of Style* recommends using sentence-style capitalization rather than headline-style capitalization when subheads consist of full sentences, we followed that style here.

Editors may change your subheads or alter where they fall on the page due to design considerations, subheads in other articles on the same or facing page, or other factors. But you can impress editors by supplying strong subheads that fit your article's content and structure. Then trust the editors' decisions to help you best reach their readers.

Yes, all this is a lot of work. No one said it was easy. (How many times have I written that in this book?) But if you take the time to "sweat" your titles and subheads, you'll show editors you're a professional, right from the start.

Besides, there are better ways to get fifteen seconds of fame than to have people laughing at you.

Chapter 45 Exercise

Try these three exercises to learn to write better titles:

1. Spend time browsing in a bookstore or your church library and list titles that capture your attention. Which ones appeal to your style? What ideas do they spark for a book idea you're considering? What patterns do you notice according to publisher?

2. Select three magazines you want to write for and study them well. Then think of an article you want to write. Look at the titles in the table of contents. Which ones appeal to your style? What ideas do they spark for the article you want to write now—or for future projects? If you find subheads, take note of the various types you find and of ways they keep the articles moving.

3. At your next critique-group gathering, use the principles in this chapter to help one another create attention-grabbing, appropriate titles for your manuscripts.

References:

Titles

The Chicago Manual of Style, Sixteenth Edition: 8.154–61
The Christian Writer's Manual of Style, Fourth Edition: pp. 88–89
The Associated Press Stylebook: See Composition Titles
Publication Manual of the American Psychological Association, Sixth Edition: 2.01, 6.29

Headlines

The Chicago Manual of Style, Sixteenth Edition: 14.204
The Associated Press Stylebook: See Headlines
Publication Manual of the American Psychological Association, Sixth Edition: 3.02–3

Subheads

The Chicago Manual of Style, Sixteenth Edition: 1.53–55, 2.56
The Christian Writer's Manual of Style, Fourth Edition: pp. 194–95

Be strong and courageous and get to work. Don't be frightened by the size of the task, for the Lord my God is with you; he will not forsake you. He will see to it that everything is finished correctly.

—1 CHRONICLES 28:20 (TLB)

Why Did the Editor Do That to My Manuscript?

46

When our children were little, "Miss Little Bits" came to me all upset one day because sibling "Miss Tinier Bits" had scribbled all over the picture Miss Little Bits had just colored so beautifully—even staying inside the lines. Ah, the joys of motherhood!

I remembered this incident as I began sketching out this chapter. Many writers have come to me at various times, wondering why I, or another conference faculty member, had "scribbled all over" their manuscripts. The conferees, sometimes in tears, thought they had presented a beautiful picture in the article or book chapter they submitted for critique. But the corrections and comments in red ink made the manuscript look as if it were bleeding all over the place. (That's why I at least use a pencil with blue or soft black lead instead of red ink. It softens the blow slightly.)

I remember the feeling when, early in my writing career, an editor accepted my article but chainsawed it so badly that I hardly recognized my precious piece in print.

In addition, sometimes editors seem inconsistent in their revisions. "I wrote *awhile* as one word on page 2," a writer says, "and the editor said it should be two. On page 4, I had it as two words, and the editor said it should be one. Argh!"

First, editors are not infallible. And, due to editing's subjective nature, one editor may edit a piece differently than another editor.

Second, one of the best ways to grow in our writing skills is to learn from the ways we're edited. Editors don't usually have time to explain revisions, but you can unearth the answers yourself.

In this final chapter, I want to give you an ongoing GPS for your writing, offering brief explanations for common editor "scribblings." Using a Q&A format, I'll review some items and present new ones.

For maximum benefit, read the questions, then—*before you read my explanations*—try to explain the principles behind each editing decision yourself.

Q. Why do editors freak out about typos? Nobody's perfect.

A. On a radio broadcast, author Chuck Swindoll read this item, purportedly from a large city newspaper:

> Notice from ABC publishing: To those who bought our book *Skydiving Made Easy*, please enter the following correction on page 12, paragraph 3, line 2. The words *State Zipcode* should say "Pull Ripcord." We regret any inconvenience this mistake may have caused.

Generally, our typos won't create life-or-death scenarios—except for our manuscripts' publishing chances. But that itself is reason enough to proofread carefully! Although spell-checkers aren't perfect either, pay attention to red squiggly lines. They're like a railroad crossing warning: Stop. Look up the word. Make sure you're right before proceeding.

When editors see tons of typos, they won't take you seriously as a writer.

Q. Why are editors' revisions inconsistent?

A. Perceived inconsistencies may indicate some glitches in our internal English language GPS (grammar, punctuation, and style).

Consider the difference between *awhile* and *a while*. Resolve the conflict by understanding each term's part of speech.

Adverb: **Ms. Scinto cavorted awhile.**

Here *awhile* modifies the verb *cavorted*, so it's an adverb, and the adverb is one word.

Noun (often following *for*): **For a while, her students played along.**

In the italicized prepositional phrase, *while* is a noun, the object of the preposition *for*. We're talking about *a* "while," two words.

For another way to remember the difference, here's a tip from Grammar Girl's online bag of tricks: "To tell the difference [between *a while* and *awhile*], you can test your sentence with other nouns and adverbs. If you can replace *a while* with another article and noun such as *an hour* or *a year*, you know you want the two-word version. If you can replace *awhile* with another adverb such as *quietly*, *longer*, or *briefly*, you know you want the one-word version."[1]

Q. Why did the editor capitalize Scripture but lowercase scriptural?

A. Consider the parts of speech. We capitalize *Scripture*, a proper noun. But *scriptural* is an adjective, so we use lowercase. Similarly, note this: anything true to the *Bible* [capitalized] is *biblical* [adjective].

Q. Why did the editor delete some prepositions?

A. Overuse of prepositional phrases induces the feeling of riding on a too-often-patched highway. Smooth the journey by cutting nonessentials and using possessives:

> OVERLY "PREPOSITIONED": The baggy britches of the student hung so low on his derriere that the photography teacher of the school was afraid of overexposure.
> SMOOTHER: The student's baggy britches hung so low that the school's photography teacher feared overexposure.

See how possessives smooth things out? We also don't need *on his derriere* (where else would his britches be—at least at that moment?). We can strengthen the verb (and cut more words) by substituting *feared* for *was afraid of*. Now we've cut the sentence from twenty-three words to fourteen. Space is precious. Use it wisely.

Q. Why did the editor switch words around so much in my manuscript?

A. Growing up with some Dutch blood in me, I often heard jokes about some Pennsylvania Dutch ancestors' propensity for transposing words, such as "Throw mama from the train a kiss."

Few writers would make such obvious errors, but editors may change word order for clarity or accuracy. Here's an example of the way word order can completely change a sentence's meaning:

> The company nearly lost $1,000.
> The company lost nearly $1,000.

The difference seems minor. But to a CFO it could mean the difference between keeping his job and losing it.

So beware. Word order may change emphasis and connotations.

Q. In Scripture quotations, why did the editor take out some ellipses and put others in?

A. In previous chapters we've said we don't need ellipses when we have deleted words at the beginning and/or end of Scripture quotations.

> ORIGINAL: Colossians 2:6 says, "So then, just as you received Christ Jesus as Lord, continue to live your lives in him."

We can usually delete transition words such as *so then, and, for,* and *therefore* at the beginning of a Scripture quotation. These words can even confuse readers, especially when they create sentence fragments.

> EDITED: Colossians 2:6 says, "Just as you received Christ Jesus as Lord, continue to live your lives in him."

We also don't usually use ellipses at the end of a quotation. But here's an example where I needed a closing ellipsis:

> **One would think that the frequent teachings of Jesus beginning with, "You have heard it said . . . but I say to you . . ." would have sunk in.**

We need the ellipsis because it indicates the various things Jesus said after those introductory words.

Q. Why did the editor say to abbreviate books of the Bible sometimes but spell them out other places?

A. We spell out Bible book names in general text but abbreviate them in parentheses:

> IN REGULAR TEXT: **Some pundits say Philippians 4:11 proves Paul wasn't from Texas because he says, "I have learned, in whatsoever *state* I am, therewith to be *content*" (KJV, emphasis added).**
>
> IN PARENTHESES: **Some pundits say Paul couldn't have been from Texas because he says, "I have learned, in whatsoever *state* I am, therewith to be *content*" (Phil. 4:11 KJV, emphasis added).**

Note: Some magazines handle this differently. Follow the style of your target publication.

Q. Why did the editor cut out or change words willy-nilly? I mean, I wrote, "As you traverse through the pages of Scripture . . ." The editor deleted the word through. What's wrong with through?

A. That correction is neither Willy nor Nilly. *Traverse through* is redundant. To *traverse* is to move through. The editor cut the deadwood and hauled it away.

Also, sometimes editors cut words simply because the article doesn't fit into the allotted space on a page. In my first staff editorial job I often had to read through articles that had been "flowed" (*over*flowed) into the design program, then cut words until everything fit. Sometimes I deleted perfectly good words. So cutting your own work to fit editors' allotted word counts can offer you a little more control about what gets chopped.

As for changing words, make sure you're using the best words and expressions.

Q. There's so much to learn! What's the best way to keep growing in my writing skills?

A. Here are a few ways:

1. Keep consulting and reviewing *this* book, *The Christian Writers Manual of Style,* and *The Chicago Manual of Style.*
2. Start or join a critique group of *working* writers (not a mutual admiration society).

3. Read broadly. Reading for pleasure can help you absorb good rhythm and flow, and reading analytically can help you build your self-editing skills. I tell the students I mentor that it's often the things we enjoy most and/or find most effective in the writing of others that can become strengths in our own writing—if we pay attention.

4. If/when you have the honor of being published, first breathe a prayer of thanks and then read through your published piece—just for the joy of reading it in print.

Next, photocopy or print out an extra copy of the article manuscript (or at least one chapter of the book) you submitted. Compare the published version with the photocopied manuscript. Using standard proofreading marks, edit the photocopy as the editor did. (Find these essential tools of our craft in appendix B.) Consider why the editor made those changes. Your critique group may be able to help you with this step.

Think of all these suggestions for growth as CEUs (continuing education units). File away in your memory bank—and put into practice—the grammar, punctuation, and style skills you've learned in this book. If you take this approach to being edited, you'll no longer feel that editors are "scribbling" all over your manuscripts.

Happy learning!

Chapter 46 Exercise

Learn from the way you're edited

For one critique session, swap manuscripts and *silently* critique each other's work, marking your revisions using standard proofreading marks (appendix B). Be prepared to justify the revisions you suggest.

Return manuscripts and discuss reasons for changes made. Use *The Chicago Manual of Style* as your authority.

If you don't belong to a critique group or class, find one or two people who have good English skills and ask them to offer suggestions for improvement.

Appendix A

Section 1 Quiz Answers: Grammar and Related Matters

Chapter 1: Defibrillate Your Verbs

Notice all the *to-be* verbs and other weak verbs highlighted here. I've made some suggestions below regarding ways we could strengthen this little vignette, but you may find better ways to wake up the piece. Give it a go.

> *Many years ago there was a little old widower who lived above a shoe-repair shop. He went by the name of W. E. Kling. He was seventy-six years old and only five feet tall. He had mustard-colored hair, his eyes were tired-looking, and he was always talking in hushed tones. He had a boring wardrobe and an equally boring dog that was always lying around on the couch. It wasn't playful at all. In one corner of the apartment was a comfortable dog bed that was donated by a neighbor; but the dog was happier, it seemed, on the couch. There wasn't much going on in the little man's life, but he was usually in fairly good spirits.*
>
> *One morning, as he walked down the stairs to his shop, his shoulders were rather low. When he sat down at his cobbler's bench, he had a gloomy look on his face. He was often teased by his sole employee, his granddaughter, Felicity. She had experienced these moods of his before, and she knew there was only one thing to do.*

Many years ago a little old widower named Wilfred E. Kling lived alone above a shoe-repair shop. At seventy-six years old and only five feet tall, he shuffled about his apartment as if trying to wear out his shoes prematurely. W. E., as he preferred to be called, spoke in hushed tones when he spoke at all. His long, mustard-colored hair fell over his tired-looking eyes, and his boring wardrobe hung on him like laundry on a clothesline.

His Dalmatian, Spot, always lying around on the couch, wouldn't even chase a ball if W. E. threw it toward him. In one corner of the apartment a donated dog bed waited to offer Spot comfy naps, but the Dalmatian preferred the couch. Little excitement invaded the diminutive man's life, but he usually maintained fairly good spirits.

One morning, however, as he walked down the stairs to his shop, his shoulders drooped, and his gloomy expression cast a pall over the whole room. His granddaughter, Felicity—his sole employee—often teased him about his melancholy, trying to raise his spirits. So now she knew what to she had to do.

Chapter 2: Resuscitate Your Nouns

1. Herkimer proudly held up the thirty-six-pound walleye he caught at Lake Shamineau.
2. Patti always wanted a blue topaz in her engagement ring.
3. Ellen unscrewed the lampshade's mermaid-shaped brass finial.
4. The EF2 tornado left us without power for six days.
5. Ramona discovered she was allergic to Splenda.
6. The wings of the ruby-throated hummingbird . . .
7. The Mendozas surprised us by bringing moo goo gai pan to our cul-de-sac's potluck.
8. Hundreds of roaches scavenged for any crumbs they could find in the long-abandoned kitchen.

9. In a huff Damaris swung her Coach tote bag over her shoulder and stomped out of the house.
10. The bed-and-breakfast owners turned a dilapidated Victorian house into a classic Painted Lady in pinks and blues.

Chapter 3: The Match Game

1. zoom
2. C
3. is
4. wins
5. wants. Either *want* or *wants* is now considered correct. CMoS 16 now prefers *want*, much to my and others' dismay.
6. C
7. C
8. There are tons . . .
9. sends
10. C

Chapter 4: Getting Tense?

1. C. Either *has dreamed* or *has dreamt* (present perfect verb) is correct. Dictionaries list *dreamed* first.
2. Should be *could have* (or *could've*). (*Could have* is a conditional verb, a term we didn't discuss. Google it.); *hadn't* [*had not*] *intervened* is correct, a past perfect tense.
3. C. *wanted* is simple past tense; *to sing* is an infinitive.
4. *was intending* is past progressive; *to repair* is an infinitive; *says* should be *said*, which is simple past tense; *have* [you] *lost* is present perfect tense.
5. *had worshiped* (note only one *p*; past perfect verb).
6. *shows* is simple present tense; *shone* should be *shown*; *has shone* is the past participle of *shine* (*has shown* is a present perfect verb).
7. C. *is serving* is present progressive.
8. C. *wrote* (simple past tense) or *writes* (simple present tense) are acceptable (though *wrote* is preferable); *has* [not] *given* is present perfect tense.
9. Modern publishing prefers *traveling* over *travelling*; *was traveling* is past progressive tense.
10. C. Either *dove* or *dived* (simple past tense) is allowed. *Dived* is the preferred term in dictionaries, and this sentence may hint at a reason. *Had dived* seems less awkward than *had dove*—at least to my ears. (Both could be correct and are past perfect tense.)

Chapter 5: Moody Verbs

1. IND
2. S, *was* should be *were*.
3. IND
4. S
5. S
6. IMP
7. S, *revised* should be *revise*.
8. S
9. IMP
10. S, *was* should be *were*.

Chapter 6: Get Your Adverbs Here!

Individual answers will vary.

Chapter 7: Are Your Adjectives on Steroids—or Just Obnoxious?

1. As written, Phillippa is selling humongous children! Possible rewrite: Phillippa is having a humongous sale of kids' items.
2. *than they* [are]. Remember to put the word *are* after *they/them* to help you remember the correct usage. *CMoS 16* says that traditional grammarians prefer this option in formal writing, but *than them* "represents common usage" (5.179). Remember to add the appropriate verb: My grandkids say I'm goofier than *they* [are].
3. Beware of the malaprop monster! *Proceed*, not *precede*.
4. *a historic battle*
5. C. In the first instance, the term *left handed* comes *after* the noun (*Steve*); but in the second instance, *left-handed* comes *before* the noun (*compliments*)—all correct.
6. *sporting a red Mohawk . . .*
7. Beware of spillage. *Less impressive and less* [implied] *shorter* is incorrect. Turn the descriptions around: *The sequel was shorter and less impressive.*
8. No commas needed in this sentence because of the repetition of the word *and* throughout; the term *deep-fried* is correctly hyphenated here.
9. *the mousy, well-intentioned political candidate*
10. In books and in magazines that use the "serial comma" (as recommended by *CMoS 16*), we need a comma after the word *punctuation.*

Chapter 8: Wrangling Pronouns

1. Error: using *their* (plural) to refer to *everyone* (singular, literally *every one*). Change to plural: Would all those *who have not passed . . .*
2. To whom does *they* refer? One catty nurse? An arrogant obstetrician? The entire heartless staff?
3. The *he or she* construction is awkward. Try something like this: Mr. Birchfield said that those students who wanted a brownnoser, extra-credit assignment should ask him.
4. Assuming Cherise isn't referring to her sister as her best friend, revise like this: Reluctantly, Cherise and her best friend *each* told *her* parents about *her* bad grades.
5. The drake came at us as if *he* thought we were threatening *his* ducklings. (Because a drake is a male duck, we use the male pronouns: *he* and *his*.)
6. *took its* cues. (*Audience* is a collective noun, acting as one.)
7. None (literally *not one*) of the magicians at the guys-only party, no matter how talented he was, could produce a rabbit out of his shoe.
8. Possible rewrite: *Individuals* who *want* to stand out in a crowd of experienced writers should make sure their manuscripts are as lean and clean as possible before submitting.
9. Tinkerbell and Clarabell each had *her* own . . .
10. We need to clarify the antecedent of *them*—Is it *skydivers* or *backpack*? And let's use a stronger verb—*contained*: Each of the skydivers had a backpack, but only *one backpack contained* a parachute.

Chapter 9: The "Case" of the Questionable Pronoun

1. *whom*, not *who*
2. *us*, not *we*

3. Because we don't see anyone else in the salon, we can assume the student is painting her own tootsies, so *herself* is correct. If she happens to be practicing her artistry on someone else, make that clear and use the pronoun *her*.
4. *me*, not *myself*
5. *I*, not *myself*
6. In dialogue if Lily habitually speaks with good grammar skills, substitute *she* for *her*. If she's more informal, leave as is.
7. *me*, not *I*
8. *his*, not *him*
9. Correct, but delete the commas surrounding *herself*.
10. *we parents*, not *us parents*

Chapter 10: The Reflexology of Pronouns

1. herself
2. No commas needed.
3. themselves
4. C
5. C, but highly unlikely.
6. C
7. *me*, not *myself*
8. Either *all over her* or *all over herself* can work here.
9. Inconclusive. We might assume what the writer meant was *call attention to himself*. But, as written, it could mean the pastor wants to avoid calling attention to someone else. If so, we need that person's name at the end of the sentence instead of the pronoun *him*.
10. C

Chapter 11: Where'd I Misplace That Modifier?

There are a number of ways you can revise these sentences to clarify their meaning, but consider the suggestions below.
1. [M] At the conference, the editors, with their pleasant smiles, seemed far more welcoming to new writers than we thought. (Note: Though this may seem to be an ambiguous modifier, clearly we don't mean that editors only welcome new writers with pleasant smiles. So the reference point is clear. It's simply misplaced, and the sentence needs to be rearranged. Adding commas also helps readers understand the sentence.)
2. [D] Because the writer was unwilling to revise, her manuscript arrived DOA on the editor's desk.
3. [D] Not knowing the outcome, we postponed the decision.
4. [D] Even when I was eight years old, this song spoke to my heart. Or: Even as an eight-year-old, I sensed the Lord speaking to my heart through this song.
5. [A] Having studied the market guides, she often got her work published. Or: Because she often studied the market guides, she got her work published. (The lack of a comma in the original creates confusion. Did she study often or get published often?)
6. [M] To pass the time during every day's bumper-to-bumper commute, I began quoting Bible verses I learned in high school.
7. [A] The crook, who repeatedly burglarized several convenience stores, had to make restitution. (Clarify whether the crook repeatedly robbed or repeatedly made restitution.)
8. [D] After I spent an inordinate amount of time looking for the misplaced red folder, my day was shot.
9. [D] (Did Omar's looks *prevent* him from being chosen, or were his looks not the criteria for his being chosen? Did he make the cast of the show or not?) Because of Omar's

looks, he was not chosen for the musical. Or: His looks weren't the reason Omar was chosen for the musical.

10. [M] According to one source, more than half of all Americans, including one in four children, are on one or more prescription medications.

Chapter 12: That Which Is Whom?

1. He berated the senators *who* blocked the bill. (R)
2. The family *that* prays together stays together. (R, no commas)
3. The cake that my grandma baked won the contest. (R) Simplify: delete *that*.
4. The editors who were at the conference gave helpful tips. (R) Simplify: The editors at the conference . . .
5. The Ten Commandments, which are not merely suggestions, guide Pete's life. (N)
6. ✓ (R) Simplify: *we heard the roaring lion.*
7. The pirates, *who* plundered every ship they encountered . . . (N)
8. ✓ (R)
9. Tanya realized the giddy couple on the tour bus was the same couple *whom* she had met on a cruise the year before. (R) Simplify: *the same couple she had met . . .*
10. ✓(N)

Chapter 13: Quell Those Qualifiers

1. *very.* Delete *very* and be more precise: rewrite to give the age at which he learned to read.
2. *appears.* Correct usage, not hedging—if the facts have not yet been confirmed. If, however, the coroner has established a time of death, cut the qualifier: *The man was murdered between eight and twelve last night.*
3. *relatively.* Here's a qualifier that hedges, but its meaning isn't clear. Relative to what? Rewrite.
4. *virtually.* In what virtual reality might we be here? Did they triple their sales or not? If not quite, use *almost.* If they exceeded triple sales, use *more than.* If they hit the tripled number on the nose, delete qualifiers.
5. *actually.* Using *actually* implies doubt he would pass at all, much less with highest marks. To keep it straightforward, eliminate the qualifier.
6. *basically.* Outside of dialogue, the word *basically* often can be cut. Because this is dialogue, using this qualifier may be one way to characterize Joan. Don't overdo it, but throwing in qualifiers like this often enough to make her distinct from other characters can work well.
7. *very,* which is overintensified here. This type of repetition might be suitable in a thank-you note. You can gush as much as your recipient can stand. But when writing for publication, first rewrite, using a more precise word than the overused, nebulous word *special.* Then delete *very.*
8. Unless this is a fiction piece and you're trying to characterize the sportscaster as someone who habitually talks like this, get rid of the contradiction presented by *kind of* and *definitely.* (And don't include too much of this type of dialogue. Remember, often less is more.) Possible rewrite, streamlining: "The runner at first [better yet: use the runner's name] looked like he was going for the steal," the sportscaster said.
9. *Almost.* I have made this pronouncement many times for its humor value, but obviously we either forgive someone or we don't. Grammatically, I should cut the word *almost* or confess that I still haven't forgiven her for putting this temptation in my way.
10. What does *basically* add to this sentence? Nothing. Cut it.

Chapter 14: Let's Split (and Other Last Words)

1. Ending preposition. All the newbie writers wanted to get into *Guideposts*. [Note how this wording also gets rid of the unnecessary weak verb *was* and shortens the sentence.]
2. Split infinitive. Editor Kolbaba really wanted to emphasize . . . (or delete *really* altogether).
3. C. *Is* isn't a preposition. It's a verb.
4. Ending preposition. I won't put up with the practice of ending a sentence with a preposition.
5. Split infinitive. Maynard G. Krebs always managed to get Dobie Gillis in trouble.
6. Ending preposition. Into how much trouble did Maynard manage to get Dobie Gillis? Or better: Rewrite altogether. (How can you quantify something like this?)
7. Ending preposition. Where are you? [*At* is a preposition, but it's not needed.]
8. Ending preposition. By whom was the novel written? Or better: Who wrote the novel?
9. Ending preposition. At the masquerade party, Craig had to remain vigilant because he didn't know what costume his nemesis had chosen to wear.
10. Split infinitive. He worked diligently to become a bestselling author. [Strengthens the verb and eliminates the unnecessary word *ultimately*.]

Chapter 15: Are You Appositive?

1. a library of sixty-six volumes
2. *Eb & Flo*
3. one aspect of the fruit of the Spirit
4. Ted's annoying habit, cracking his knuckles loudly in public, made Delia cringe.
5. We appreciate the deep teaching of Ronald Godlyman, pastor of Hopeville Church.
6. Holley tried to resist her greatest temptation, chocolate fudge, but she finally ate the whole package in one sitting.
7. In the Disney movie *The Little Mermaid*, Scuttle—a seagull—finds something shiny in the sea and gives it to Ariel, the mermaid princess. Not knowing what the thing is, Scuttle calls it a dinglehopper. Ariel uses the dinglehopper, a fork, for a comb.
8. C. No commas around *Jane Seymour* because she definitely was not his only wife.
9. C.
10. C, but put *My Fair Lady*, the larger work, in italics (as shown). "A Hymn to Him," a song, should be in quotation marks—as should the catchphrase quotation, "Why can't a woman be more like a man?"

Chapter 16: What Could Be Worst?

1. kinder, C
2. more frustrated, C. Even though it seems like this could be the ultimate of frustration, thus a superlative, it's actually comparing only two elements: *how frustrated I am now* and *the worst frustration I've ever felt*.
3. most ridiculous, S
4. second-ugliest, S
5. *fewer*, not *less*
6. *most winsome*, not *winsomest*
7. *more awkward*, not *awkwarder*
8. assuming Aaron is an editor, this should be any *other* editor
9. *fewer*, not *less*
10. ✓(N)

Chapter 17: Wanna Go Out for a Spell?

1. *stationery*: writing paper (*stationary* means unmovable)
2. *among*: three or more (*between* indicates only two choices)
3. *horde*: a great number (*hoard*: action of a pack rat)
4. *past*: adverb, how he zoomed (*passed* is a verb—McQueen *passed* Mater)
5. *led*: past tense of the verb *to lead* (*lead* [sounds the same as *led*] is a heavy metal)
6. *lie*: to recline (*lay*: to put or place; requires a direct object—to place what? Also the past tense of *lie*)
7. *than*: a comparison (*then* concerns time)
8. *anecdotes*: stories (*antidote*: what Snow White needed to counteract the poison apple)
9. *could have*: verb (*could of*: no legitimate usage)
10. *used to*: formerly (*use to*: What can we *use to* remember these examples?)

Section 2 Quiz Answers: Punctuation and Related Matters

Chapter 18: That's What *He* Said

1. C
2. Watch out for long dialogue tags such as this one, and remember that few things happen simultaneously. She's only saying five words, but how long would it take for her to do all the things she's supposedly doing while she says them? Put the action beats before or after what she says. For example: Hailey curled her hair, donned her dress, and headed downstairs to wait for her prom date. "Everything has to be perfect," she said.
3. Hank pulled Petunia's pigtails. "You're a dork," he said.

   "Well, you're not exactly Mr. Wonderful." (Note the inserted closing quotation marks that were missing.)

   "At least I know how to throw a football." He tossed a perfect spiral down the field.

   Running after the ball, she caught it cleanly and fired it back. "I can do that too." Her throw bonked him on the head.
4. Better to save the word *stated* for police or other officials' "statements." Sounds stiff and unnatural here. Good place for *said*: . . . Mother said, sniffing the aroma.

   Another possibility:

   "The pie is out of the oven." Mother sniffed the aroma. (Note the period, not comma, before the closing quotation marks.)
5. "I can't take any more of this frivolity." She laughed. (We can't laugh a sentence, so use a period instead of a comma in the dialogue.)
6. No comma between *asked* and *warily*.
7. In this case, *suggested* is an appropriate synonym for *said*. However, *retorted* is a strong word, usually with a connotation of a rather sharp response. So use *replied* or *said*. Better yet, delete the dialogue tag if there are only two people in the scene.
8. "You never let me finish my sen—"
9. Here's a possible rewrite to break up a long piece of dialogue (I've inserted interaction and reaction with/from the teacher as well):

   The teacher asked Waldo to recite his piece from *The Merchant of Venice*.

   "The quality of mercy is not deranged," Waldo began his slaughter of Shakespeare. "It droppeth as the gentle brain from heaven upon the place bequeathed. . . ."

   The teacher covered his face with his hands as the fiasco continued.

"'Tis [don't miss the apostrophe] Mighty Mouse like the throned monarch butterfly—better than his cronies."

10. Joanna said, "I published an article in *FarmFriendly* magazine. The article is called 'Confessions of a Cowbell Player.'"

Chapter 19: Hyphen Hyperactivity

1. C
2. un-Christlike
3. Ambiguous. Clarify. Was there an extra pillow? Then use a comma: *Rowena snuggled into the extra, soft pillow.* Was the pillow softer than usual in addition to its hunger-inducing fragrance? Then use a hyphen: *the extra-soft pillow.*
4. antitrust
5. The *nonbelievers* left the *snake-oil* salesman's presentation, laughing out loud.
6. geopolitical (no hyphen)
7. The well-traveled business exec felt exasperated when he saw that his wife planned to take two large suitcases for a five-day vacation.
8. no hyphen with an *ly* adverb; hence, *thinly sliced*
9. sixth- (Don't forget the hyphen followed by a space here.)
10. C. (As it should, right?)

Chapter 20: Compound Infractions

1. I (*Nonfiction* formerly used a hyphen, now it doesn't. Note that a few publications still use a hyphen.)
2. I and C. *Selfless* (one word), *self-conscious* (hyphenated)
3. I (one word): *reoccupied*
4. I (one word): *eyewitnesses*
5. I (one word): *alongside*
6. C
7. C
8. I (one word): *postmodern*
9. C
10. I (hyphenated): end-time; C

Chapter 21: The Inside Scope

1. Colon, not semicolon.
2. C
3. Technically correct, and the two clauses are related. But let's streamline and create two separate sentences to accommodate readers' shortened attention spans: *The economist reported that the price of helium is rising for inexplicable reasons. Therefore, balloon sales and helium-canister rentals—solely to distort people's voices at parties—are tanking.*
4. C. Using the letter *b* to designate the second part of the verse in Luke is acceptable here to isolate a particular part of the verse the preacher used. But generally we don't need such designations.
5. C; some publications will use the two-letter postal abbreviations for states, such as Iowa's *IA.*
6. Most book publishers use no colon unless what precedes it is a complete sentence. Some magazines will use the colon.
7. C

8. Use a colon after *settings* to introduce the list. Then to avoid the confusion, separate the items with semicolons, like this: Valentine, Nebraska; Romeo, Colorado; and Bridal Veil, Oregon.

9. No colon needed. Use a comma after *such as*.

10. The first reference needs a colon instead of a semicolon. (Personal note: I have become fanatical about checking the accuracy of all Scripture references ever since.)

Chapter 22: Stamp Out Apostrophe Abuse

1. I. Change to *Grishams*. The plural of the name *Grisham* is *Grishams*. No possessive. No apostrophe.

2. I. No reason for an apostrophe here. Just slap a lowercase *s* on the end, making *PINs*. (PIN stands for *Personal Identification Number*, so *PIN number* is redundant.)

3. I. Change to *boys'*. The dormitory by definition is for boys, plural, and they at least *act* like they own the place.

4. I. Change to *Beverly's*. Two girls cannot wear the same outfit at the same time, so each needs her own apostrophe.

5. C. (The word is not *perservere*, but *persevere*. Because I've used this illustration twice in this chapter, you may surmise—correctly—that this is one of my pet peeves.)

6. I. Change to *people's*. This word is similar to *children's*. *People* is the plural of *person*, so we use the apostrophe and then the *s* to indicate possessive.

7. C

8. I. Change to *Charles's*.

9. I. Turn that beginning single quotation mark around so it becomes an apostrophe. (Type two apostrophes at the beginning of the number and delete the first one. Then delete the apostrophe before the *s*: *'70s*.

10. I. Change to *ATMs, TVs*.

Chapter 23: Capital Crimes and Misdemeanors

1. *godly*

2. *professor's*

3. *grandfather's; Scriptures*

4. *captain; Navy; Pledge of Allegiance*

5. *proposal; Hitchhiker's; Guide; Spiritual; Disciplines*

6. *iPads* (no hyphen), lower case *i* even to begin a sentence; lowercase everything else capitalized here.

7. C

8. Check your target publication to see if it capitalizes deity pronouns. If so, capitalize *his*.

9. Capitalize *senator*

10. Lowercase the entire word DON'T, and use italics for emphasis if needed.

Chapter 24: Commatose

Once upon a time, a bright young woman, Sunny Diamante, who scored extremely high on her SATs, was accepted at several prestigious universities. She chose to study English at Harvard University in Cambridge, Massachusetts, with an eye toward teaching at the college level.

Sunny and her roommate clicked instantly. They were both bookworms from small towns. They loved the same books, music, and sports. During the first semester, they even fell in love with the same guy, their freshman comp professor.

He himself looked like he'd barely graduated college. They eventually learned he was a child prodigy who finished high school by the time he was twelve. He was actually younger than they were. Though he had his doctorate, he certainly didn't look old enough.

Before they finished their freshman year, each woman had written a romance novel about a college student and a young English professor with chiseled features, long eyelashes, and curly black hair that dangled over his sky-blue eyes.

Chapter 25: In This Corner . . . Italics versus Quotation Marks

1. *Oklahoma!* features the song "Oh, What a Beautiful Mornin'." (Note: The exclamation point is part of the title of this musical. And with the dropped *g*, creating *Mornin'*, we put the period after the apostrophe, followed by the closing quotation marks.)
2. . . . Mark tells us about a time that a teacher of the religious law asked Jesus which of the commandments was most important. [Scripture quotation begins here:] "'The most important one,' answered Jesus, 'is this: "Hear, O Israel: The Lord our God, the Lord is one. Love the Lord your God with all your heart and with all your soul and with all your mind and with all your strength." The second is this: "Love your neighbor as yourself." There is no commandment greater than these'" (Mark 12:29–31).

   Note: In this case, we need the initial double quotation marks to indicate that we're quoting from the Bible, so that means we have to reverse each of the quotation marks inside and finish with doubles again. The standard advice to cut and paste from a trusted Bible site, such as BibleGateway.com, still holds true. But remember to reverse the quotation marks.

   To simplify your life—and communicate more clearly—streamline the quotation: Jesus replied, giving the top two commandments: "Love the Lord your God with all your heart and with all your soul and with all your mind and with all your strength" and "Love your neighbor as yourself."
3. My all-time favorite movie is *The Princess Bride.*
4. This is a tricky one. It depends on the meaning. If Mom is saying *she herself* can't have any cookies, then we need quotation marks: *Mom said, "I can't have any . . . trip."* If Mom is saying *the daughter* can't have any, we don't use quotation marks here. We could also revise this way: *Mom said that I can't have any.*
5. I've been reading through *The One Year Chronological Bible.* Another tricky one. Although the Bible is one of the book titles we don't italicize, this is a particular book with a title trademarked by Tyndale, so italicize the entire name (note lack of hyphen in the title as well).
6. Luci Shaw, in her book *The Crime of Living Cautiously*, wrote, "Are you feeding your fears or fueling your faith?"
7. Comedian Steven Wright asked, "Why isn't the word *phonetically* spelled with an *F*?"
8. The editor said yes to my book proposal!
9. . . . he noticed the Wet Paint sign.
10. . . . her first children's book, *Roni Rabbit's* Really *Ridiculous Rocket.* [Delete italics for emphasis when rest of title is italicized.]

Chapter 26: Gimme a Break!

1. Dashes would work better here. Replace both commas with dashes.
2. Use parentheses, not brackets.
3. We need a dash after *impress*, not a comma. Remember: when you open a door, so to speak, with parentheses, brackets, and dashes, be sure to close them when you leave that thought.

4. Substitute a single dash for the hyphen: *Jennie created a masterpiece—a sculpture I will never understand but a masterpiece nonetheless.*
5. theses, or commas here because the conversion to modern-time sensibility isn't in the original. The brackets indicate that we're adding something for clarification.
6. C
7. Ken tapped his fingers on the table and said wistfully, "I wish . . ." First, we can't use a dash because that indicates an interruption, which we don't see here. (Consult chapter 18 for more on punctuating dialogue.) Second, putting the word *wistfully* beforehand not only saves words but helps us, as readers, know how Ken said it before we see what he said. That's especially helpful for adults reading aloud to each other or to a child.
8. C
9. Use en dash instead of hyphen.
10. Use en dash, not em dash. (Careful proofreading required.)

Chapter 27: Diagnosis Terminal

1. Period, not question mark.
2. Startling enough to merit an exclamation point.
3. Startling, yes. But use question mark, not both.
4. Depends. Period if it's an assumption. Question mark if it's a question.
5. Hold period till end of sentence, not end of quotation.
6. C
7. Who directed the musical *Mama Mia!*? Title includes exclamation point. Rare instance of correct double-terminal punctuation. (Note: only the exclamation point—not the question mark—is italicized.)
8. You would be justified in using an exclamation point rather than a comma after the word *closer*. But then you wouldn't need the dialogue tag, *he hollered*. The punctuation does the trick.
9. C. This is a shortened version of a longer question, such as *Have you ever seen anything like that?* But we can assume, I think, that it's spoken more in disbelief than as a question requiring an answer.
10. Only one question mark needed—the one inside the quotation marks.

Chapter 28: Watch Out for "Slash"-ers

1. journalist-politician. This person isn't a journalist *or* a politician. This person is a journalist *and* a politician, so use the hyphenated term *journalist-politician*.
2. Insert space before and after the solidus.
3. Change the backward slash to forward slash. Better yet, reword the sentence to avoid *him/her*—e.g., *When editors ask you to submit something, don't fail to send it to them.*
4. and/or
5. secretary of membership
6. three-fourths
7. . . . Battle of Baltimore that began on the evening of September 13, 1814, and raged on into the early morning hours of September 14.
8. Change to plural (*garbage collectors*). Or if you're writing about one particular garbage collector, you might use that person's name and the appropriate-gender pronoun: *When garbage collector Ana Bouquet comes home, she makes a big stink.*
9. C
10. C. Technically, this is correct. However, we might create a more helpful sentence like this: *The forward slash, virgule, diagonal, slant, oblique, or solidus—all these words refer to the same mark (/)—can be a useful tool.* Here's another possible rendering: *The forward slash (/) can be a useful tool. It's also called a virgule, diagonal, slant, oblique, or solidus.*

Chapter 29: Paint-by-Number Writing

1. nineties
2. three, third
3. twelve
4. C
5. 90 percent
6. 80% (no space)
7. First John (dialogue)
8. C (note: hyphenated adjective: *good-quality*)
9. 9/11-anniversary article (note: hyphenated adjective)
10. Spell out *one* and *nine* (dialogue).

Chapter 30: Getting Possessive

1. Theirs
2. Gideon's
3. Gideons
4. Gideons'
5. his
6. Browns
7. your
8. it's
9. his
10. its, browsers'

Chapter 31: "Quotable Quotes for 2000, Alex"

1. The transitional word *But* is not necessary. Delete. Then insert the omitted period at the end of the sentence.
2. Two problems here: (1) The opening quotation mark is missing. (2) We don't include the verse numbers in the text we've copied and pasted from a Bible software program. So delete the superscript number (^{2}).
3. There's nothing wrong, essentially, with this quotation. However, it would be helpful for the reader not to have to wait until the end to find out who wrote this. You could introduce the quotation this way: Oswald Chambers wrote, "The author or speaker from whom you learn the most . . ."

    But it often creates a nicer flow if you bring in the author attribution at a natural break in the wording—such as when someone reading aloud might take a breath, like this: "The author or speaker from whom you learn the most," wrote Oswald Chambers, "is not the one who teaches you something you didn't know before . . ."
4. . . . when he wrote, "Pride goes before . . . a fall" (Prov. 16:18 NIV)? This verse is often misquoted as "Pride goes before a fall," leaving out some words. Here's the whole verse: "Pride goes before destruction, a haughty spirit before a fall." So if you're going to leave out a section of the verse, insert ellipses. But it seems there's good reason to quote the whole verse.
5. C
6. By using an ellipsis, we've cut out a significant part of this conditional promise. Jesus stipulates the condition that we must ask *in his name*. And he repeats that phrase in the beginning of verse 24. So we have misrepresented the promise by leaving out what we did with the ellipsis.
7. one hundred
8. Trick question. Omit quotation marks at the beginning and end of block quotations.

9. According to *CWMS 4*, you may quote about 300 words[1] cumulatively from a book and 100 words from an article—providing that's not a large percentage of the work from which you're quoting. To "borrow" 100 words from a 350-word article, for example, would not be fair use. Write your own stuff!

10. Accuracy, clarity, integrity, and correct formatting.

Chapter 32: Citation Citings

1. Answers will vary. Check *The Chicago Manual of Style* or *The Christian Writer's Manual of Style* for helpful examples.

Chapter 33 Handling Scripture Carefully and Correctly

1. Use an arabic numeral, not a roman numeral: *1 Samuel*, not *I Samuel*. Then delete the word *But* at the beginning of the quotation. It's a transition word that distracts when we aren't given what comes before it.

2. Because the word *that* precedes the quotation, the first word of the verse should not be capitalized.

3. No period before the closing quotation marks; it only goes after the reference in parentheses.

4. Check the wording. The word *in* does not appear in the New King James Version. And the word *His* is capitalized in this translation.

5. Check the wording. We need to add a comma after *wisdom*. And delete the comma between the reference and the version cited.

6. The comma is missing after the word *wrote*.

7. We can't use the numeral 2 at the beginning of a sentence. Spell it out: *Second Corinthians 5:17 says . . .*

8. Writers sometimes use *David* and *the psalmist* interchangeably. This particular psalm was written by Moses. So you might recast the sentence this way: *Moses, that great leader of Israel, wrote, "Satisfy us . . .*

9. Because we have already identified John as the author and his first epistle as the source of the quotation, all we need in the parentheses is the chapter, verse, and translation: *(4:4 NKJV)*. Also insert the missing closing quotation marks before the reference.

10. When copying and pasting from an electronic Bible program, delete the verse numbers, such as the [2] here. Then the designation in parentheses should be the following: *(vv.* [not *vss.*] *1–2 NLT)*.

Section 3 Quiz Answers: Style, Usage, and Other Considerations

Chapter 34: Stylin'

Answers will vary.

Chapter 35: Don't Use That Tone with Me

1. When we receive the Lord Jesus Christ as our Savior, he forgives all our sins.

2. Giving God first place in our lives helps us to . . .

3. When we consistently read the Bible and pray, our faith will grow deeper.

4. As we obey the command of Jesus to go and tell others about him, we're helping to build his kingdom.

5. Eating a healthy, balanced diet will give us more energy and prevent . . .

6. If we want to be true disciples of Jesus Christ, he calls us to take up our cross every day and follow him. And he promises that yoking ourselves to him actually lightens our burdens (Matt. 11:28–29).

7. C.

8. There might be a place for this kind of confrontational writing, but if you want to soften it, you might write something like this: If you know you need to forgive someone, and you've been putting it off, you'll finally find peace if you take that step right now. Why wait?

9. In conversation this might work. In some homes, this might even be the only way to motivate a teenager. But in writing, we usually aim for a kinder, gentler approach toward our readers, showing benefits instead of laying down edicts—something like this: "God's Word warns us against laziness and promises to reward humble service with a "Well done, good and faithful servant!" (Matt. 25:23).

10. If we let go of our sin and follow God in everything, he will give us a freedom we have never known before.

Chapter 36: Tight Writing

1. *Apprehensive* and *anxious* are essentially the same thing. Pick *one*! In addition, we can streamline *interview for college* by saying *college interview*.

2. Eleven donuts remain.

3. Blend the ingredients, pour into a greased pan, and put into an oven preheated to 350 degrees. (This version is streamlined, but instructions like these frustrate me. First tell me to preheat the oven, then do the greasing and blending—in order.)

4. The painting disappeared.

5. The unscrupulous financial planner's goal was to abscond with his clients' life savings and head for the Cayman Islands.

6. Or better yet: The unscrupulous financial planner intended to abscond . . . . (Now we've strengthened the to-be verb *was*.)

7. Besides Jordan's start time being incomprehensible to me, we can avoid redundancy by deleting either *a.m.* or *in the morning*, not both.

8. We're clearly in Erin's point of view. So we can say this: Erin crouched beside the fire escape across the street from the jewelry store. The burglars ran out the store's side door, and she scrammed.

9. A kind editor might try to soften criticism with qualifiers such as *a bit*. But either the children's book was too cutesy for that publishing house or it wasn't. Delete *a bit*.

10. Pick one. *Eager* is the better choice because *anxious* can have connotations of fear or anxiety. You can also improve this sentence by moving the last phrase closer to its antecedent: *eager to impress the girls at the diving meet*.

11. Eliminate the word *completely*. It's impossible to surround something *partially*.

Chapter 37: Spit-Polished Writing

1. farther. We use *farther* to indicate concrete distance, *further* for abstract concepts such as *for further review*.

2. implied. Cassandra may have only *inferred* (her perception) that the editor thought the manuscript was putrid, or the editor may have *implied* it (in not-so-subtle hints perhaps).

3. virtually

4. Either option is acceptable, but *liable* is often used when indicating an undesirable outcome, and I believe this sentence would qualify.

5. nauseated

6. famous
7. Both are technically correct. Ironically, they mean the same thing. But use *flammable* to avoid confusion. *Inflammable* might be construed as *not flammable*.
8. horde
9. more than
10. in case. (If you're *not* hungry, does the chocolate cake cease to exist?)

Chapter 38: Got Rhythm?

1. Answers will vary. Discuss with your critique group.
2. We could vary the sentence structures several ways, but here's one example that tightens the paragraph a little in the process:

> A few kooky conferees played a practical joke on Ginger, their favorite magazine editor. After writing a manuscript filled with grammatical errors and inserting Ginger's byline, they filled out a cover sheet for a manuscript critique to see how a faculty member would respond to such a terrible submission from a respected editor. Sensing the ruse, the book editor laughed and tossed the manuscript. Ginger never found out, disappointing the conferees.

Chapter 39: Flow Gently, Sweet Manuscript

1. C. Good use of short sentences—even sentence fragments—in this snippet from a vaudeville comedy sketch, sometimes known as "Niagara Falls." (Worth looking up for its entertainment value.)
2. Redundant. Pick one: use either *thankfulness* or *gratitude*, not both.
3. Good transition device, indicating these things must be done in order. However, put the ideas in similar format. We wouldn't use the word *firstly*, so don't use *secondly*. Use *first, second, third* . . .
4. Here we have too many simple, subject-then-verb sentences: *Gunther tried . . . . He loved . . . . She was . . . . They were . . . . months passed. . . . He (barely) slept . . . . He was . . . .*

   Okay, this is rather sappy, but I'll try a rewrite, varying sentence lengths and construction:

   > After Brunhilda walked out on him, Gunther couldn't get her out of his mind. Devastated, he barely slept for three months. From the moment they met, he knew he was in love. They were perfect for each other.

5. C. This works, but there's probably a cause-and-effect relationship here, right? So one of the following might be better:

   > After the Supreme Court made a questionable ruling, huge crowds . . .

   > Because the Supreme Court made a questionable ruling, huge crowds . . .

   > Huge crowds marched . . . after (or because of) the Supreme Court's questionable ruling.

6. Nice use of the "glory of threes," but put it in parallel form: *price, floor plan, and location.*
7. C. Appropriate, short sentences convey the tension and action.
8. A case could be made that this long sentence captures the reader's "overwhelmed" feeling. However, breaking up the lengthy diatribe probably works best, something like this greatly simplified version:

   > Those trying to live healthy lives have a difficult time knowing what to eat. One day butter is bad for you. The next, margarine is suspect. Then, recommendations that olive oil is best are followed by food gurus extolling the virtues of coconut oil. How can a person know what to believe?

9. We have a lot of material lumped together here, and we don't find out what all these phrases refer to till we get to the end. Recommendation: Cut the number of elements in this sentence. (You can always discuss the omitted elements in another section.) Then turn the sentence around, using bullets to call attention to each of the points, and streamline everything, something like this:

> Our nation has become vulnerable for several reasons:
> - lack of vigilance regarding possible homegrown terrorists
> - lack of military funding
> - lack of sensitivity to the strategies of the devil
> - lack of courage to speak up when our lawmakers, in effect, try to over-turn God's laws

10. Here we have a rather choppy feel to a scene characterized by a key word—*sprawling*. So we can stretch it a bit, using some longer sentences and variations in sentence structure to convey that feel more effectively, maybe something like this:

> Diana sprawled on the lush, green lawn—the lawn of a grand castle, of all things. Staring up at the thin, wind-swept clouds, she praised God that she finally felt free and that the horrors of her past were just that—past, never to keep her awake at night, never to be dredged up again.

Chapter 40: Come to Your Senses

Answers will vary.

Chapter 41: Putting the Transit into Transitions

Answers will vary.

Chapter 42: Beware the Jargonaut

Answers will vary.

Chapter 43: Exclusive All-Inclusives

1. Jesus died for all *humanity* or all *people*.
2. We catch this error more easily if the word used is *waitress*, but both males and females are now called *servers*.
3. Is it important to the reader (and to the story) that the minister is black? Would the readership prefer the term *African-American*? And do we know for sure the minister is male?
4. To me we're still girls, and I will continue calling us that in conversation. However, if I were writing about them, it would be better to refer to my colleagues as *women*.
5. Christian jargon: What does it mean that God blessed Justin? In what ways?
6. Use *actors* instead of *actresses*.
7. Don't be too quick to assume the nurse is a woman. Verify. I've benefited from the care of some great male nurses.
8. Christian jargon: *Because Jesus paid the penalty for our wrongdoings, we don't fear eternity.* (You can explain more, depending on the audience and space allowed.)
9. In this example the writer may simply be pulling words from a Greek New Testament online, and readers can get lost in the "funky" letters and unfamiliar terms. If we want to focus on the possible reason that Jesus used two different words, we can point out the differences in meanings (which we don't get here).
10. The flight attendant could be male.

Chapter 44: Touché, Clichés!

Answers will vary.

Chapter 45: Worth the Sweat

Answers will vary.

Chapter 46: Why Did the Editor Do That to My Manuscript?

Exercise outcomes will vary.

Appendix B

Learn these industry-standard proofreading marks. They can help you decipher an editor's corrections. You can use these symbols to revise your own work on hard copy (manuscripts printed out) because it's easier to spot errors on hard copy than on screen. And you can use these symbols to mark your critique group members' manuscripts for suggested improvements.

<u>The Iliad</u>	Underline words to be set in italics.
the bible	Capitalize.
the company President	Make lower case.
film festival	Transpose letters or words.
Please stay a while.	Close up space.
Please stay for awhile.	Separate. Two words.
the kumquats	Delete.
¶	Begin new paragraph.
6 people saw it	Spell out.
goofy the attorney	Insert material above.
the tree jacaranda	Insert material below.
When he finished he left.	Insert comma.
She phoned Dr Schmitt.	Insert period.
This is mine he said.	Insert quotation marks.
"Its his," she agreed.	Insert apostrophe.
He's weird she thought.	Insert space.
They quickly surrendered.	Restore to original (ignore changes). Place dots beneath the word(s) to be restored.

Appendix C

Resources

Reference Works in Print Form

Some of these resources are officially out of print but available used at amazon.com or barnesandnoble.com.

Alpha Teach Yourself Grammar and Style in 24 Hours, Pamela Rice Hahn and Dennis E. Hensley, PhD, MacMillan

AP Stylebook
The standard for newspapers and some magazines

Chicago Manual of Style, Sixteenth Edition, University of Chicago Press
The standard for most book publishers and some magazines

Chicago Manual of Style Guidelines (based on sixteenth ed.), BarCharts, Inc., Quick Study Academic

Christian Writer's Manual of Style, Fourth Edition, Robert Hudson, general editor, Zondervan
Based on the *Chicago Manual of Style* (*CMoS 16*), this reference work is smaller and much easier to use. This book also covers Christian and other religious terms more completely than *CMoS 16*.

Diagramming Sentences, Deborah White Broadwater, Mark Twain Media

The Elements of Style, Wm. Strunk and E. B. White, Fourth Edition, Longman

The Little Red Writing Book, Brandon Royal, Writer's Digest Books

Garner's Modern American Usage, Bryan A. Garner, Oxford University Press

Grammar Desk Reference, Gary Lutz and Diane Stevenson, Writer's Digest Books

The Grammar Girl Devotional, Mignon Fogarty (not Christian oriented but good quick tips)

Grammatically Correct, Second Edition, Anne Stilman, Writer's Digest Books

Merriam Webster's Collegiate Dictionary (buy the most recently published edition)

Proofreading Secrets of Best-Selling Authors, Kathy Ide, Lighthouse Publishing of the Carolinas

Random House Webster's Pocket Bad Speller's Dictionary

Online Grammar Resources

Chicago Manual of Style Online (fee-based subscription):
http://www.chicagomanualofstyle.org/subscription_opts.html
Subscription includes periodic newsletter emails with Q/A helps

www.apvschicago.com

www.copyright.cornell.edu/resources/publicdomain.cfm

www.grammarly.com

www.quickanddirtytips.com/grammar-girl

Note: If you google almost any grammar question you have, such as *lay v. lie*, you'll find many sites clarifying the issue. Just be sure the site you choose as your authority is a reliable one, such as university sites or writersdigest.com or about.com or a site ending in .edu. Check more than one listing to verify. Chat rooms are *not* reputable grammar sites. An example of shared ignorance, they are often, quite frankly, wrong.

Joyce's Three Favorite Books on the Writing Craft

The Magazine Article: How to Think It, Plan It, Write It, Peter Jacobi, Indiana University Press
On Writing Well, William Zinsser, Harper Perennial
Writing for Story: Craft Secrets of Dramatic Nonfiction, Jon Franklin, Plume [publisher]

Magazines Covering the Writing Craft

Christian Communicator magazine
The Writer magazine
Writer's Digest magazine

Resources for Handling Scripture

How to Read the Bible for All It's Worth, Gordon D. Fee and Douglas Stuart, Zondervan
Insight's Bible Handbook and other resources from Insight for Living Ministries, http://insight.org/resources/bible
Living by the Book: The Art and Science of Reading the Bible (book and workbook), Howard G. Hendricks, William D. Hendricks, Moody
Searching the Scriptures: Find the Nourishment Your Soul Needs, Charles R. Swindoll, Tyndale
Walk Thru the Bible (many materials) for a comprehensive understanding of the Bible: www.walkthru.org.store
What the Bible Is All About: Revised-NIV Edition Bible Handbook, Henrietta Mears, Regal

Endnotes

Start Here

1. British spelling of *grey* (rather than *gray*) à la Agatha Christie's Belgian detective, Hercule Poirot.

Page vii

1. Howard B. Grose, "Give of Your Best to the Master," 1902.

Chapter 3. The Match Game: Subjects and Verbs

1. Robert C. Pinckert, *Pinckert's Practical Grammar* (Cincinnati: Writer's Digest Books, 1986), 93.

Chapter 4. Getting Tense? Avoiding Verb Tense Errors

1. British spelling of *grey* (rather than *gray*) à la Agatha Christie's Belgian detective, Hercule Poirot.

Chapter 7. Are Your Adjectives on Steroids—or Just Obnoxious?

1. G. K. Chesterton, *The Man Who Was Thursday* (Radford, VA: Wilder Publications, 2007), 7.
2. Bill Barker, "Picturesque Speech," *Reader's Digest*, September 1997, 23.
3. Bryan A. Garner, *Garner's Modern American Usage*, 3rd ed. (New York: Oxford University Press, 2009), 1.

Chapter 9. The "Case" of the Questionable Pronoun: Pronoun Case

1. Also called nominative case.

Chapter 10. The Reflexology of Pronouns: Reflexive Pronouns

1. Gary Lutz and Diane Stevenson, *The Writer's Digest Grammar Desk Reference* (Cincinnati: Writer's Digest Books, 2005), 157.

Chapter 12. That Which Is Whom?

1. Robert Hudson, *The Christian Writer's Manual of Style, Fourth Edition* (Grand Rapids: Zondervan, 2016), 571.

Chapter 14. Let's Split (and Other Last Words): How to Handle Infinitives and Final Prepositions

1. 246.
2. *The Christian Writer's Manual of Style, Fourth Edition*, 358.
3. http://public.wsu.edu/~brians/errors/churchill.html.
4. *The Christian Writer's Manual of Style*, 358.

Chapter 17. Wanna Go Out for a Spell? Spelling and Usage

1. 549.
2. 290.
3. Published in the *Journal of Irreproducible Results* (January–February 1994): 13. Reprinted ("by popular demand") in the *Journal of Irreproducible Results* 45, no. 5/6 (2000): 20. *Journal of Irreproducible Results*, Box 234, Chicago Heights, IL 60411. Used by permission of the author.

Chapter 18. That's What *He* Said: Punctuating Dialogue

1. 634.
2. 368.

Chapter 19. Hyphen Hyperactivity: When to Use Hyphens

1. Some editors' house style prefers "co-authored," also "co-worker," so study your target publication—and be consistent.
2. Gary Lutz and Diane Stevenson, *The Writer's Digest Grammar Desk Reference* (Cincinnati: Writer's Digest Books, 2005), 294–95.

Chapter 21. The Inside Scope: Colons and Semicolons

1. 128.
2. 327.
3. Dave Barry, "A Journey into My Colon—and Yours," *Miami Herald*, February 22, 2008, 1A.
4. Robert C. Pinckert, *Pinckert's Practical Grammar* (Cincinnati: Writer's Digest Books, 1986), 63–64.

Chapter 23. Capital Crimes and Misdemeanors: Capitalization

1. 446.
2. As you can see, I had to acquiesce to my publisher's style in this book.

Chapter 24. Commatose: All about Commas

1. Note: *M&M's* (with an apostrophe) is correct per the Mars trademark.

Chapter 29. Paint-by-Number Writing: Proper Expression of Numbers

1. Variations between my original columns and the material in this book reflect that difference in style manuals because I have used *CMoS 16* and *CWMS 4* as my standards here, noting, at times, where some newspaper/magazine styles differ. I have also taken counsel from colleagues and made alterations accordingly.

Chapter 30. Getting Possessive: Showing Possession

1. 298.

Chapter 31. "Quotable Quotes for 2000, Alex": Handling Quotations Correctly

1. 175.
2. 189.

3. Oswald Chambers, *My Utmost for His Highest* (New York: Dodd, Mead & Company, 1935), 350.
4. A. W. Tozer, *Born after Midnight* (Harrisburg, PA: Christian Publications, 1959), 59.

Chapter 32. Citation Citings: Footnotes, Endnotes, and Other Source Citations

1. *The Chicago Manual of Style* is even more comprehensive and is highly recommended by the editors of this book.

Chapter 33. Handling Scripture Carefully and Correctly

1. 333

Chapter 34. Stylin': What Is Style?

1. *The Applause of Heaven* (Nashville: Thomas Nelson, 1996), 73.
2. *Bird by Bird* (New York: Anchor, 1994), 26.
3. *The Crime of Living Cautiously: Hearing God's Call to Adventure* (Downers Grove, IL: InterVarsity, 2005), 41.
4. *Confessions of a Prayer Wimp: My Fumbling, Faltering Foibles in Faith* (Grand Rapids: Zondervan, 2005), 113.
5. *The Silmarillion* (New York: Del Rey, 2002), 116.
6. *The Big Sleep* (New York: Vintage Books, 1992), 3.
7. George Plimpton, ed., *Writers at Work: The Paris Review Interviews*, 2nd series (New York: Penguin, 1963), 156.

Chapter 37. Spit-Polished Writing

1. Though I've found this quote in various permutations, the one I've used seems to be the most reliable: from Mark Twain in a letter to George Bainton, October 15, 1888, cited in *The Quotable Mark Twain* by R. Kent Rasmussen (New York: McGraw Hill, 1998), 18.
2. Mark Twain, "Spelling and Pictures" (address, Annual Dinner of the Associated Press, Waldorf-Astoria, New York, September 18, 1906, quoted in the *New York Times*, September 20, 1906), twainquotes.com: http://www.twainquotes.com/19060920.html (January 26, 2017).
3. *New Kid Catastrophes* (Carol Stream, IL: Tyndale Kids, 2011), 110.

Chapter 38. Got Rhythm?

1. Kirk Livingston, "Stop the World, I Want to Get Off," *Pursuit* VI, no. 4 (1998): 4. Used by permission of the author.

Chapter 39. Flow Gently, Sweet Manuscript

1. I also recommend using the Gunning Fog Index to assess the readability of your manuscript. See an explanation at Writing Information & Tips, Elizabeth Bezant's website, http://www.writing-information-and-tips.com/fog-index.html.
2. Peter Jacobi, *The Magazine Article: How to Think It, Plan It, Write It* (Cincinnati: Writer's Digest Books, 1991), 13.

Chapter 40. Come to Your Senses: Captivating Readers with Sensory Detail

1. I've told this story in *The 500 Hats of a Modern-Day Woman*; but it illustrates this point well, so I repeat it here.

2. *Charlotte's Web* (New York: HarperCollins, 2012), 139.
3. *Murder Makes Waves* (New York: Avon, 1997), 132.
4. *The Question That Never Goes Away* (Grand Rapids: Zondervan, 2014), 18.
5. *Rose* (New York: Ballentine, 1996), 280.
6. *The Silver Chair* (New York: Collier, 1970), 13.
7. Ibid., 202–3.
8. Created by Joyce K. Ellis, all rights reserved. For permission to reprint, contact her through www.joycekellis.com.

Chapter 41. Putting the Transit into Transitions: The Importance of Smooth Transitions

1. Jacobi, *The Magazine Article*, 13.

Chapter 42. Beware the Jargonaut: Purging Jargon from Your Writing

1. Barna Group and American Bible Society, "The State of the Bible Report 2014," http://www.americanbible.org/uploads/content/state-of-the-bible-data-analysis-american-bible-society-2014.pdf.
2. Kenneth Berding, *Bible Revival: Recommitting Ourselves to One Book* (Wooster, OH: Weaver Book Company, 2013), 19.
3. "Survey Describes the Spiritual Gifts That Christians Say They Have," Barna Group website, February 9, 2009, https://www.barna.org/barna-update/faith-spirituality/211-survey-describes-the-spiritual-gifts-that-christians-say-they-have#.VnRWGZVIhlY.

Chapter 43. Exclusive All-Inclusives: Avoiding Gender and Other Types of Exclusivity

1. Hebrews 2:15 NLT [1996 edition].
2. Rusty Wright, "Paris Hilton and What We Want," Probe Ministries website, January 10, 2007, http://www.probe.org/paris-hilton-and-what-we-want/.
3. *The Chicago Manual of Style, Sixteenth Edition* (Chicago: University of Chicago Press, 2010), 301.
4. Ibid.

Chapter 44. Touché, Clichés!

1. Jane Rubietta, *Finding Your Promise: From Barren to Bounty—the Life of Abraham* (Indianapolis: Wesleyan Publishing House, 2015), 15.
2. Randy Singer, *The Advocate* (Carol Stream, IL: Tyndale, 2014), 44.

Chapter 45. Worth the Sweat: We're Entitled to a Great Title and Engaging Subheads

1. Roger Palms, *Effective Magazine Writing: Let Your Words Reach the World* (Colorado Springs: Shaw Books, 2000), 142.

Chapter 46. Why Did the Editor Do That to My Manuscript?

1. Mignon Fogarty, "Grammar Girl #547 '"A while' versus 'Awhile'?" Last updated December 15, 2016. *QuickAnd DirtyTips.com:* http://www.quickanddirtytips.com/education/grammar/while-versus-awhile (January 26, 2017) .

Section 2 Quiz Answers: Punctuation and Related Matters

1. 174–75.

Index

Q

Acknowledgments

First, I must thank my parents for setting a good example in our home, tuning my ear to good English usage as I was growing up.

Then I must thank Joanne Kilsberg—my high school English, journalism, and Spanish teacher—who not only fanned the flame of my love for writing but also gave me a firm foundation in Spanish language skills that I continue to build upon and use wherever God gives me opportunity. Learning a second language helps us better learn our own.

I must also acknowledge my indebtedness to my aunt and role model, Claire Lynn—the mother of eight children who still found time to write. She lovingly urged me to use my God-given gifts for him.

Many thanks to Norm Rohrer, founder of the original Christian Writers Guild, who helped me explore many paths of helping others through writing. He has encouraged me greatly over the years as a mentor and friend, always closing his correspondence with the word *Onward*!

My thanks also to Margaret Anderson and her book, *The Christian Writer's Handbook* (now out of print), which taught me much and emphasized the importance of writing Christian materials with excellence. Though she has gone on to heaven, her legacy lives on in many of us.

Much gratitude to James L. Johnson, a pioneer, role model, and early mentor to me, who, from a human perspective, went to his eternal reward much too soon.

Deep gratitude to my longtime mentor Jerry Jenkins, who, in turn, gave me the privilege of mentoring writing students for many years through the Jerry B. Jenkins Christian Writers Guild.

Unending thanks go to Lin Johnson, editor of the *Christian Communicator*, for believing in the GPS column for that publication, for encouraging me to compile my more than five years of columns into a book, and for praying me through the process. She is a great editor and friend.

Thanks also to my critique group—Alice Bostrom, Lois Holmes, Rita Kroon, and Sharon Sheppard—for their encouragement and helpful feedback on my columns and this collection.

Without the prayers of my prayer partners—Sharon Sheppard and Phyllis Hedberg—I think I might have quit writing many times over the years. How grateful I am for their prayers and for their kindness in the big task of keeping me accountable.

I'm so grateful, too, for Jane Rubietta, a great cheerleader God has put in my life, for her prayer support and encouragement.

Thanks to Ann Byle, who helped me connect with Credo House Publishers to fulfill my long-held dream of publishing this book. Her enthusiasm and encouragement have meant so much to me.

Endless thanks to Tim Beals, publisher at Credo House, who jumped into this project with both feet and has shepherded it to completion. I can never adequately thank him for his belief in me and in this project.

Thanks, also, to Andy Sloan for his detail-oriented editing expertise, and to the rest of the staff at Credo for their commitment to excellence.

My deepest gratitude and love to my husband, Steve, whose loving support, encouragement, and proofreading skills mean the world to me. How I thank the Lord for the gift Steve is to me.

Above all, my gratitude belongs to God, my strength and joy, without whom I can do nothing! May this book bring encouragement to writers for his glory.